A Barfield Reader

A Barfield Reader

Selections from the Writings of Owen Barfield

Edited and with an Introduction by

G. B. Tennyson

Floris Books

First published in 1998 by Wesleyan University Press
in the United States of America
First published in the United Kingdom in 1999 by Floris Books

British Library CIP Data available

ISBN 0-86315-286-4

Printed in the United States in America

Contents

Contents / vii

Preface

With characteristic self-deprecation, Owen Barfield used to say that he always wrote the same book, was always "the same old Barfield, saying the same old thing." If that were true, a selection from his writings would not be necessary or at least would present no particular challenge. But in fact Barfield's "same old thing" is extraordinarily rich and varied, expressed in a wide variety of modes and genres, and spanning more than eighty years of the century now drawing to a close. The real challenge is to represent his writing and thinking adequately in a single volume. It is that challenge that the present anthology seeks to address.

The idea for an undertaking like the present one was first suggested to the Wesleyan Press, Barfield's longtime publisher, by a (to me) unknown Barfield reader and enthusiast, to whom I herewith express my thanks. The notion was then passed on to me by Wesleyan just at the time when I was completing the final editing on the documentary video "Owen Barfield: Man and Meaning." A concern with representing an overview of Barfield's thoughts was therefore fresh in the mind. Barfield himself was a still vital ninety-five at the time. Thus, a selection from his lifetime of writing clearly seemed to be an appropriate way to mark his upcoming centenary. In the event, sadly, he passed from the scene, aged ninety-nine, just short of a year before publication. Fortunately, he was available to be consulted on the contents and to give his approval to the main outline and selections for this collection.

Not surprisingly, there was a subtle kind of truth in Barfield's modest claim to have been writing the same book over and over: it lay in his consistency of vision, however, rather than in any sort of repetition. It led me to see that the way to present a selection from his writings was not in terms of chronology but in terms of central ideas, somewhat as we had done in the video, but now for the anthology in greater and more readerly depth. Thus I resolved to provide selections large and small clustered about leading Barfieldian concepts. The devil, of course, was in the details, especially the selection of short passages to supplement and illuminate the larger selections. Again, the "same old thing" proved to be more various, beautiful, and new than Barfield himself had ever allowed. But with time and reflection it became possible to cull at least some of the best from the ample body of work that Barfield has left us. The hope is that the selection succeeds in presenting Barfield's enormously insightful ideas in accessible form. In all the selections internal cross-references to other parts of the text have been omitted.

An additional aim of this anthology is to show the range of Barfield's writing, the fact that, although best known for his literary and philosophical prose, he was also an inventive and gifted writer of fiction and poetry. Joining the creative dimension of his writing to the more purely intellectual, this collection aims to enable the reader, first time or veteran, to see Barfield steadily and whole. It is a reader for readers. It is thus not only a presentation of the best of Barfield but also a tribute to his genius.

In compiling this anthology the editor has incurred several debts of gratitude, the first being to Barfield himself for his help and cooperation. Others who have been supportive of this endeavor include my fellow literary trustees, Walter Hooper, Thomas Kranidas, and Shirley Sugerman. Walter Hooper deserves special thanks for his help to me over many years and many visits, for his ministrations to Owen Barfield, and for his preservation of the literary remains that we believe will yield yet further treasures. I have also had the support of Mr. Barfield's surviving family, especially Alexander Barfield, and I am very thankful for it. I am grateful to the staffs at the Walhatch and at the Chequers Inn, Forest Row, for their many courtesies over the years of my visits to Owen Barfield. Others in Forest Row also stimulated my work, particularly Josephine Spence and Simon Blaxland-de Lange. In the wider world of Barfield admirers I have been heartened by the support and unfailing good cheer of Jane Hipolito, and also by various forms of encouragement from Lionel Adey, Samuel Bickford, Allan Christensen, James Cutsinger, Jan Edwards, John Kurzweil, Michael Logsdon, George Michos, Stephen Miles, Dale Nelson, James Prothero, Philip Rand, John Rateliff, Roger Stronstad, Carl Swift, Peter Taylor, Dale Trela, William Watt, and by the members of the Southern California C. S. Lewis Society. My collaborators on the video mentioned above also deserve my thanks, especially Ben Levin and David Lavery. In a very material way I have been aided by support from the Committee on Research of the University of California, Los Angeles.

In the actual production of this work the staff at Wesleyan University Press have been exceedingly obliging, particularly Editor-in-chief Suzanna Tamminen who helped initiate and sustain this project. Thanks also to Director Thomas Radko and Editor Matt Byrnie. Sincere thanks to consultants Gertrude Reif Hughes and Douglas Sloan. At the University Press of New England I was aided by the fine skills of the staff. The cover design is based on a drawing by Louis Soria that first appeared in *The World and I* in 1990 to accompany my essay "Owen Barfield: First and Last Inklings." My thanks to the artist and the publication.

I was once chidden by Owen Barfield for insufficient respect for Milton. I argued that respect was hardly due a regicide. Barfield replied that the issue was poetry not politics. He was (probably) right. Thus nothing befits Barfield's passing and my work on this volume better than these lines from that very poet that Barfield so loved and respected:

> Dear son of memory, great heir of fame,
> What need'st thou such weak witness of thy name?

Encino, California   G.B.T.

Owen Barfield: A Life in Thought

In an essay on his lifelong friend C. S. Lewis, Owen Barfield[1] discerned "five C. S. Lewises each more or less separate from the other.[2] There were the three defined by Lewis's publications–literary critic, fiction writer, religious apologist—and then another two associated with Lewis's biography—the pre- and post-conversion Lewises. Elsewhere, and often in conversation, Barfield contrasted himself with this multifaceted figure, saying that he was "always the same old Barfield, always saying the same old thing."[3] True in one sense, perhaps not so true in another. For one can also readily discern at least five Owen Barfields. There is the literary critic, the anthroposophist, the philosopher; and one can easily add poet and fiction writer, although these latter are not well known aspects of his work. Even biographically there is a parallel in that Barfield, too, underwent a profound change in outlook earlier in the same decade as Lewis's much noted conversion, albeit there was no single dramatic and defining moment as Lewis records of himself on that grim night in Magdalen College in 1929 when he knelt and admitted that "God was God."[4] With Barfield the change was more gradual and evolutionary, but like a conversion, it released intellectual and creative energies that led to a lengthy and varied writing career that spanned almost the entire twentieth century. Even if it is a characteristically modest Barfield assessment to describe all of his work as saying the same old thing, it is more accurate to say that all of Barfield's works are intertwined and that each enriches the other, that the later Barfield fulfills the promise of the earlier and is Barfield come of age. The aim of this selection is to acquaint readers with all the Barfields, early and late, wise and yet ever wiser.

Arthur Owen Barfield was born on 9 November 1898 in Muswell Hill, North London, the fourth of four children, two boys and two girls, of the solicitor Arthur Barfield and his wife, Elizabeth Shoults Barfield.[5] Barfield's two sisters were a decade older than he, and his brother almost four years older. Such facts as are known about Barfield's early life paint a picture of a comfortable, middle-class, semi-suburban life in a family with pronounced intellectual and artistic interests. Barfield's mother, known as Lizzie, was keenly musical. She taught her husband to play the piano and the entire family to participate in musical evenings, leading Owen Barfield in later life to say to the surprise of many of his readers that if he had to give up all but one art, he would save music. Barfield's mother was also a suffragette who attended rallies and even spoke at some, though evidently out of commitment rather than from any passion for attention. Barfield stresses that she was a loving mother, strongly intellectual but without the stridency that comes so easily to many who take up causes. It appears indeed that the Barfields in general held positions on intellectual rather than emotional grounds and that a natural reserve prevented them from becoming zealots. There was in the Barfield family a distrust of fervor or visibly displayed emotion. Those who appeared especially enthusiastic were called "affected," so the dominant tone of the Barfield family life was one of cool and balanced intellect. This led Barfield himself to suspect "anything in the nature of what seemed like powerful emotional experience, in terms of such things as poetry, as being a kind of self-deception." The need to join emotion to intellect was a major factor leading to Barfield's ultimate philosophic position. His writings reflect that cool and balanced intellect of the Barfield household, but they also touch emotional and imaginative depths not dreamt of in his parents' philosophy.

The parental distrust of zeal and affectation was also reflected in the Barfield family's attitude towards religion. Though both parents had been born Congregationalists, the Barfields as a family had no formal religion and observed no regular church attendance; nor did they have their children baptized. Nevertheless, like proper Victorians, they refrained from outside activities, especially sports, on Sunday mornings. (The Barfield house boasted a tennis court in the rear, which was the main area of Sunday prohibition.) They were benign, enlightened agnostics and not militant freethinkers who denigrated religion.

Owen Barfield believed that his parents probably met at some Congregationalist church event or social activity and were in due course married in a Congregationalist church. But they "threw it off like so many people of their generation in their adult life." Certainly no rigorous religious views were imposed on the Barfield children. Of course, it would not have been possible to grow up in a middle-class English household at the turn of the century without a general awareness of at least the broad doctrines of Christianity. Further, one of the family entertainments was the reading aloud of Victorian novels, from which at the very least a diffuse kind of religion would have filtered down, if nothing more than Dickens's "Philosophy of Christmas," Dickens being a constant source of material for family readings, one especially favored by the senior Barfield. Indeed, the major feasts like Christmas were certainly noted in the Barfield household, and the exchange of gifts and visits with relatives on both sides of the family were regular features of the holiday. Moreover, the senior Barfield had what his son later called something like "reverence" for the Gospels and tolerated no flippancy about them or about Christianity in general.

Perhaps for this reason, although the life of the young Barfield was free of any kind of religious rigor, he recalls becoming aware by the end of his Highgate years that he had ceased to believe and was effectively an agnostic, which indicates that in youth he perceived himself to be some sort of Christian.

Because the three older children were already well along in school when it came time to begin Owen's education, Lizzie Barfield undertook to tutor him herself at home for the first few years. When he was eight, he was enrolled as a day student in Highgate School, which his brother Harry was already attending. Barfield explains that the curriculum was divided into modern and classical. Harry had been placed on the modern side while Owen was placed on the classical. Barfield says he does not now know why they were thus assigned, but one suspects that the school authorities detected from the start a more literary disposition in Owen and a more technical inclination in Harry. They appear to have been correct, for the older brother went on to become an engineer and the younger to become a writer. In his own words, Owen Barfield had the "ordinary classical education that public schools provided in those days." But from the late twentieth-century perspective, this would have been a rich and challenging curriculum, heavy in Latin and Greek grammar and literature, and now virtually unobtainable.

A half-century before Barfield attended Highgate, the young Gerard Manley Hopkins had been a student there, and earlier yet the "Sage of Highgate," Samuel Taylor Coleridge, had been buried in the crypt, a fitting association for Barfield, who would come to be a profound interpreter of Coleridge's ideas.[6] Towards the end of Barfield's Highgate years, the future Poet Laureate John Betjeman, eight years younger than Barfield, was enrolled at the school. Given the age difference, Barfield and Betjeman did not know one another at that time, but they became friendly acquaintances in later years. At Highgate they shared the instruction of at least one of the teachers and very probably shared the same headmaster as well.

Barfield recalled the Highgate headmaster as somewhat forbidding as he interviewed him for admission and concluded grudgingly, "Well, he can read anyhow"; while Betjeman recalls an even more forbidding headmaster posing to him the question, "How many half-crowns in a pound?" to which Betjeman did not know the answer. He was admitted nevertheless. It sounds like the same headmaster. More certainly they both encountered literature under the tutelage of a Miss Long, an encounter Betjeman memorialized in his blank verse autobiographical memoir, *Summoned By Bells*, when the teacher introduced him to the poetry of Poe, who was described in a footnote as having "died of dissipation." Thus, "And what is 'dissipation,' please, Miss Long?" asked the boy Betjeman.[7]

Interestingly, Betjeman recalls his greatest boyhood trauma as that of being bullied by other schoolboys who would throw him into the bushes and call him a German spy (Betjeman's Highgate days fell during the First War and his schoolfellows assumed that the Dutch surname Betjeman was a German one), whereas Barfield recalled his greatest childhood unhappiness as being afflicted with stammering, a problem that lingered on for many years and spoiled any chance of his having a career as a lecturer, even though he became a very successful one in America many decades later.[8]

Miss Long's occasional excursions into literature were, of course, not the mainstay of the classical curriculum at Highgate, and Barfield recalls in the upper forms only casual once-a-week chats on the subject under the direction of one of the masters. More important than any instruction in modern literature was Barfield's meeting at Highgate with Alfred Cecil Harwood, who was to remain a lifelong friend and in the nineteen-twenties to become a fellow advocate of the ideas of Rudolf Steiner. Harwood was Barfield's "First Friend," to use C. S. Lewis's term for the one who agrees with you about everything and is a kind of alter ego.[9] At Highgate the two Barfield brothers were known officially as Barfield One and Barfield Two[10] as a way of distinguishing them in reference, but the two friends, Owen and Cecil were known unofficially as "Barwood and Harfield" as a way of referring to the identity of their ideas and attitudes.

In December 1916 both Barfield and Harwood won classical scholarships to Oxford, Barfield to Wadham College, Harwood to Christ Church, but both had to postpone entry because of service in the war, Harwood as an infantry officer, Barfield as a wireless officer in the Signal Corps. Barfield served mainly in Belgium, using what was by modern standards a still rudimentary form of communication, that is, Morse code signalling by radio transmission, which he describes as largely unreliable. His duties allowed him time for extensive reading, which increasingly turned towards poetry and English literature. After release from the service in the summer of 1919, he went up to Oxford in October to take up the scholarship he had earlier won; but, because of his increased interest in English literature, he transferred from the program called Greats (philosophy, history, classical languages) to English literature. Harwood also took up his scholarship, as earlier in the year C. S. Lewis, also returned from the war, had taken up his at University College. It was in the fall of 1919 that Barfield and Lewis met. They became friends almost immediately and remained so until Lewis's death in 1963.[11]

Barfield and Lewis pursued their respective studies at the heightened pace necessitated by the pressure of an enlarged Oxford during the immediate postwar years, and from 1923 on they pursued as well a philosophical debate about life and meaning that was to influence the thought and writings of each in future years. This ongoing exchange came to be known as the "Great War" in jocular reference to the more celebrated one of that name in which each had lately participated. During the Oxford years the exchanges were entirely verbal, often engaged in as they took long walks through the countryside. After Barfield had moved to London in the mid-twenties the debate continued in epistolary form.

The full story, including the surviving written aspects of it, has been illuminatingly recounted in Lionel Adey's *C. S. Lewis's 'Great War' with Owen Barfield* (1978)[12] and offers an unusual insight into the early thinking of these two extraordinary figures. A practical consequence of their association was that Lewis allowed that Barfield had cured him of "chronological snobbery," the idea that anything that was outdated was therefore invalid. For his part, Barfield acknowledged that Lewis had helped him to see the value of logic in reasoning as a curb on the unbridled imagination.

It was in Oxford in 1923 that Barfield surprised and dismayed Lewis by becoming an Anthroposophist and follower of Rudolf Steiner, thereby precipitating the "Great War." In embracing Anthroposophy Barfield was once again in the company of his First Friend, Cecil Harwood, who would devote his life to the advancement of Steinerian ideas and become a founder of a Steiner school called Michael Hall. Years later in *Surprised by Joy* Lewis described his unhappiness with Barfield's decision, but it is clear that much of his concern had to do with Barfield's adoption of a religious position at all, as it challenged Lewis's own faltering grasp on agnosticism.[13] Lewis was to adopt his own theistic position before the decade was out and his full acceptance of traditional Christianity by 1931.

Although Barfield made clear in many places the degree of his indebtedness to Steiner's holistic thought and has even translated and participated in translations of Steiner works, he nowhere recorded a full account of his personal experiences in coming to so momentous a resolution as the adoption of Anthroposophy as a creed.[14] Perhaps even autobiographically, he preferred evolution to revolution. It does seem clear, however, that as his studies in literature deepened during the Oxford years, particularly in the early twenties when he stayed on after the conventional B.A. to undertake a B. Litt. Degree, he saw in the nature of poetry and in the deepest nature of language itself that there were elements that no materialist philosophy could explain. He had also arrived independently at ideas about language, metaphor, and the imagination that turned out to be congruent with those he encountered in Rudolf Steiner.

It would appear that the encounter with Steiner's ideas, and eventually personally with Steiner himself, came about from Barfield's, and then Harwood's, interest in folk dancing, which led first Barfield then Harwood into membership in the English Folk Dance Society in their second year at Oxford. The year following the completion of their Oxford degrees Barfield and Harwood lived in a thatched country dwelling called Bee Cottage in Beckley outside Oxford (still standing and relatively little changed), close enough for frequent visitors to come and for continued pursuit of their interest in folk dance and meetings in Oxford. Through their association with the English Folk Dance Society they went on a summer tour of Cornwall and southwestern England in 1922 and met among the participants Maud Douie and Daphne Olivier. Maud Douie was a professional dancer who had earlier worked with Gordon Craig. The Honorable

Daphne Olivier, a graduate of Cambridge, was the daughter of a former governor of Jamaica.[15] Barfield was to marry Maud in 1923 and Harwood was to marry Daphne in 1925.

It was Daphne Olivier who had already encountered the works and ideas of Rudolf Steiner and had heard him lecture. Because of her enthusiasm Barfield and Harwood attended some lectures on Anthroposophy, read a good deal about it, discussed it with others already involved, and, as at Highgate, the Barwood-Harfield team found themselves in general concord on Steiner's ideas. By 1923 both had joined the Anthroposophical Society, Barfield, by his own recollection, "a few weeks or months before" Harwood. It was Harwood, however, who was to devote his life to Steiner causes and whose personal encounter with Steiner Barfield wrote of as of a conversion, citing in evidence two Harwood poems written within a month of each other, one before, one after, Harwood's hearing and meeting Rudolf Steiner personally in Torquay in August 1924, about a year after his commitment to Anthroposophy: "Read now together [the poems] reveal, they positively proclaim, that in the month or so that elapsed between them the soul from which they sprang had reached and passed the nadir of its spiritual adventure in this life; while the second of the . . . poems . . . evinces already a prophetic awareness of its being such a turning point."[16]

Though "turning point" and "conversion" mean etymologically much the same thing, the former carries less emotional freight than the latter, which bears in Western thought always the imprint of the Damascus Road experience, but Barfield appears to interpret Harwood's experience as indeed a Pauline conversion. In Barfield's own case one finds no such dramatic language. It was more like a confluence of reading, reflection, thinking, and personal influences that constituted for him the turning point. Lewis depicts his own conversion as that of one pursued by God, cornered, and finally conquered; to show his reluctance he says that his search for God would be like speaking of the mouse's search for the cat, and he calls himself "the most dejected and reluctant convert in all England."[17] Barfield, by contrast, one must imagine, was indeed searching and knowing he was searching, but he was more cat than mouse, and a cat looking for a place be at home in rather than for a victim. When he found what he was looking for, he saw it was strangely familiar, though perhaps now, to adapt T. S. Eliot's phrase in "Little Gidding," "he knew the place for the first time."

By 1925 the young Barfield couple had taken a flat in London in order to facilitate Barfield's pursuit of a literary career. He worked part time for a journal called *Truth* and wrote independently on his own projects. The Barfields continued to spend part of the week in the country near Oxford in the village of Long Crendon where they had resided just after marriage in 1923 and where Barfield would continue to write at his own works. Here too he was within easy reach of further engagement in "Great War" discussions with Lewis. Although Barfield had published some substantial articles, a number of reviews, and even some poetry and fiction as an undergraduate and immediately thereafter, it was during this period of the mid-twenties that his first published books appeared. From the standpoint of the later emergence of Lewis and Tolkien and others, it is interesting that Barfield's first book was a fairy tale, *The Silver Trumpet* (1925). He was not to do much more in this vein, but the fact of his early interest suggests an intuitive feel for a literary mode that was to characterize and bring great fame to the group that would later be known as the Inklings. Barfield was an Inkling *avant la lettre*.[18]

More characteristic of what we think of as Barfield's lifetime achievement was the appearance in 1926 of his *History in English Words*, a far more original and profound work than its somewhat prosaic title suggests. Two years later came the even more provocative *Poetic Diction*. The leading ideas of these two works had their genesis in Barfield's Oxford literary studies (*Poetic Diction* was a refinement of his B. Litt. thesis) and in his debates with C. S. Lewis, as will become evident later in the presentation of Barfield's thought and in the selections from the works themselves. From the biographical standpoint, it would seem that Barfield was now well launched on a literary career. But it was not to be. Although his early works received respectful attention from the literary world (both *History in English Words* and *Poetic Diction* have remained continuously in print), they did not provide sufficient resources for Barfield to devote his full time to writing. Additionally, Barfield's solicitor father had recently lost through death the services of his brother in his London office. There was pressure for Owen Barfield to join the parental firm and to enter the law. He did so in 1929, and for the following almost thirty years Owen Barfield's chief energies were directed to the demands of a full time position as a London solicitor.

The years that followed Barfield's move into the legal profession are years he has called "colorless," referring evidently to their relative lack of literary activity and absence of any major work from his pen. From a domestic point of view they were colorful enough. They saw the adoption over the years of three children, two sons, one daughter, and the attendant pursuit of a full family life, a good deal of it spent in the semi-rural commuter area of Kent, south of London. Nor were these years totally devoid of literary endeavor. Barfield continued active in Anthroposophical circles, contributing often to the leading journals of the movement—*Anthroposophy, Anthroposophical Movement,* and *The Golden Blade*—and delivering lectures to various groups. Many of these were collected in *Romanticism Comes of Age* (1944, expanded edition 1966), which thus serves as his most sustained tribute to Rudolf Steiner. The more imaginative works he was able to produce during this period include the verse drama *Orpheus*, written in the mid-thirties, performed once in Sheffield in 1948, but not published until 1983, and the brilliant (and for Barfield cathartic) *This Ever Diverse Pair* (1950), technically a fiction but in fact simply *sui generis*.

On the social level Barfield continued his visits to Oxford and his association with Lewis and the Inklings as well as taking whenever possible the annual walking tour, a tradition that he, Harwood, and Lewis following, had begun in the twenties.[19] He was for a time a member of a London group that met weekly for lunch and included T. S. Eliot. He enjoyed other literary associations as well, among them a friendship with Walter de la Mare, whose poetry strongly appealed to Barfield.[20] An important personal landmark was reached during this period when in 1949 Barfield was baptized in the Church of England, prompting a hearty "Welcome, welcome, welcome" from the same C. S. Lewis who had been so alarmed in the early twenties by Barfield's move to theism through Anthroposophy.[21] Of course, by the late forties Lewis was the internationally acclaimed Anglican Christian apologist and author of *The Screwtape Letters* and very much in a position to extend welcome into his own communion. So, although the colorless years were not quite so stark as Barfield recalled them, what has made them seem so in retrospect is what they surely did, namely, prevent Barfield's total dedication to writing.

By the late fifties Barfield was able to retire from legal practice and to devote himself to writing and lecturing. The outpouring that followed in the next twenty-odd years was impressive indeed. For many it is the works of this second career, begun when Barfield was sixty, that introduced him to a wider public, beginning at first in America with a kind of cult status gained chiefly by *Saving the Appearances* (1957, first published in America in 1965) and leading to broad recognition of his intellectual eminence through invitations to serve as visiting professor and guest lecturer at universities throughout North America. At last the timing was right, for Barfield's unconventional ideas appealed to counter-culture anti-materialists and thoughtful academics alike. As time went on Inklings enthusiasts became aware of his writings, both for their connection with Lewis and Tolkien and for their own sake. American followers of Rudolf Steiner also played a major role in increasing awareness of Barfield's accomplishment.[22] The extraordinary richness of Barfield's thought began to be appreciated in ever-wider circles of American intellectual life.

As a consequence of Barfield's new freedom to devote himself entirely to writing, thinking, and lecturing, he created an additional body of work of rare quality. From this period stem such titles as *Worlds Apart* (1963), *Unancestral Voice* (1965), *Speaker's Meaning* (1967), *What Coleridge Thought* (1971), *The Rediscovery of Meaning* (1977), and *History, Guilt and Habit* (1979), along with reissues, second editions, prefaces, afterwords, and most recently two collections of Barfield's previous writings, *Owen Barfield on C. S. Lewis* (1989) and *A Barfield Sampler* (1993).

This last title reminds us that there is the unsung aspect of Barfield's work, unsung because mostly unknown and unavailable. Both he and C. S. Lewis began their literary careers with the expectation of writing primarily poetry.

Both published some poetry early on and sporadically throughout their writing careers, but both also gradually gave up the hope of being recognized as important poets. Both also published fiction, but only Lewis would gain popularity in this area and that not for more than two decades after their undergraduate years. Barfield's most ambitious work of fiction, a novel titled "English People" has remained unpublished.[23] He continued to write but not publish poetry throughout his career. Nevertheless, the lifelong concern with what has come to be called creative writing, and which Barfield prefers to call "forgetive writing," worked to keep his focus literary and his philosophy humane.[24] He never ceased to be responsive to the "felt change of consciousness" that only literature can bring that he first described in *Poetic Diction* in the nineteen-twenties.

For much of the period of Barfield's post-legal career he lived in Kent, first in South Darenth, later and chiefly at the house named Orchard View, not far from Dartford, looking out upon a wold that had long since lost its orchard but retained a certain enchantment lent by the sense of unfolding distance. It was a peculiarly English setting, comforting, mannerly, harmonious, as though to confirm Barfield's own assessment of himself as being "very English." At the same time, the scene evoked a sense of *Sehnsucht* or longing (the concept that Barfield taught C. S. Lewis) with its undulating hills meeting the sky at an almost but not quite unreachable remove. This too corresponds to an essential dimension of Barfield that is not so much English as Romantic, and German Romantic at that. It is that aspect of his work that ponders and leads the reader to ponder the mystery and wonder of being, and it lies at the heart of his philosophy.

Barfield's wife died in 1980, and in 1986 he moved to the retirement residence The Walhatch in Forest Row in East Sussex. He died there on 14 December 1997 after a short illness, aged ninety-nine.

Both in Orchard View and at the Walhatch, Barfield enjoyed the attentions of a stream of visitors and admirers, especially from America, but increasingly also from England where his public has been developing apace. Victorian designations being no longer in fashion, Barfield was not called the Sage of Orchard View, or the Sage of Forest Row, though such unofficial honorifics would have been entirely in order. Neither a cryptic Coleridge moving in a mazy motion and speaking obscurely, as Carlyle had it, of "om-m-mject" and "sum-m-mject," nor even less an irascible Carlyle himself tyrannizing neighbors about the annoying sounds of cock-crowing or reproving Americans for their manifold follies, Barfield as Sage—of Orchard View or of Forest Row—instead demonstrated those qualities of gentle but intellectually rigorous guidance that made C. S. Lewis call him "the wisest and best of my unofficial teachers." Many of these qualities are seen to advantage in *Owen Barfield: Man and Meaning* where just a few years before his death he was captured in reminiscence, reflection, and commentary in such a way that one can appreciate Lewis's other private tribute when he wrote in his early diaries, "Barfield towers above us all."[25]

Notes

1. Biographical materials on Owen Barfield are scarce. The sketch that follows draws on several published sources and on unpublished interviews and conversations the editor has had with Barfield over the years. The published sources are "A Conversation with Owen Barfield," by Shirley Sugerman in *Evolution of Consciousness* (1976), "Afterword: Owen Barfield: A Biographical Note," by Marjorie Lamp Mead in *The Silver Trumpet* (1986), three "Conversations on C. S. Lewis" in *Owen Barfield on C. S. Lewis* (1989) (hereafter cited as *OB/CSL*), interviews in the journal *Towards*, and the video *Owen Barfield: Man and Meaning* (1995). Full bibliographical information on these sources and on the works by Barfield cited in shortened form in these notes can be found in the bibliographies at the end of the Introduction. Unless otherwise noted, quotations from Barfield come from the video and interviews conducted during the filming, or from the Sugerman and Mead sources. Works not included in the Bibliography are cited in full in these notes.
   2. "The Five C. S. Lewises," in *OB/CSL*.
   3. Barfield has made this or similar remarks at various times, most recently in *Owen Barfield: Man and Meaning*.
   4. C. S. Lewis, *Surprised by Joy* (New York: Harcourt, 1955), p. 228.
   5. The house still stands, as does the later Barfield dwelling on Athenaeum Road in Whetstone, North London. Both can be seen in *Owen Barfield: Man and Meaning*.
   6. Coleridge spent his last years, from 1816 to 1834, in Highgate, under the care of the physician James Gillman. It is from those years that much of Coleridge's philosophic work stems. Visited and consulted by literary and intellectual society, Coleridge was dubbed the "Sage of Highgate" by Carlyle (who was himself later to be known as the "Sage of Chelsea") in a not altogether flattering but brilliantly evocative portrait in Carlyle's *Life of John Sterling* (1851).
   7. John Betjeman, *Summoned by Bells* (Boston: Houghton Mifflin, 1960), pp. 24–25. Betjeman attended only the Highgate Junior School before enrolling at Marlborough School, evidently because the family had moved from Muswell Hill to Chelsea. In Barfield's last year at Highgate, one of the schoolmasters was a reluctant T. S. Eliot, who left for his better-known post at Lloyd's Bank after only one year at Highgate. During that year Betjeman presented a collection of his verse for Eliot's opinion. Eliot did not care for it, but much later the two became friends. Another Betjeman-Barfield connection also occurred in the years after Highgate when Betjeman became an undergraduate at Magdalen College and had C. S. Lewis for his tutor. The two did not get along. See Walter Hooper, *C. S. Lewis: A Companion and Guide* (1996), pp. 629–631; hereafter cited as *CSL*.
   8. Between the mid-sixties and the mid-eighties Barfield spent terms as visiting professor at Drew University (twice), Brandeis University, the University of Missouri, the University of British Columbia, and SUNY, Stony Brook. During that period he also lectured and participated in conferences at various universities and Steiner institutions. He was both subject of and participant in conferences devoted to his work, most notably at Woodstock, Vermont, at Drew University, at Baruch College, CUNY, and at California State University, Fullerton.
   9. *Surprised by Joy*, pp. 199–200. Lewis' own First Friend was Arthur Greeves; his Second Friend, the one "who disagrees with you about everything" and is "not so much the *alter ego* as the antiself," was Owen Barfield.
   10. This corresponds to the usage common at other public schools that designated such siblings as "Major" and "Minor."
   11. See *Surprised by Joy*, *OB/CSL*, and Hooper's *CSL*. Lewis claimed that Barfield "changed me a good deal more than I him."
   12. This penetrating and thoughtful treatment of the ideas of Lewis and Barfield is based mainly on surviving letters and documents in the Wade Collection at Wheaton College, Illinois. Many of these are undated, but Adey posits that the epistolary and written portions of the "Great War" that

continued the verbal discussions of the Oxford years ran from 1925 to about 1930, with the main group of letters falling between 1925 and 1927. Adey concludes that "Barfield's thought is both more original and more profound" than Lewis's. Adey has recently expanded his study of Lewis in *C. S. Lewis: Writer, Dreamer, Mentor* (1988), which includes a treatment of the "Great War" and of Lewis's rejection of Anthroposophy (pp. 30–39), as well as other references to Barfield.

13. *Surprised by Joy*, pp. 205–209. Lewis writes: "First Harwood . . . , and then Barfield, embraced the doctrines of Steiner and became Anthroposophists. I was hideously shocked." According to Barfield, the order was first Barfield and then Harwood. On the Barfield-Harwood embrace of Steinerism vis-à-vis Lewis, see also Cecil Harwood, "About Anthroposophy" in *C. S. Lewis at the Breakfast Table*, ed. James T. Como (New York: Collier Books, 1979), pp. 25–30.

14. His most extensive treatment of the matter appears in the Introduction to the second edition of *Romanticism Comes of Age* (1966).

15. See Hooper's *CSL*, pp. 676–678.

16. "Introduction," *The Voice of Cecil Harwood*, ed. Owen Barfield (1979), p. 10. Barfield also wrote about his First Friend shortly after Harwood's death in 1975 in "Cecil Harwood," *Anthroposophical Quarterly*, 21 (Summer 1976).

17. *Surprised by Joy*, pp. 228–229.

18. A fugitive, brief reminiscence by Barfield seems to confirm this judgment. In "The Inklings Remembered" (not listed on the contents page but printed as an inset on pages 548–549 of G. B. Tennyson's "Owen Barfield: First and Last Inklings," *The World and I* [April, 1990], pp. 541–555), Barfield dissents from the common view that the Inklings began in 1933, pointing out that there were "quite a few meetings—enough to constitute a 'series'—in Lewis' rooms in the twenties between Lewis, Tolkien, and myself, sometimes together with Colin Hardie and at least one with Nevill Coghill. I think it was these foregatherings that ultimately turned into the Inklings, though it may well be that the name was not adopted until 1933." For further information on the Inklings, see Humphrey Carpenter, *The Inklings* (1979) and Hooper, *CSL*, pp. 765–766 and *passim*. Carpenter gives the date 1933 for the beginning of the Inklings, but in *CSL* Hooper gives the dates of the Inklings as 1930–1949. The name itself was taken over from another, unrelated group that disbanded in 1933, which is doubtless the reason for using that as the starting date for the group surrounding Lewis.

19. In the original three-part 1979 version of the video "Through Joy and Beyond," Barfield and Walter Hooper retrace a walking tour in Derbyshire that Barfield and Lewis had taken in 1935. The currently available version of the video is considerably reduced and omits the tour, but part of the conversation with Barfield that occurred on the tour is printed in the book by Walter Hooper that is not a transcript of the video but that arose from the experience of filming it and that is also titled *Through Joy and Beyond*. Another part of the conversation is printed as "Early Days with C. S. Lewis" in *OB/CSL*.

20. Barfield had published a few pieces on de la Mare in the twenties and thirties, and the two became friends in 1939 when de la Mare joined the Athenaeum Club in London where he and Barfield were able to engage in discussions of poetry and philosophy. See Theresa Whistler, *Imagination of the Heart: The Life of Walter de la Mare* (London: Duckworth, 1993), esp. pp. 395–96.

21. Recorded by Hooper in *CSL*, p. 623. Lewis's "Welcome" came in a letter of 23 June 1949, and was followed by the statement, "No, of course it won't mean the end of the Great War." But Barfield has maintained in various places that once Lewis accepted Christianity he refused to engage in any further "Great War" exchanges with Barfield. See especially the essay "Lewis and/or Barfield" and the interview "C. S. Lewis: A Retrospect," both in *OB/CSL*.

22. The roster of Barfield's prominent American admirers includes Saul Bellow, Howard Nemerov, Marshall McLuhan, and Norman O. Brown. It was from the world of Anthroposophy that the Barfield-oriented journal *To-Wards* emanated, founded and edited by Clifford Monks, initially of the Highland Hall School in Northridge, California, later of the Rudolf Steiner College in Fair

Oaks, California. Barfield often said that he had no British public, but that may be putting it too strongly. He certainly has had British admirers. In addition to the Inklings and dedicated Anthroposophists, who might be thought to be partial, Barfield early enjoyed the esteem of T. S. Eliot, who accepted his fiction for the *Criterion,* and subsequently that of Walter de la Mare, Cyril Connolly, and William Empson, among others, and of W. H. Auden, who wrote an appreciative introduction to a reissue of *History in English Words.* In recent years more and more British scholars have been citing Barfield's work; the numbers seem likely to grow.

23. The best account of Barfield's creative writing can be found in the Introduction to *A Barfield Sampler* and in prefatory remarks to the prose selections in that volume.

24. In *Owen Barfield: Man and Meaning*, Barfield called for the adoption of the obscure word *forgetive* in place of the widely used *creative.* The word appears to have been coined by Shakespeare and means, as Barfield put it, "creative but not quite with the metaphysical claim to supernatural creation." He counts it as similar to Tolkien's "sub-creation." In 2 *Henry IV* Shakespeare has Falstaff praise the virtues of wine in a lengthy disquisition in which he says: "A good sherris sack . . . makes [the brain] apprehensive, quick, forgetive, full of nimble, fiery, and delectable shapes" (IV, iii, 107). From this, the OED notes, *forgetive* came to mean "apt at 'forging,' inventive, creative."

25. *All My Road Before Me: The Diary of C. S. Lewis, 1922–1927* (1991), p. 67.

The Forgetive Mind

Barfield has said that his entire literary endeavor has been based on the concept of the evolution of consciousness and the ideas that flow from it. Therefore, understanding this idea is essential to understanding the basis of Barfield's philosophy. The evolution of consciousness is a concept that has its challenges for even the informed reader, as it goes against the grain of much contemporary thought. Barfield developed his belief in the evolution of consciousness in studying poetic diction and in reflecting upon the nature and development of language. One could say it is the study of etymology raised to the level of philosophy.

In examining the changes in words and word meanings over time Barfield came to the realization that words and language *evolve*, not in a crude Darwinian way from simple to complex but in the sense of growing, enlarging, and to use the Coleridgean term, "desynonymizing," which is to say differentiating themselves into a variety of separate meanings. Conventional thinking about language origin and development held that language arose first from a series of primitive sounds used to designate physical objects and elementary feelings. From these sounds, or roots, speakers built up larger and more complex words and concepts and transferred some of these to intangible things. This transference stage postulates that, after the root word stage, language proceeded to a metaphorical period during which the simple, concrete root ideas were transferred metaphorically to abstract or intangible notions.

The example that Barfield has used often to illustrate this kind of thinking about language is the word *breath* or *wind*. In Greek and Latin it is also the word for *spirit—pneuma* and *spiritus* respectively. It is held that humans first noted and named the physical wind and physical breath and then applied the word for this physical thing to the idea of the intangible thing called *spirit*. As he studied words Barfield came to question this kind of model for the evolution of language. He found that the farther back one went in the study of language the more complex not the more simple it became. The word for *wind* and *spirit* is the same because earlier people had perceived the two together, as a unity. Thus he writes:

> the study of the history of meaning . . . assures us definitely that such a purely material content as 'wind,' on the one hand, and on the other, such a purely abstract

xxvi / **The Forgetive Mind**

content as 'the principle of life within man or animal' are both *late* arrivals in human consciousness. Their abstractness and their simplicity are alike evidence of long ages of intellectual evolution. So far from the psychic meaning of 'spiritus' having arisen because someone had the abstract idea, 'principle of life . . .' and wanted a word for it, the abstract idea 'principle of life' is itself a *product* of the old concrete *meaning* 'spiritus,' which contained within itself the germs of both later significations. We must therefore, imagine a time when 'spiritus' or πνευμα, or older words from which these had descended, meant neither *breath* nor *wind*, nor *spirit*, nor yet all three of these things, but when they simply had *their own old peculiar meaning*, which has since, in the course of the evolution of consciousness, crystallized into the three meanings specified—and no doubt into others also, for which separate words had already been found by Greek and Roman times. (*Poetic Diction*, pp. 80–81)

From this example alone one can begin to see the way in which Barfield's thought evolved. He discerned in the study of words a development, an evolution, of thought from an earlier unity to later differentiation. That earlier unity, he recognized, represented also a different perception on the part of earlier human beings, who perceived the world as a greater unity than moderns do. This meant therefore that human consciousness had evolved as had language, indeed that the two evolved together, and that the evolution of language was the demonstration of the evolution of consciousness. A further consequence of this understanding was to realize that earlier forms of perception reflected a different relationship with the external world from that which moderns have. He called that relationship "Original Participation," and that term as well as "Final Participation" have become Barfieldian bywords, both being specific types and stages of the overarching Barfieldian concept of "Participation" in general. All relate to language and to the evolution of consciousness.

That Barfield was able to see words and language in his particular way had also much to do with the issues that he and C. S. Lewis debated in their personal "Great War," which was taking place during the same years that Barfield was developing his thinking about language and the evolution of consciousness. The surviving materials that led to Adey's scholarly account of the "Great War" make it plain that the nub of the Barfield-Lewis debate was on the question of epistemology, the nature of knowing. Although, as his later fiction would show, Lewis had an exceptionally rich imagination, he was intellectually committed to a thoroughgoing rationalism as the only grounds on which we can know anything. Barfield, by contrast, was persuaded that the faculty of Imagination was also a faculty that enabled us to know. Here we see the influence of Barfield's reading and pondering literature, especially Romantic literature, as opposed to philosophy proper, for it was through what he called "sharp" experiences from reading poetry that he began to recognize that something deeper than transient pleasure was involved in poetic language.

The something deeper was the enlargement of our awareness and hence of our understanding. It was brought about by what Barfield was to call a "felt change of consciousness" produced by certain passages of poetry. The most powerful of such passages in turn almost always involved metaphor, the carrying over of one meaning to another to bring forth a new meaning. Thus Metaphor becomes for Barfield a central concept in his thinking, not merely a decorative device used by writers to please and delight. Moreover, metaphor being a vehicle by which we enlarge our consciousness, it is therefore a vehicle that enlarges meaning, another frequently encountered term in Barfield's writing. Meaning itself, Barfield argues, is not something arbitrarily assigned by reason but is pre-existent, so to speak, because Mind precedes Matter. Another way that Barfield put this concept was to say, or have a character representing the Logos in *Unancestral Voice*, say that "Interior is anterior." Moreover, it is the Imagination that enables us to grasp, that is, to participate in Meaning in the first place.

This exalted view of imagination will be for many reminiscent of the Romantics and their conviction that we participate in Meaning through the Imagination. Wordsworth spoke of the mind as half-creating and half-perceiving; Coleridge said "we receive but what we give." Similar ideas can be found in two other strong influences on Barfield—Goethe and Steiner. Barfield says that the mind must go some distance in meeting the external objects of the world, which he sometimes calls the "particles" but more often simply "the Unrepresented," before these can have any significance. There must be an interior notion in the human mind of an object if that object is to have any reality; otherwise the external world would be a sea of undifferentiated lights and colors. And what enables the human mind to make its discriminations is the exercise of the Imagination, not a series of logical deductions from rational postulates. The obvious illustration is the example of childhood learning, which proceeds as an imaginative rather than as a logical exercise, as anyone who has ever watched a child develop can attest. On a simpler but more easily understood level, one can think of drawings and patterns of so-called optical illusions whereby the same image can take on two different shapes or reverse itself, depending, as it is said, on how you look at it. How you look at it is something going on in the mind, not a change in the external object nor in the structure of the human eye. Perhaps imaginative illusion would be a better term. Likewise, the Imagination must come into play in those drawings that "conceal" other figures, such as animals or people, that only reveal themselves to the viewer when you ponder the drawing and the shapes seem suddenly to come into being. Again, physically nothing has changed; imaginatively much has.

But, one will ask, what is this faculty of the Imagination that plays so central a role in learning and understanding and where does it come from? Barfield's answer is very like the one Coleridge advanced in his famous statement in the *Biographia Literaria* that students of literature used to know almost by heart:

"the living Power and prime Agent of all human perception, and as a repetition in the finite mind of the eternal act of creation in the infinite I AM." Elsewhere I have rendered this typically Coleridgean and typically high-sounding statement as follows:

> Coleridge is saying that the limited human mind (the finite mind) in exercising the Imagination repeats and recapitulates what the unconstrained divine mind (the infinite I AM) is eternally engaged in by creating and sustaining the universe. The universe would not be there if God did not imagine it and continue to imagine it. Put even more simply, the Imagination is what the mind does when it functions at all, and it does so by virtue of participation in the Logos—in other words, by the grace of God. Also, though Barfield will develop this concept more fully later, the Imagination works through polarity, the holding in creative tension of opposed, though not contradictory ideas. Through metaphor, the mind demonstrates the creative tension in polarity and brings forth new meaning. (Tennyson, "Owen Barfield: First and Last Inklings")

It is clear that acceptance of the Coleridgean concept of the Imagination as explicated above also means the acceptance of much else in Romantic philosophy, not least the idea of an omniscient and omnipotent intelligence at the heart of reality. One can see why these notions would be disturbing to the earnest atheist or agnostic that Lewis was striving to remain for most of the nineteen-twenties. When Barfield added Steinerian thought to the mix, he added what Lewis dismissively called the "occult," following Steiner's use but not his understanding of the word. It is rather what Barfield would call the "spiritual" or, also following Steiner, "spiritual activity." For Steiner's thinking is distinctly traditional in terms of accepting the centrality of God and also that of the Incarnation as a great turning point in human history, but it shows as well the influence of Eastern thought and of Steiner's earlier association with theosophy in its emphasis on the need for contemporary people to cultivate the capacity to commune with the spirit world from which the dominant materialistic philosophy has estranged them. This is a holistic position that is quite compatible with Barfield's revivified Romanticism and with much of the thought of Goethe, Steiner's intellectual mentor.

Barfield's achievement has been to make all of these ideas accessible to contemporary readers in a way that neither Steiner nor even Coleridge could, the former because he is so often abstruse in a highly Teutonic way that is baffling and even off-putting to many English-speaking readers, the latter because he so often seems to meander, indeed seems to be writing permanently in a digressive and fragmentary mode. Barfield likened his mission to Coleridge's. Coleridge, Barfield says, "anglicized the German philosophical inspiration" of the Romantic Movement. Barfield has continued that work and added to it the anglicizing of Steiner's philosophy. Like both Coleridge and Steiner, Barfield begins with wonder, wonder at the glory of language and the range and diversity of reality. At the same time Barfield rightly describes his work as having a "certain element of bringing down to earth" the abstruse ideas of Romanticism and Anthroposophy. He thinks this capacity for bringing ideas down to earth is especially English and that his own Englishness has been essential to what he has done.

Another way of explaining Barfield's achievement is to point out that by having come to his ideas through literature, especially poetry, and especially English poetry, Barfield expresses these ideas in a literary way rather than as a philosopher writing for other philosophers. He thus opens up a broad avenue that can be entered onto by virtually all reasonably well-educated readers. This is surely what has kept *Poetic Diction* in print for more than two-thirds of a century. Even the later, more purely philosophic and speculative works are grounded in a literary sensibility and draw heavily on Barfield's profound literary knowledge, providing a point of contact for the general reader to enter into the distinctive world of Barfield's thought. In the introduction to the third edition of his *Poetic Diction*, Barfield wrote retrospectively of that work that despite its unassuming title "it claims to present, not merely a theory of poetic diction: and not merely a theory of poetry, but a theory of knowledge." When we look at his entire body of work, we can properly say that it presents not merely a theory of knowledge but a theory of meaning and a theory of being.

A Barfield Glossary

The ideas that are associated with Barfield are, of course, best appreciated by reading Barfield whole, but because this is an anthology, it may be helpful to isolate those leading ideas and the uniquely Barfieldian terms associated with them to facilitate understanding when the reader encounters them in the selections that follow. Hence I offer here in alphabetical arrangement a baker's dozen of major Barfield terms and concepts that appear throughout his work and in the passages presented in this collection. The quoted passages within some of the definitions are Barfield's own comments on these concepts as he offered them in *Owen Barfield: Man and Meaning*, with an occasional passage from one of his works or interviews. Some readers may prefer to move directly to the Barfield selections and to return to these terms as they are encountered in reading and to use them as a reference resource.

Collective representations. These are the ideas, images, and perceptions that are broadly shared by all humans, those commonly held ways of looking at the world that make possible general communication: "everything . . . that the ordinary human being, in common with his fellow human beings, sees." Thus when one says, in whatever language, that he sees a cat on a mat or hears a dog bark anyone can grasp and share the idea.

Evolution of consciousness. The idea that human mental awareness, consciousness, has not been static but has developed over time. Barfield's study of words and language and their changes over time led him to the conviction that "it wasn't just people in the past who think like us but have different ideas, but who didn't think like us altogether at all. They had a different kind of thinking." The evolution of consciousness involves a progressive separation of the individual from the external world, although they coexist interdependently in polarity.

Figuration. The mental activity necessary to transform sense perception into a representation or a "thing" in the familiar world. The Imagination is the primary agent operating in Figuration. In treating the representations as independent of our own minds and approaching them analytically we are engaged in what Barfield calls *alpha-thinking*. When we reflect upon the representations and their relation to our own minds we are engaged in what he calls *beta-thinking*.

Imagination. The chief mode by which the human mind apprehends reality and through which it expands knowledge and awareness. "The Imagination is a form . . . of perception, if you like, a way of apprehending reality which cannot be reformulated in terms of logical sequences. It's not a rule of logic and reason, but it's not unreal for that reason." The rational faculty can increase understanding, but it cannot increase knowledge; only the Imagination can increase knowledge and expand consciousness.

Interior is anterior. Another way of saying that mind precedes matter. It is what is inside, what is essentially mental that exists before what is material comes into being. On the macrocosmic level, it means that the divine Logos created the physical world ("In the beginning was the Word"); on the microcosmic level, it means that the human mind must first exercise the interior function of the Imagination before the external world can have any meaning for it.

Meaning. The totality of signification, both abstract and concrete, that words and language convey and that, in Barfield's view, is accessible only through an act of the aesthetic Imagination. Meaning descends from the Mind or Logos and is initially an undivided perception, gradually separating into inner and outer, self and not-self, but continuing to retain the whole content of a word or group of words.

Metaphor. Metaphor is the new meaning that is revealed by the comparison of two images. "A metaphor is not the same as the meaning of the individual words; it's something between two meanings. And it can only be apprehended by the imagination, and not by the logical brain. But it's not unreal for that reason." The new meaning revealed by metaphor is itself a portion of Meaning in the larger, spiritual sense.

Mind (Logos). Not the human brain, which is however a necessary physical agent and receptor for human beings, but a pre-existent, immaterial entity from which meaning is derived. The Greek "Logos," meaning both "Mind" and "Word," is much the same as Barfield's concept of Mind. "I don't think that the mind is something that goes on in the brain. I think the brain was originally formed by the mind, or by Mind—not any particular component of Mind—and then used the brain to produce the subjective picture of the world in which we live."

Myth. For Barfield what we call myth was originally neither a metaphorical creation of poets or story-tellers, nor an early attempt to explain phenomena of nature, nor yet a projection of inner ideas onto the external world, though from our perspective it may comprehend all these. He calls what has come down to us as myth "the ghost of concrete meaning," because what we see as myth was originally experienced or lived by human beings. The primary meanings in myth were "given by Nature" and therefore could not be *known* by their first recipients but only experienced. We can no longer create Myth in that original sense, but in the highest reaches of literature we encounter the work of the mythopoeic imagination which can lift the modern consciousness to a mythic plane.

Participation. The way in which individual or collective minds take part in universal Mind. Barfield differentiates two kinds of Participation, Original and Final. *Original participation* was the mode of imaginative interaction between man and nature that "people took for granted as happening. That is why they were able to perceive mythical beings in trees and animals." The remnants of such participation are still with us but entirely unconscious in human beings while being the dominant mode of "mental" activity in animals. *Final participation* is Barfield's term for a future stage of human consciousness in which we participate in the reality given by Nature and Mind but knowingly and with the full self-consciousness that evolved out of Original Participation. "By developing the imagination . . . we could get back an awareness of participation which we no longer have, without losing our independent self-consciousness."

Polarity. Also sometimes referred to as *polarity of contraries*. The interdependent and mutually fructifying forces of objective being and consciousness. The two can be distinguished in thought but not divided one from the other. They are necessary sides of the same coin. The one force is poetic and expansive, the other prosaic and specifying; one is the world of objects, the other the world of the self. They "exist by virtue of each other *as well as* at each other's expense." On their interaction depends the evolution of consciousness.

Thinking about thinking. Barfield's expression, like beta-thinking, for his lifelong concern with how the mind works. Thus the "form" of a poem is not the shape it has on the page but a shared form "in the consciousness of the poet and his readers." In an effort to understand how such a sharing can come about, Barfield found himself thinking about how thinking takes place and in turn calling upon his readers to do the same, so that they will recognize that thinking is something beyond the mere physical activity going on in the brain. Barfield believes that the study of words reveals more about thinking than any other approach. He distinguishes thinking about thinking from the history of thought.

Unrepresented. Everything that is conceived to exist independently of consciousness, everything that is "out there" whether we recognize it or know it or not. Sometimes referred to by Barfield as the "particles." The converse of the Unrepresented is the Represented, which is what we collectively perceive and recognize as phenomena, and which is drawn from the Unrepresented.

A Barfield Chronology

1898	Owen Barfield born 9 November in Muswell Hill, North London.
1906–1916	Attends Highgate School. Meets lifelong friend A. C. Harwood.
1917–1919	During World War I serves in the Signal Service of Royal Engineers, stationed mostly in Belgium.
1918	Enters Wadham College, Oxford. Meets C. S. Lewis.
1921	Graduates with First Class Honors in English. Begins work on B. Litt degree.
1922	Encounters the philosophy and writings of Rudolf Steiner.
1923	Joins the Anthroposophical Society. Marries the dancer Maud Douie.
1925	Publishes first book, *The Silver Trumpet,* a fairy tale for children.
1926	Publishes *History in English Words.*
1927	B. Litt. thesis accepted by Oxford.
1928	Publishes *Poetic Diction.*
1929	Moves to London. Begins work in father's law firm, Barfield and Barfield. Adopts first of three children; others adopted in 1935 and 1945.
1934	B. Litt. degree awarded by Oxford.
1944	Publishes *Romanticism Comes of Age.*
1948	The play *Orpheus* performed in Sheffield. Published 1983.
1950	Publishes *This Ever Diverse Pair.*
1957	Publishes *Saving the Appearances.*

1959   Retires from legal practice.

1963   Publishes *Worlds Apart.*

1964   Serves as Visiting Professor at Drew University, the first of several such appointments at North American universities extending into the eighties.

1965   Publishes *Unancestral Voice.*

1967   Publishes *Speaker's Meaning*, composed of lectures delivered at Brandeis University.

1970   Publishes *The Case for Anthroposophy*, translation of selections from Rudolf Steiner's *Von Seelenrätseln.*

1971   Publishes *What Coleridge Thought.*

1977   Publishes *The Rediscovery of Meaning and Other Essays*, a collection of twenty essays from the fifties into the seventies.

1979   Publishes *History, Guilt and Habit*, lectures delivered in British Columbia.

1980   Death of Maud Douie Barfield.

1983   Publishes *Orpheus.*

1985   Publishes *The Year Participated*, translation of Rudolf Steiner's *Seelenkalender.*

1986   Moves from Orchard View to the Walhatch, Forest Row.

1990   Publishes *Owen Barfield on C. S. Lewis*, comprising his writings and interviews on C. S. Lewis.

1993   Publishes *A Barfield Sampler*, a selection of his poetry and fiction.

1995   Subject of documentary video *Owen Barfield: Man and Meaning.*

1997   Death of Owen Barfield, 14 December in Forest Row, East Sussex.

Bibliography

Books by Owen Barfield

The first date, given in parentheses, for each book is that of initial publication. Subsequent information is that of the most recent reprint or revised edition. This list is chronological by date of first publication. Only books written, edited, or translated by Owen Barfield are included. For a bibliography of all of Barfield's writings up to 1975, see G. B. Tennyson, "The Works of Owen Barfield," in Sugerman, *Evolution of Consciousness*, pp. 225–239. There is as yet no published bibliography of articles after 1975.

The Silver Trumphet. (1925) Longmont, Colo.: Bookmakers Guild, Inc. 1986. Edited with an Afterword by Marjorie L. Mead. With illustrations by Josephine Spence.

History in English Words. (1926) Edinburgh: Floris Books, 1985. Reprint of 1967 revised edition containing a Foreword by W. H. Auden.

Poetic Diction: A Study in Meaning. (1928) Middletown, Conn.: Wesleyan University Press, 1973. Third edition with an Afterword by the author.

Romanticism Comes of Age. (1944) Middletown, Conn.: Wesleyan University Press, 1986. Second expanded edition.

This Ever Diverse Pair. (1950) Edinburgh: Floris Books, 1985. Reprint of first edition with an Introduction by Walter de la Mare.

Saving the Appearances: A Study in Idolatry. (1957) Middletown, Conn.: Wesleyan University Press, 1988. Second edition with an Introduction by the author.

Worlds Apart: A Dialogue of the Sixties. (1963) Middletown, Conn.: Wesleyan University Press, 1971.

Unancestral Voice. (1965) London: Faber and Faber, 1965.

Speaker's Meaning. (1967) Middletown, Conn.: Wesleyan University Press, 1967.

The Case for Anthroposophy: Being Extracts from Von Seelenrätseln By Rudolf Steiner. (1970) London: Rudolf Steiner Press, 1970. Selected, translated, arranged, and with an Introduction by Owen Barfield.

What Coleridge Thought. (1971) Middletown, Conn.: Wesleyan University Press 1971.

The Rediscovery of Meaning and Other Essays. (1977) Middletown, Conn.: Wesleyan University Press, 1977. Reprint 1985.

History, Guilt, and Habit. (1979) Middletown, Conn.: Wesleyan University Press, 1979. Foreword by G. B. Tennyson.

The Voice of Cecil Harwood: A Miscellany. (1979) London: Rudolf Steiner Press, 1979. Edited by Owen Barfield.

Orpheus: A Poetic Drama. (1983) West Stockbridge, Mass.: The Lindisfarne Press, 1983. Edited, with an Afterword by John C. Ulreich, Jr.

The Year Participated, Being Rudolf Steiner's Calendar of the Soul *Translated and Paraphrased for an English Ear.* (1985) London: Rudolf Steiner Press, 1985. Translated by Owen Barfield.

Owen Barfield on C. S. Lewis. (1989) Middletown, Conn.: Wesleyan University Press, 1989. Edited, with an Introduction by G. B. Tennyson.

A Barfield Sampler: Poetry and Fiction by Owen Barfield. (1993). Albany, N.Y.: State University of New York Press, 1993. Edited by Jeanne Clayton Hunter and Thomas Kranidas, with an Afterword by Owen Barfield.

Books, Articles, Research Sources about Owen Barfield

The following selected listing is arranged alphabetically by author or research source and is limited to works that are primarily about Barfield or that contain substantial sections or materials treating Barfield. Articles that appeared in *To-Wards* are not listed separately, as the journal itself is devoted to Barfield. Likewise regular updates on Barfield that appeared in *Seven* are not listed separately, but some individual articles are.

Adey, Lionel. *C. S. Lewis's "Great War" with Owen Barfield.* University of Victoria: English Literary Studies, 1978. No. 14 ELS Monograph Series.

———. "A Response to Dr. Thorson," *CSL: Bulletin of the New York C. S. Lewis Society,* 15, no.1 (1984), 6–10.

———. *C. S. Lewis: Writer, Dreamer, and Mentor.* Grand Rapids, Mich.: William B. Eerdmans Publishing Company, 1998.

Avens, Roberts. *Imagination Is Reality: Western Nirvana in Jung, Hillman, Barfield, and Cassirer.* Irving, Tex.: Spring Publications, Inc., 1980.

Brown, Norman O. *Apocalypse and/or Metamorphosis.* Berkeley: University of California Press, 1991.

Carpenter, Humphrey. *The Inklings: C. S. Lewis, J. R. R. Tolkien, Charles Williams, and Their Friends.* Boston: Houghton Mifflin, 1979.

Colbert, James. "The Common Ground of Lewis and Barfield," *CSL: Bulletin of the New York C. S. Lewis Society,* 6, no. 10 (1975), 15–18.

Flieger, Verlyn. *Splintered Light: Logos and Language in Tolkien's World.* Grand Rapids, Mich.: William B. Eerdmans Publishing Co., 1983.

Fulweiler, Howard W. "The Other Missing Link: Owen Barfield and the Scientific Imagination," *Renascence: Essays on Values in Literature,* 46 (1993), 39–55.

Grant, Patrick. *Six Modern Authors and Problems of Belief.* New York: Harper and Row, Inc., Barnes and Noble Import Division, 1979.

Hipolito, T. A. "Owen Barfield's *Poetic Diction,*" *Renascence: Essays on Values in Literature,* 46 (1993), 3–39.

Hooper, Walter. *C. S. Lewis: A Companion and Guide.* New York: HarperSanFrancisco, 1996.

———. *Through Joy and Beyond: A Pictorial Biography of C. S. Lewis*. New York: Macmillan, 1982.

Hunter, Jeanne Clayton, "Owen Barfield: A Change of Consciousness," *The Nassau Review*, 4 (1984), 93–101.

———. "Owen Barfield: Christian Apologist," *Renascence: Essays on Values in Literature*, 36 (1984), 171–179.

Knight, Gareth. *The Magical World of the Inklings: J. R. R. Tolkien, C. S. Lewis, Charles Williams, Owen Barfield*. London: Element, 1991.

Kranidas, Thomas. "C. S. Lewis and the Poetry of Owen Barfield," *The Bulletin of the New York C. S. Lewis Society*, 12, no. 2 (1980), 1–2.

———. "The Defiant Lyricism of Owen Barfield," *Seven: An Anglo-American Literary Review*, 6 (1985), 23–33.

Lavery, David. "The Owen Barfield Web Site." An Internet site devoted to Owen Barfield. Established and maintained by David Lavery at http://www.mtsu.edu/~dlavery/toc.htm

Lewis, C. S. *All My Road Before Me: The Diary of C. S. Lewis, 1922–1927*. Ed. Walter Hooper. Foreword by Owen Barfield. New York: Harcourt Brace Jovanovich, 1991.

———. *Surprised by Joy: The Shape of My Early Life*. New York: Harcourt, Brace & World, 1955.

Miller, Ruth. *Saul Bellow: A Biography of the Imagination*. New York: St. Martin's Press, 1991.

Morris, Francis J. and Ronald C. Wendling. "Coleridge and the 'Great Divide' between C. S. Lewis and Owen Barfield, *Studies in the Literary Imagination*, 22 (1989), 149–159.

Nemerov, Howard. "Introduction," *Poetic Diction: A Study in Meaning*, by Owen Barfield (New York: McGraw-Hill, 1964), 1–9.

Potts, Donna. *Howard Nemerov and Objective Idealism: the Influence of Owen Barfield*. Columbia: University of Missouri Press, 1994.

Reilly, R. J. *Romantic Religion: A Study in the Work of Owen Barfield, C. S. Lewis, and J. R. R. Tolkien*. Athens: University of Georgia Press, 1971.

Schenkel, Elmar. "Interview mit Owen Barfield," *Inklings-Jahrbuch für Literatur und Ästhetik*, 11 (1993), 23–38.

Seven: An Anglo-American Literary Review. An annual devoted to the work of George MacDonald, G. K., Chesterton, C. S. Lewis, J. R. R. Tolkien, Charles Williams, Dorothy L. Sayers, Owen Barfield. Published by Wheaton College, Illinois. 1980–continuing.

Sloan, Douglas. *Insight-Imagination: The Emancipation of Thought and the Modern World*. Westport, Conn.: Greenwood Press, 1983.

Sugerman, Shirley, ed. *Evolution of Consciousness: Studies in Polarity*. Middletown, Conn.: Wesleyan University Press, 1976. [A *Festschrift* containing an interview, three tributes, thirteen essays, and a bibliography of Barfield's writings to 1975.]

Tennyson, G. B. "Owen Barfield and the Rebirth of Meaning," *Southern Review*, 5 (1969), 42–57.

———. "Owen Barfield: First and Last Inklings," *The World & I*, April 1990, 540–555.

———. "On Location, Without Tears," *California Political Review*, 5, no. 1 (1994), 30–33.

————, producer. "Owen Barfield: Man and Meaning." [Documentary Video] Encino, Cal.: OwenArts, 1995.

————. "The Rebirth of Wonder," *The Catholic World Report*, June 1997, 35–36.

Thorson, Stephen. "Knowing and Being in C. S. Lewis 'Great War' with Owen Barfield," *CSL: Bulletin of the New York C. S. Lewis Society*, 15, no. 1 (1983), 1–9.

————. "Reply" [to Lionel Adey], *CSL: Bulletin of the New York C. S. Lewis Society*, 15, no. 5 (1984), 10–11

————. "Lewis and Barfield on Imagination," *Mythlore*, 17, no. 2 (1990), 12–18, 32.

To-Wards. A Journal devoted to the work of Owen Barfield, Coleridge, Goethe, and Rudolf Steiner. Published and Edited by Clifford Monks. Northridge and Fair Oaks, Cal. 1977–1989. Ceased publication.

Wade Collection. Wheaton College, Illinois. Repository of materials relating to the seven authors addressed by the annual publication, *Seven*, cited above.

Language and Literature

Both as writer and thinker Barfield grounds his thought in language and literature. It is the subject of his earliest writing and remains throughout his career the seedbed from which his thinking grows. It was during his Oxford years that he realized that he had "very sharp" experiences in reading poetry and as a result began pondering intensely the nature of these experiences. He determined that they lay in "a felt change of consciousness" brought about by the way in which the language of poetry alters our awareness and ultimately our knowledge. This led to a concentrated study of the development of language and the nature of poetic diction. Such study led in turn to his interest in the nature of imagination, of meaning, of perception, and of the evolution of consciousness. The following selections represent Barfield's characteristic thinking, early and late, about language and literature, imagination and perception, poetry and the poet. The titles of short passages have been supplied by the editor.

from *Poetic Diction*

Metaphor

I

In the West, since Plato's time, the study of language has been developed mainly by grammarians and logicians. It is true that about a hundred and fifty years ago a more historical conception of philology suddenly began to spread rapidly over Europe. But the emphasis was still, until recently, on the external *forms* of words. The result is, as far as I am aware, that no really profound study has yet been made of *meaning*—that is to say, of the meanings of individual words. This subject—Semantics, as it is now commonly called—makes its first, embryonic appearance as a cautionary chapter following the chapter on Terms in a logical textbook, and it is not until long after that it acquires a separate existence, and even a hint of wings, in the work of writers like Archbishop Trench, Max Müller, and, today, Mr. Pearsall Smith.

The extraordinarily intimate connection between, language and thought (the Greek word λόγος combined, as we should say, both meanings) might lead one to expect that the philosophers at least would have turned their attention to the subject long ago. And so, indeed, they did, but with a curiously disproportionate amount of interest. The cause of this deficiency is, I think, to be found in the fact that Western philosophy, from Aristotle onwards, is itself a kind of offspring of Logic. To anyone attempting to construct a metaphysic in strict accordance with the canons and categories of formal Logic, the fact that the meanings of words change, not only from age to age, but from context to context, is certainly interesting; but it is interesting solely because it is a nuisance.

I will try to make this clearer by a comparison. The financial mysteries of 'inflation' and 'deflation' may likewise be said to 'interest' the practising merchant. But that interest is, for the most part, of a limited sort. Since money is the very basis of all his operations, he has, I think it can be said, an instinctive distaste for the mere possibility that money-units themselves should be found to have only an arbitrary 'subjective' value—that they should prove to be simply

5

cross-sections of an endless process taking place in time. If that is true, all is lost. The dykes are opened. Like magic, he sees shrewd practical maxims turning into rarified academic theories, and a comparatively simple and intelligible system of acknowledged *facts* ('the economic verities') having to be rigged with all sorts of super-subtle reservations and *ceteris paribus*'s, before it will bear the faintest relation to contemporary realities.

What money is to the conservative economist, words are to the conservative philosopher. For the conception of money as a 'symbol of barter' and the conception of words as the 'names of things' are, both alike, not so much untrue as 'out of date'; and for the same reason: not because the advance of science has revealed avoidable ancient errors, but because the facts themselves have changed. Once upon a time money really was an immediate substitute for barter, and once upon a time words could really be the expression on the face of concrete reality. Error—or, at best, waste of energy—is in both cases the fruit of unwillingness to recognize essential change. The spell of the immediate past proves too strong; and, just as the stubborn economist, with his eyes fixed on that past, turns his back on all new-fangled nonsense and nails his colours stoutly to the mast of *stabilization*, so the philosopher waves aside the study of meaning and still maintains a desperate faith in the ancient system of *definitions*. In both instances, it may be that somewhere—deep down in the unconscious—a voice has cried *Lass mich schlafen*!

Whatever the cause, nearly all that has hitherto been said on the semantic aspect of language has been said from one point of view only. And from that point of view it has been said wonderfully well. The original twist was given by the Father of Logic himself, when he included in his *Organon* a brief treatise *De Interpretatione*, and since then the conception of language as the prime material of logical constructions has been developed many times with infinite delicacy. It is difficult, for example, to praise too highly the limpid clarity of the third book of Locke's *Essay on the Human Understanding*; and even as recently as the last century Mr. Bosanquet found memorable things to say in the opening chapters of his *Logic*. It may be that other modern philosophers have done as well, or better.

We have had, then, to the full, language as it is grasped by logical mind. What we have not had—or what we have only had in hints and flashes—is language as it is grasped by poetic mind. The fundamental difference between logical and poetic mind (which has very little to do with the fashionable contrast between Poetry and Science) will appear farther in the course of this book, wherein I have myself attempted to sketch the way in which a poetic understanding would approach the problem. I have, however, made no attempt to write what I should so much like to see written—a true, poetic history and philosophy of language. On the contrary, it has been my object to avoid (except perhaps in two of the Appendices) entering deeper into the nature of language than is absolutely necessary, in order to throw on 'Poetry', in the usual literary sense of that word, the kind of light which, I think, needs to be thrown.

2

The most conspicuous point of contact between meaning and poetry is *metaphor*. For one of the first things that a student of etymology—even quite an amateur student—discovers for himself is that every modern language, with its thousands of abstract terms and its nuances of meaning and association, is *apparently* nothing, from beginning to end, but an unconscionable tissue of dead, or petrified, metaphors. If we trace the meanings of a great many words—or those of the elements of which they are composed—about as far back as etymology can take us, we are at once made to realize that an overwhelming proportion, if not all, of them referred in earlier days to one of these two things—a solid, sensible object, or some animal (probably human) activity. Examples abound on every page of the dictionary. Thus, an apparently objective scientific term like *elasticity*, on the one hand, and the metaphysical *abstract*, on the other, are both traceable to verbs meaning 'draw' or 'drag'. *Centrifugal* and *centripetal* are composed of a noun meaning 'a goad' and verbs signifying 'to flee' and 'to seek' respectively; *epithet, theme, thesis, anathema, hypothesis*, etc., go back to a Greek verb, to put', and even *right* and *wrong*, it seems, once had the meanings of 'stretched' and so 'straight' and 'wringing' or 'sour'. Some philologists, looking still further back into the past, have resolved these two classes into one, but this is immaterial to the point at issue.

'Nihil in intellectu', wrote Locke, 'quod non prius fuerit in sensu.' And Anatole France, in his *Jardin d'Épicure* has adorned this theory of thought with a characteristically modern jumble of biological, anthropological, and etymological ideas:

> Et qu'est-ce-que penser? Et comment pense-t-on? Nous pensons avec des mots; cela seul est sensuel et ramène à la nature. Songez-y, un metaphysicien n'a pour constituer le système du monde, que le cri perfectionné des singes et des chiens. Ce qu'il appelle spéculation profonde et méthode transcendante, c'est de mettre bout à bout, dans un ordre arbitraire, les onomatopées qui criaient la faim, la peur et l'amour dans les forêts primitives, et auxquelles se sont attachées peu à peu des significations qu'on croit abstraites quand elles sont seulement relachées.
>
> N'ayez pas peur que cette suite de petits cris éteints et affaiblis qui composent un livre de philosophie nous en apprenne trop sur l'univers pour que nous ne puissions plus y vivre. Dans la nuit où nous sommes tous, le savant se cogne au mur, tandis que l'ignorant reste tranquillement au milieu de la chambre.

Later on, in an imaginary dialogue between a metaphysician and an etymologist, the latter kindly offers to resolve into its elements the sentence 'L'âme possède Dieu dans la mesure où elle participe de l'absolu'. When he has finished with it, it reads: 'Le souffle est assis sur celui qui brille, au boisseau du don qu'il reçoit en ce qui est tout délié'.

3

Anatole France's etymologist, then, sees language as beginning with simple, purely perceptual meanings, and building up, by metaphor, a series of meanings which pretend to be 'abstract,' when they are really only vague. Now it will at once be seen that the conception of the primitive mind, on which this imagination is based, would make it correspond exactly with the state of consciousness into which the reader was asked to throw himself . . . as the result of a fictitious 'stroke'. So that the process by which the words mentioned above have acquired the meanings which they now possess would, on this view, be identical with the process by which Shelley was able to write:

My soul is an enchanted boat . . . (Ext. V)

To carry the illustration further: should the feeling and idea which these lines embody ever become sufficiently well-known and widespread, one can easily perceive how in a few hundred, or in a few thousand years, the word *boat*, or perhaps the phrase *enchanted boat* might lose its present meaning and call up to the minds of our posterity, not a vessel, but the concept 'soul' as enriched by Shelley's imagination. A new word, abridged perhaps to something like *chambote*, might grow into being. Language actually abounds, as we shall see, in meanings, and is not lacking in words, which have come into it in just this way.

We are tempted to infer that, as language grows older, it must *necessarily* become richer and richer as poetic material; it must become intrinsically more and more poetic. The bald sentence: 'Le souffle est assis sur celui qui brille, au boisseau du don qu'il reçoit en ce qui est tout délié', is palpably prosaic, and its original can only begin to arouse imagination and feeling at whatever point in time *âme* begins to add to its material meaning a vague suggestion of 'something like breath indeed, but more living, sentient, inward—a part of my Self', and *Dieu* to acquire the signification of 'something like sky, yet more living, corresponding, therefore, to something in me'. Thus, from the primitive meanings assumed by the etymologist, we are led to fancy metaphor after metaphor sprouting forth and solidifying into new meanings—vague, indeed, yet evocative of more and more subtle echoes and reactions. From being mere labels for material objects, words gradually turn into magical charms. Out of a catalogue of material facts is developed—thanks to the efforts of forgotten primitive geniuses—all that we know today as 'poetry'.

Was it really like this? To have observed a resemblance between, say, a straight stick and an inner feeling, and to have used the name of the stick to describe the feeling is indeed to have made a long step forward. From now onward—so we perhaps imagine—upon the chaotic darkness in which it first awoke, human consciousness begins to cast its own brilliant and increasing light. It flings its beams further and further into the night. 'With the beginning of language', writes Ludwig Noiré, a disciple of Max Müller, 'the period of spiritual creation began; the light glimmered feebly and inconspicuously at first which now illumines heaven and earth with its rays—the divine light of reason . . .' and he adds, still more enthusiastically:

the first step is herewith hewn, by the joint toil of reason and speech, in the hard rock, where a second and then others must follow, till aeons hence the lofty summit is reached, and reason enthroned on high sees all the beneath as the theatre where her might and glory is displayed, and ventures forth upon new flights through the unexplored realms of heaven not even here without a clue, any more than at the hour of her birth, afforded by her own—but now purely ideal—constructions.

And Shelley: 'Metaphorical language marks the before unapprehended relations of things and perpetuates their apprehension until words, which represent them, become, through time, signs for portions or classes of thought, instead of pictures of integral thoughts.'

Here again we seem to have a picture of language becoming, intrinsically, more and more poetic; for who could make poetry out of a disjointed list of unrelated percepts? And what is the very essence of poetry if it is not this 'metaphorical language'—this marking of the before unapprehended relations of things?

4

Yes, but is it poetry, or reason that is being exalted? Shelley, in the passage just quoted, seems hardly to distinguish the one from the other. Let us actually examine the sentiments of those who have thought historically, not on language, but on poetry itself. 'As civilization advances', said Macaulay, 'poetry almost necessarily declines.' Peacock's *Four Ages of Poetry*, notwithstanding its irony at the expense of 'progress', is a genuine dirge on the gradual murder of the Muse by that very Reason, whose 'divine light' the philologist was constrained to hymn. Mr. Courthope, in his *Liberal Movement in English Literature*, qualifies a similar opinion by the subtle distinction: 'As civilization advances, the matter for poetic creation diminishes, while the powers of poetic expression are multiplied'. And even to Shelley, who wrote with the express purpose of refuting Peacock, it is in 'the infancy' of society that 'every author is a poet, because language itself is poetry'. There is no need to go further for examples. They are found everywhere. Thus the general view is the exact opposite of what one would be led to expect. Indeed, nothing in the world seems so likely to turn a man into a *laudator temporis acti* as an historical survey of poetry. Even today it remains a moot point among the critics whether the very first extant poet of our Western civilization has ever been surpassed for the grandeur and sublimity of his diction.

Yet if language had indeed advanced, by continual accretion of metaphor, from roots of speech with the simplest material reference, to the complex organism which we know today, it would surely be *today* that every author is a poet— today, when a man cannot utter a dozen words without wielding the creations of a hundred named and nameless poets. Given the necessary consciousness of this (i.e. an historical knowledge of, and feeling for, language),[1] our pleasure in such a sentence as—for example—'I simply love that idea' should be infinitely more sublime than our pleasure—as far as the language itself is concerned—in reading Homer. How is it then that, in actual fact, we find this almost universal consciousness that the golden age of poetry is in the *infancy* of society? Bearing in mind our conclusion that *pleasure* in poetic diction depends on the difference between two planes or levels of consciousness, we can indeed see why language, at an early stage, should delight us. But what follows? If this theory of the growth of language, by means of metaphor, from simple perceptual meanings to complex psychic ones is a correct theory, it follows that our pleasure in such relatively primitive diction ought to be of a poor and unsatisfying nature, compared to our pleasure in the diction of a modern writer who wields these wonderful meanings. It should be more akin to the pleasure we take in such primitive locutions as Example I, where the change of consciousness is effected by contraction rather than expansion—as for example, by emphasizing those purely external, pictorial relations of things, which sophistication—saving the painter's case—too often induces us to ignore. Is this true? We know at once that it is not. We know from first-hand experience that resemblances between the Greek poetry of Homer's day, or even the Anglo-Saxon of the author of *Beowulf*'s, and, say, pidgin-English—though tell-tale—are yet in point of value so slight as to be almost negligible. We find, in fact, that this old poetry has the knowledge-value, as well as the pleasure-value, and has it in a high degree.

Now, to the genuine critic, the spiritual fact of his own aesthetic experience, when once he knows inwardly that it is purged of all personal affection,[2] must have at least equal weight with any reported historical or scientific facts which

---

1. Language reserves one satisfaction for the observer, all the more lively because it is not sought after: the satisfaction, namely, of feeling a metaphor, whose value has not hitherto been understood, suddenly open and reveal itself. Bréal; *Semantics*, p. 129.

2. That is to say, when he knows that his pleasure arises from the *proper activity* of imagination and not from any incidental suggestion of pleasurable sensation—in the case of metaphor, when it is the pure *content* of the image, and not only the *reference*, which delights.

may be placed beside it. Beyond that, it must be his aim, as it is the aim of all knowledge, to reconcile or relate conceptually all the elements included in his perceptual experience; among this latter he must number his own aesthetic reactions.

5

Since, then, ancient poetry is simply ancient language at its best, we must now try and discover why it is that this best ancient language, when it is compared with the best modern language, so often appears, not simply as naïve, but, on the contrary, as endued with an extraordinary richness and splendour. Where, we must ask, is the fallacy in that proud conception of the evolution of language from simplicity and darkness to complexity and light?

It should be remembered that we are here dealing, not with 'poetry', which includes the creative activity itself, but with 'poetic diction'—that is to say, with the language of poetic compositions, as we actually find them written in different ages. Someone might come forward and say: But this is nonsense. You are leaving out of account the one thing that really matters and making a mystery of what is left. When people say that Homer has never been surpassed, they mean precisely what they say—that he has never been surpassed. His poetry is sublime because he himself was sublime, and if there has been no such great poetry since, it is because there has been no such great man; or, at any rate, if such a man has lived, he cannot have turned his attention to poetry.

The reply to such an objection would be threefold: (i) It has already been pointed out that there are certain elements in poetic diction which are clearly *not* traceable to any identifiable individual. (ii) Homer is in any case a bad example to choose, as his individual existence is disputed. (iii) This problem of the responsibility of individuals for poetic value is just one of the most important questions which a theory of poetic diction has to attack. To make any assumptions beforehand would be to beg it. The only way to start with an unprejudiced mind is to take actual examples of poetic diction . . . and to work backward from them to their sources. This method does not exclude the possibility of arriving *eventually* at the conclusion expressed in the objection—that the poetic element in language is, and always has been, the result of individual effort, but we have certainly not arrived at that conclusion yet. The question will come up for discussion, in fact, in its proper place.

A hundred and fifty years ago Dr. Hugh Blair wrote in his *Lectures on Rhetoric*:

> We are apt, upon a superficial view, to imagine that those modes of expression which are called Figures of Speech are among the chief refinements of Speech, not invented till after language had advanced to its late periods, and mankind were

brought into a polished state; and that then they were devised by orators and rhetoricians. The contrary of this is the truth. Mankind never employed so many Figures of Speech, as when they had hardly any words for expressing their meaning. For, first, the want of proper names for every object, obliged them to use one name for many; and, of course, to express themselves by comparisons, metaphors, allusions and all those substituted forms of Speech, which render Language figurative. Next, as the objects with which they were most conversant, were the sensible, material objects around them, names would be given to these objects long before words were invented for signifying the dispositions of the mind, or any sort of moral and intellectual ideas. Hence, the early language of men being entirely made up of words descriptive of sensible objects, it became, of necessity, extremely metaphorical . . .

Now this appears to be conception of language which, since the time of Locke, has been held by most people who have troubled to write on the subject. Yet it proves (unless one stretches the meanings of such words as *metaphor* and *trope* intolerably far) to be quite unreasonable. For how it is arrived at? In this way: (i) The theorist beholds metaphors and similitudes being invented by poets and others in his own time. (ii) Examining the more recent history of language, he finds many examples of such metaphors having actually become a part of language, that is to say, having become meanings.[3] (iii) Delving deeper still into etymology, he discovers that all our words were at one time 'the names of sensible objects', and (iv) he jumps to the conclusion that they therefore, at that time, had *no other meaning*.[4] From these four observations he proceeds to deduce, fifthly, that the application of these names of sensible objects to what we now call *insensible* objects was deliberately 'metaphorical'.

In other words, although, when he moves backwards through the history of language, he finds it becoming more and more *figurative* with every step, yet he has no hesitation in assuming a period—still further back—when it was not figurative at all! To supply, therefore, the missing link in his chain of linguistic evolution, he proceeds to people the 'infancy of society' with an exalted race of amateur poets. Thus, Max Müller in his *Science of Language* speaks with confidence of the 'metaphorical period', describing how:

> *Spiritus* in Latin meant originally blowing, or wind. But when the principle of life within man or animal had to be named, its outward sign, namely the breath of the mouth, was naturally chosen to express it. Hence in Sanskrit asu, breath and life; in Latin *spiritus*, breath and life. Again, when it was perceived that there was

3. So M. Bréal (*Semantics*): 'There is the same difference between the tropes of language and the metaphors of poets as between a product in common use and a recent conquest of science'.

4. See Blair, quoted above: and compare Locke (*Human Understanding*, III, i. 5): '*Spirit*, in its primary signification, is breath, *angel* a messenger', etc., etc.

something else to be named, not the mere animal life, but that which was supported by this animal life, the same word was chosen, in the modern Latin dialects, to express the spiritual as opposed to the mere material or animal element in man. All this is a metaphor.

We read in the Veda, ii. 3, 4: 'Who saw the first-born when he who had no form (lit. bones) bore him that had form? Where was the breath (asuh), the blood (asrik), the self (atma) of the earth? Who went to ask this from any that knew it?'

Here breath, blood, self are so many attempts at expression what we should now call 'cause'.

It would be difficult to conceive anything more perverse than this paragraph; there is, indeed, something painful in the spectacle of so catholic and enthusiastic a scholar as Max Müller seated so firmly on the saddle of etymology, with his face set so earnestly towards the tail of the beast. He seems to have gone out of his way to seek for impossibly modern and abstract concepts to project into that luckless dustbin of pseudo-scientific fantasies—the mind of primitive man. Not only 'cause', we are to suppose, was within the range of his intellection, but 'something', 'principle of life', 'outward sign', 'mere animal life', 'spiritual as opposed to mere material', and heaven knows what else. Perverse; and yet for that very reason useful; for it pushes to a conclusion as logical as it is absurd, a view of mental history, which, still implicit in much that passes muster as anthropology, psychology, etc.—even as ordinary common sense—might easily prejudice an understanding of my meaning, if it were ignored without comment.

The truth is, of course, that Max Müller, like his predecessors, had only been able to look at 'meaning', and the history of meaning, from one imperfect point of view—that of abstraction. For in spite of frequent flights of imagination, the main road of his approach to language was the regulation one from philosophical logic or logical philosophy. Thus, he was an enthusiastic disciple of Kant—even to the Herculean extent of translating the *Critique of Pure Reason* into English. The full meanings of words are flashing, iridescent shapes like flames—ever-flickering vestiges of the slowly evolving consciousness beneath them. To the Locke-Müller-France way of thinking, on the contrary, they appear as solid chunks with definite boundaries and limits, to which other chunks may be added as occasion arises. Nevertheless, it is a mistake, and a mistake that is commonly made, to underrate Max Müller's semantic flights. The marvel is that with his materials and antecedents he was able to fly so high. Thus, even to this very question of metaphor he has an interesting contribution to make. We find him drawing a novel distinction between *radical* and *poetical* metaphors:

I call it a radical metaphor when a root which means to shine is applied to form the names, not only of the fire or the sun, but of the spring of the year, the morning light, the brightness of thought, or the joyous outburst of hymns of praise. Ancient languages are brimful of such metaphors, and under the microscope of the etymologist almost every word discloses traces of its first metaphorical conception.

From this we must distinguish *poetical* metaphor, namely, when a noun or verb, ready made and assigned to one definite object or action, is transferred poetically to another object or action. For instance, when the rays of the sun are called the hands or fingers of the sun. (*Science of Language*, p. 451)

Language and Poetry

I

Thus, a history of language written, not from the logician's, but from the poet's point of view, would proceed somewhat in the following manner: it would see in the concrete vocabulary which has left us the mythologies the world's first 'poetic diction'. Moving forward, it would come, after a long interval, to the earliest ages of which we have any written record—the time of the *Vedas* in India, the time of the *Iliad* and *Odyssey* in Greece. And at this stage it would find meaning still suffused with myth, and Nature all alive in the thinking of man.

The gods are never far below the surface of Homer's language—hence its unearthly sublimity. They are the springs of action and stand in place of what we think of as personal qualities. Agamemnon is warned of Zeus in a dream, Telemachus, instead of 'plucking up courage', meets the goddess Athene and walks with her into the midst of the hostile suitors, and the whole earth buds into blossom, as Zeus is mingled with Hera on the nuptial couch.

Millions of spiritual beings walk the earth. . . . And these august beings, speaking now from the mouths of the characters, and again passing and repassing invisible among them, dissolve into a sort of *largior aether*, which the Homeric heroes breathe all day; so that we, too, breathe it in the language they speak—in their ῥοδοδάκτυλος ἠώς, their ἱερὸν ἦμαρ in the sinewy strength of those thundering epithets which, for all their conventionality, never fail to impart life and warmth to the lines.

Meanwhile, the historian would note how the antipoetic, or purely rational, had begun to take effect. He would find meanings splitting up in the manner previously described and language beginning to change its character, to lose its intrinsic life. He might note, also, that the increased action of this principle was accompanied by the birth of hitherto unknown antitheses, such as those between truth and myth, between prose and poetry, and again between an objective and a subjective world; so that now, for the first time, it becomes possible to distinguish the *content* of a word from its *reference*.

He might then, perhaps, look to the history of philosophy for some indication of the moment at which the ascending rational principle and the descending poetic principle (for, in certain respects, we can think of them as of two buckets in a well) are passing one another. If so, I think he would fix on the prominence in men's minds of the metaphysical problem of 'universals'. For when the number of general ideas arrived at by abstraction . . . is rapidly increasing, and yet there is still a strong sense of the old, concrete, unitary meanings, it is natural that the coexistence of two kinds of universal should arouse confusion. Are universals real beings, it is asked, or mere classifying abstractions in the minds of men, evolved for the convenience of quick thinking? The latter (Nominalist-Conceptualist) verdict, if applied indiscriminately to *all* universals, may be compared with the error, . . . by which an adult thinker reads his own generalizations into a child's mind.

Thus the old, instinctive consciousness of single meanings, which comes down to us as the Greek myths, is already fighting for its life by Plato's time as the doctrine of Platonic Ideas (not 'abstract', though this word is often erroneously used in English translations); Aristotle's logic and his Categories, *as interpreted by his followers*, then tend to concentrate attention exclusively on the *abstract* universals, and so to destroy the balance; and then again the forms and entelechies of Aristotle are brought to life in the poetry of Dante as the Heavenly Hierarchies; and, yet again, Nominalism, with its legacy of modern empirical philosophy and science, obscures men's vision of all but the abstract universals.[1]

Thus would he find the general progress obscured and varied by all sorts of particular forces operating in the history of civilization. For example, if he chose the Aryan community of speakers as his canvas, he would have to consider, on the one hand, the history of Aryan language and Aryan consciousness as a whole, and, on the other, the rise and decay—within that single entity—of the various national languages and national spirits among which it has been distributed. Each of these, he would probably find, repeats in its own compass, and in varying degrees, the broad lines of evolution of the whole. Within certain

1. Naturally, this sketchy account must be met half-way, and with considerable delicacy of apprehension, if it is to have any truth and meaning. Any rigidly regular development of the two principles is out of the question. Innate differences between mind and mind, together with the increasing intercommunication of record thought and its transmission from past to present, are always at work to spread the process. The two principles themselves, however, and their historical development, are none the less realities because, like the aesthetic values, they do not force themselves on the attention of the percipient, but await the exertion of his own imaginative activity.

limits, we should be brought to see that, in poetic character, the Latin language is to the Greek as the later stages of Greek are to its own earlier stages; and, also, as the later stages of English are to its earlier stages.

2

For example, there is a certain half-spurious element in the appreciation of poetry, with which everyone will be familiar, when one takes delight, not only in what is said and in the way it is said, but in a sense of difficulties overcome—of an obstreperous medium having been masterfully subdued. It is a kind of architectural pleasure. One feels that the poet is working in solid masses, not in something fluid. One is reminded by one's very admiration that 'words are stubborn things'. In English literature Milton's verse presents a particularly striking example of what I mean; and I select a quotation almost at random, hoping that it will make my meaning clear:

> Fall'n Cherube, to be weak is miserable
> Doing or Suffering: but of this be sure,
> To do ought good never will be our task,
> But ever to do ill our sole delight,
> As being the contrary to his high will
> Whom we resist. If then his Providence
> Out of our evil seek to bring forth good,
> Our labour must be to pervert that end,
> And out of good still to find means of evil.

It is demonstrable that this architectural element in poetic diction is something which only arises at a certain stage in the development of a language. It is there in the iambics of the Attic dramatists, but not in Homer's hexameters; yet it is not entirely foreign to the spirit of the hexameter, for it is conspicuous in Virgil:

> At regina dolos (quis fallere possit amantem?)
> Praesensit motusque excepit prima futuros,
> Omnia tuta timens. Eadem impia Fama furenti
> Detulit armari classem cursumque parari.

Indeed Virgil's poetry is an excellent example. It is in his most famous and most often-quoted passages that we find that exquisite hint, as it were, of the jig-saw puzzle; and, along with it, that exact use of quantitative values and the marvellous interweaving of these with the different stresses which would normally be given to the sentences, in accordance with their emotional content.

This subtle music is the very life of the *Æneid*. But it is a life that is imparted by Virgil himself, in his arrangement of the words, rather than one inherent in the Latin language. There is quite another kind of life in the *Iliad*—that of the old Greek language itself. Compare the vigour and brilliance of Homer's epithets with the best equivalents that Virgil could find for them: *celer* for πτερόεις, *curvæ naves* for νῆες ἀμφιελίσσαι, *flumine pulchro* for καλλρρόῳ ποτάμῳ, etc. And we find the same contrast—a contrast, as it were between movement and rest—working itself out in broader curves in the descriptions of the shields (*Iliad*, xviii and *Æneid*, viii, 607–731), where Homer instinctively translates the description of motionless objects into action, while Virgil finds it natural to employ the static mode of 'here is . . .', 'there is . . .'.[2]

There is a strong tendency in the Greek language, with its reckless profusion of double epithets, its looser word-order, and its nervous, restless twitchings of grammatical particles, to make itself felt as a living, muscular organism rather than as a structure; and it is quite in harmony with this that the terminology of grammar, most of which is derived from Greek, should have originated in so many cases as physical or physiological metaphor.[3] In Horace's Sapphics and Alcaics, on the other hand, the architectural element practically reaches its zenith. And again, if we turn to the history of English, I do not think we can say that we find this architectural element at all pronounced until the seventeenth century. It strikes us, for instance, in Milton and in the Metaphysicals, and frequently afterwards, but hardly in Chaucer or Shakespeare.

To characterize further the difference between what I have ventured to describe as the *fluid* type of poetry and the later, *architectural* type: in the later, elisions tend to become less frequent, whilst (in verse) the number of syllables in a single foot or time-interval grows less easily variable. Another test is this: it is much harder to convey the *full* effect of poetry of the architectural type with the *voice*. The eye seems to be necessary as well, so that the shape of a whole line or period can be taken in instantaneously. The actual sounds have grown more fixed and rigid and monotonous; the stresses accordingly are more subtle, depending upon the way in which the emotional meaning—as it were—struggles against this rigidity; and this produces a music different indeed, but none the less lovely because it is often audible only to the inward ear. The fluid type of verse, on the other hand, is made for reciting or singing aloud and probably gains more than it loses by this method of delivery.

3

It is especially interesting that we find this transition of poetry from an organic to a relatively structural character reflected in the formal history of language itself.

2. Moreover, Homer shows us Hephaestus *actually fashioning* the shield, whereas Virgil speaks as a spectator examining the finished product.
3. E.g. πτῶσις, ἄρθρον, συνδέσμος, etc.

For assuming that Jespersen's view of the direction of progress is correct, we can trace the change from a flexional state, in which word-*order* is relatively unfixed and unimportant, towards a final state in which word-order is fixed and so essential to the expression of meaning that a slight change may actually reverse the sense—as in the English sentence 'The Gentlemen beat the Players'. Of known languages, Chinese is again, apparently, the furthest developed in this direction. To the poet or critic, a language which has reached this last stage presents the appearance of a kind of crystallization, the semantic elements requiring to be rearranged in a series of kaleidoscopic jerks. Whereas in a language still at the 'flexional' stage the meaning, vaguer in its outlines, but more muscular and alive, can afford to leave even the words themselves as though still in motion. The reader has not the same sense of their being set and fixed in their places.

Here it is worth remarking on a phenomenon in the history of philology which comes in for some ridicule at the hands of Jespersen. I mean the pronounced tendency to refer to the flexional type of language as 'strong' and the analytic type as 'weak'. In the same way the loss of inflexions has long been regarded in philological circles as a symptom of 'decay' or 'senility'. Jespersen attributes the origin of this incorrigible philological prejudice to pedantic preoccupation with Latin and Greek; its maintenance he assigns to blind tradition. He sums up in a masterly manner the enormous advantages in point of economy and lucidity which the analytic language possesses over its flexional ancestor and pronounces himself unable to see any meaning in the use of such a word as 'senility' in such a connection.

In my view, however, this well-worn terminology of the philologists springs from a kind of true instinct for poetic values. Mr. Jespersen, in his *Progress in Language*, builds argument upon argument to prove that the historical development of language is indeed 'progressive' and not a kind of falling away from grace, as his predecessors held. These arguments are absolutely convincing and require no comment, as long as we remember that, to the author, 'progress' in the history of consciousness does not merely include, but is synonymous with an increasing ability to think abstract thoughts. This fact grows more and more apparent as one reads on, until at last one realizes that, where Coleridge failed, Mr. Jespersen has succeeded in 'taming down his mind to think poetry a sport or an occupation for idle hours'. But I have already referred to the summary manner in which the distinguished Danish philologist dismisses this side of his subject.

The poetic historian of language, therefore, would certainly have to consider such a question as the following: is there some period in the development of a language at which, all other factors being excluded, it is fittest to become the vehicle of great poetry; and is this followed by a kind of decline? We might suppose that at a certain stage the rational, abstracting, formal principle will have stayed and confined the primal flow of meaning to an extent which is just exquisite; that this is the moment of all moments for the great poet to step in; and that in a century or so the balance will have been destroyed, the formal principle have run ahead, so that in the greatest poetry we shall have henceforth that Miltonic flavour—delightful indeed, but perhaps a thought less divine—of cyclopean achievement and rest after labour. It can hardly be doubted that this period would be found to bear *some* recognizable relation to that point of balance between the rational and the poetic, to which I referred earlier in the chapter. But I may not put all this forward as more than a suggestion; for the poetic history of language which I have attempted to sketch upon air would need for its actual bringing down to earth a far wider culture and an acquaintance with a great many more languages and literatures than I can lay claim to. *Faciant meliora potentes.*

The Making of Meaning

I

It is, then, impossible—on an absolutely unprejudiced interpretation of experience—not to recognize two different sorts of poetry, the later of which, having arisen out of the former by imperceptible gradation, exists side by side with it and eventually tends to replace it. 'The poetry', says Hegel, 'of ages in which the prosaic spirit is already developed is essentially distinct from that of primitive epochs, among peoples whose imagination is still wholly poetic.'[1]

We have, however, already seen that that earlier kind of poetry—the instinctive kind, if we choose to call it so—lives on to some extent in the meanings of words, even after the other has begun to replace it; so that in any particular poem it is still a question of disentangling the two elements . . . And when we have done so, we shall find that, in the later kind of poetry, for which the individual poet is increasingly responsible—in which, as we saw, he has in certain respects to fight *against* language, making up the poetic deficit out of his private balance—in this kind it is perfectly true to call the poet the creator, or re-creator of meaning itself.

1. *Philosophy of Fine Art.* Oswald Spengler, in *The Decline of the West*, has a great deal to say on the whole nature and meaning of this 'prosaic spirit', tracing its increasing expression in nearly every walk of life, in the historical development both of our own civilization and of the great civilizations of the past.

For, if re-creation is strictly the more accurate term, yet creation, besides being established in current aesthetic terminology, is more truly fitted to the majesty of the idea. Surely no critic with enough metaphysical wit to be interested in the question at all would deny that 'creation', as an aesthetic term, signifies, not some fantastic 'creation out of nothing', but the bringing farther into consciousness of something which already exists as unconscious life? It is no disservice, then, to this frightfully abused word to emphasize its real connotation.

Now apart from the actual invention of new words (an art in which many poets have excelled), the principal means by which this creation of meaning is achieved is—as has already been pointed out—metaphor. But it must be remembered that *any* specifically *new* use of a word or phrase is really a metaphor, since it attempts to arouse cognition of the unknown by suggestion from the known. I will take an example: the painter's expression *point of view* was a metaphor the first time it was used (probably by Coleridge) with a psychological content. This content is today one of its accepted meanings—indeed, it is the most familiar one—but it could only have become so *after* passing, explicitly or implicitly, through the earlier stage of metaphor. In other words, either Coleridge or somebody else either said or thought (I am of course putting it a little crudely) '*x* is to the mind what *point of view* is to an observer of landscape'. And in so doing he enriched the content of the expression 'point of view' just as Shakespeare enriched the content of 'balm' (and of 'sleep', too) when he called sleep the 'balm of hurt minds' ('sleep is to hurt minds what balm is to hurt bodies'). Reflection will show that the 'new' use of an epithet—that is to say, its application to a substantive with which it has not hitherto been coupled—is also a concealed metaphor.[2]

In the present chapter I shall attempt to trace a single, predominantly 'literary' example of the continuous creation of meaning in the above sense.

2

English schoolboys are generally taught to translate the Latin verb 'ruo' by one of two words, *rush* or *fall*. And it does indeed 'mean' both these things; but,

2. Thus, when Blake wrote:

> Then I made a rural pen
> And I stained the water clear ...

his semantic act can be seen, in retrospect, to have contained *implicitly* the judgement: 'These hitherto unapprehended attributes are to my pen what the attributes connoted by the epithet *rural* are to the objects to which that epithet is customarily applied'.

But to say that it contained this judgement implicitly is not to say that it was equivalent to this judgement. On the contrary; for logical judgements, by their nature, can only *render more explicit* some one part of a truth *already implicit in their terms*. But the poet makes the terms themselves. He does not make judgements, therefore; he only makes them possible—and only he makes them possible.

because it means both and because it also means a great deal more, neither rendering alone is really an adequate equivalent. In the classical contexts themselves it nearly always carries with it a larger sense of swift, disastrous movement—'ruit arduus aether' of a deluge of rain, and again, 'Fiat Justitia, ruat coelum'. Why is this? The Greek ῥέω, 'to flow', and similar words in other European languages (whether philologists admit a lineal connection is a matter of comparative indifference for periods so remote), suggest that the old rumbling, guttural 'r', which our modern palates have so thinned and refined, once had its concrete connection with swift, natural movements such as those of torrents or landslides.[3]

Now the conscious realization by men that such motions, with the noise that accompanies them, are often the prelude to disaster, may or may not have been the cause why 'ruo' came to convey in such a lively manner the notion, not only of movement, but also of *collapse*. If so, then we are already at the 'metaphorical' stage, and the transition from 'given' to 'created' meaning has begun, even before the first recorded use. If not, then an older single meaning ('rush-fall-collapse') has begun, under the influence of the rational, to split up into this treble meaning of the Latin word—which is subsequently going to require *three separate words* for its expression. In any case it is noticeable that, when the substantive 'ruina' came to be formed, it contained this last part only of the meaning of the verb—in other words, the older meaning, whether still wholly 'given' or containing by now a 'created' element, was now being further restricted, hardened, *arrested*, under the influence of the rational principle. And another change soon took place: it could now mean, not only the falling itself, but *the thing fallen*. It is like watching a physical process of crystallization.

Guy de Maupassant said somewhere: 'Les mots ont une âme; la plupart des lecteurs, et même des écrivains, ne leur demandent qu'un sens. Il faut trouver cette âme qui apparaît au contact d'autres mots. . . .' It will, I think, appear that this 'soul', latent in words, and waiting only to be discovered, is for the most part a kind of buried survival of the old 'given' meaning under later accretions; or, if not of the 'given' meaning itself, then of an old 'created' meaning which has been buried in the same way. For created meanings, once published, are as much subject, of course, to the binding, astringent action of the rational principle as the original given meanings. Like sleeping beauties, they lie there prone

3. Boiardo, in the *Orlando Innamorato*, uses the Italian equivalent, on two consecutive pages, to express (i) a swiftly flowing river ('L'acqua che al corso una *rovina* pare') and (ii) a fall in battle:

'E ben credette d'averlo conquiso,
'E *rovinarlo* a quel sol colpo al piano'

while a few pages further on we find it (iii) describing a man galloping off on horseback:

'Allor ne andava lui con gran *rovina*,
'Spronando il buon destriero a piu potere.'

and rigid in the walls of Castle Logic, waiting only for the kiss of Metaphor to awaken them to fresh life. That words lose their freshness through habit is a more humdrum way of saying the same thing; and it will do well enough, as long as we remember that 'habit' is itself only a familiar name for the repetition of the identical, and that the repetition of the identical is the very essence of the rational principle—the very means by which the concrete becomes abstract—the Gorgon's head itself.

The words 'au contact d'autres mots' (which remind us of the tag from the *Ars Poetica*: 'notum si callida verbum Reddiderit *iunctura* novum . . .') are particularly important. For this 'contact' with other words is *the precise point at which the potential new meaning originally enters language*. And it is by quotations illustrating such 'contacts' that I am trying to trace the gradual loss of ancient meaning, given or created, from the word 'ruin', the recovery of part of it, and the positive gain which, thanks to individual poets, arises out of that sequence of loss and recovery.

In Latin, then, the four letters 'r-u-i-n' never lost the power to suggest *movement*. In certain contexts they may seem to modern readers to possess a purely static and material reference; but if so, it is because those readers are of the kind described by Maupassant as demanding only a 'sens', a definable meaning. The *soul* of such a word as 'ruina' is really inseparable from motion.

> Si fractus illabatur orbis,
> Impavidum ferient ruinae

says Horace; the world is still falling when the stanza ends.

3

Before 1375 the word *ruin* with the meaning 'a falling' has come, via France, to England, and we find Chaucer using it in that sense. Thus, Saturn, in the *Knight's Tale*, boasting of his powers, proclaims to Venus:

> Min is the ruine of the highe halles,
> The falling of the toures and of the walles.

Here is the word in poetic use, mobile and vigorous enough, but without its modern subtlety, because in English it has as yet no *solid* associations to give it weight and deepen its private significance. It is simply a useful Latin word. So, too, we may notice that Gower, about the same time, is employing the word almost in its exact classical sense:

> The wal and al the cit withinne
> Stant in ruine and in decas,

where we should now say 'stand in *ruins*', and think at once, not of a process or a state (which is Gower's meaning) but of the actual fragments of masonry. 1454 is the date of the first recorded instance of plural use with a definitely material reference—*ruins*—and it is probable that by Spencer's time the meaning was quickly spreading over the special area which it was to cover during the eighteenth century. He writes, it is true:

> The late ruin of proud Marinell,

meaning Marinell's disastrous defeat in battle, and uses the word twenty-one times in this older sense; but he also uses the modern plural thirteen times, and speaks of

> The old ruines of a broken towre.

These two lines alone are enough to show that already, before the end of the sixteenth century, the English word, with the double set of associations which it was now beginning to acquire, had a 'soul'; though no one had quite found it; no one, that is, had realized it in consciousness. For it was not in the nature of English poetry before the seventeenth century to 'add' meaning to words in this way, by evoking their hidden quality. Thus, Spenser, who made all English into a language of his own, half-creating in his poesy another Spenserian world, which never quite touches the real one, gave little of *permanence* to language. As creator of language, Spenser was fantastic rather than imaginative.[4]

4

By this time, however, English meaning had suddenly begun to ferment and bubble furiously round about a brain in a Stratford cottage; witness the sheer verbal exuberance of *Love's Labour's Lost*. Many of its words were to suffer an extraordinary change before the century was out, however slowly that change might become apparent. In some cases the new energy in them was not to be released until the nineteenth century—even later. But the energy was there. There is a new English Dictionary hidden between the pages—or is it between the lines?—of the First Folio. Shakespeare stands supreme over the other poets of the world in the one great quality of abundant life; and this he gave to words, as he gave it to Falstaff and Sir Andrew Aguecheek. He made more new words than any other English writer—but he also made new meanings. We are at present concerned only with the word *ruin*; let us listen, then, to Salisbury's

4. He seems, however, to have invented the useful epithet, *blatant*, though he himself never employed it outside the conventional title of the 'Blatant Beast'.

words, when he is confronted with Arthur's body lying huddled on the stones, where the fall has killed him:

> It is the shameful work of Hubert's hand,
> The practice and the purpose of the King;
> From whose obedience I forbid my soul,
> Kneeling before this ruin of sweet life . . .

'Les mots ont une âme . . .' No synonym would do here; the phrase

> Kneeling before this ruin of sweet life

is one—a tiny work of art. In Spenser's line

> The late ruin of proud Marinell

you could substitute *fall* or *disaster*, if the syllables would scan. But Shakespeare has felt the exact, whole significance of his word. The dead boy has *fallen* from the walls; the sweet life, which was in him too, has crumbled away; but wait—by Shakespeare's time the word was beginning to acquire its other meaning of the actual remains—and there is the shattered body lying on the ground! He has, indeed, found a soul in the word.

It seems to have been one which appealed dearly to his imagination, for we find the transitive verb in one of the loveliest lines from the sonnets:

> That time of year though may'st in me behold
> When yellow leaves, or none, or few do hang
> Upon those boughs which shake against the cold,
> Bare ruin'd choirs, where late the sweet birds sang.

But it was in *Antony and Cleopatra*, near the end of his work, that he made the boldest stroke of all, writing quietly but magnificently:

> The noble ruin of her magic, Antony.

There is a new word. Yet Shakespeare had not done it *all* with his own hands. The transitive verb 'to ruin' had been invented already, by 1585, before he started to write, and, without the new habit of thought which this use of them was forming in himself *and in his hearers*, he could not have used the four letters passively with such effect. For a poet must take his words as he finds them, and his readers must not realize too acutely that fresh meaning is being thrust upon them. The new meaning must be *strange*, not incomprehensible; otherwise the poetry of the whole passage is killed, and the fresh meaning itself will be still-born.

5

The word *ruin*, then, has grown with Shakespeare's help into a warm and living thing, a rich piece of imaginative material ready at hand for anyone who has the skill to evoke its power. Now, early in the seventeenth century, it had been used for the first time as an intransitive verb, taking the place once and for all of an older verb, to *rue*, which had the same meaning, but never probably (since it had not been used by the poets) the same suggestive power. Grimstone, in a *History of the Siege of Ostend* (1604), wrote: 'They suffered it to burn and ruin'; while Sandys, in a verse paraphrase (!) of Job, has:

> Though he his House of polisht marble build,
> Yet shall it ruine like the Moth's fraile cell.

It was natural that Milton, with his bookish sense of the philological history of his words, should come forward to perpetuate this use. To the noun *ruin* he added nothing; what he did was to help 'fix' its Latinity by *never once* using it in its modern material sense. So that when Satan

> yet shone, majestic though in Ruin,

he exerted only a negative, if deepening, influence on the history of the world. It is the terrific phrase:

> Hell heard the insufferable noise, Hell saw
> Heaven ruining from Heaven

which is important. For it is preserving that old content of large and disastrous movement, which Wordsworth, Milton's devout disciple, has finally recovered for us into the language.

But there is all the eighteenth century in between; and during that time *ruin*, like most words other than domestic and civic and scientific terms, seems to have possessed a greatly diminished power of suggestion. These latter words, of course, grew. Pope, for instance, found out a kind of soul in the word *engine*, when he used it in the *Rape of the Lock* of a pair of scissors:

> He takes the gift with reverence, and extends
> The little engine on his fingers' ends.

But the others—especially those purporting to be descriptive of Nature—must have felt uncomfortably stifled, and many of them, as we have seen, actually lost much of their poetic vitality. The question was, in each case, whether any poet would arise to restore it.

Dryden wrote:

So Helen wept, when her too faithful glass
Reflected to her eyes the ruins of her face.

But after that, until the coming of Wordsworth, it is all tumbledown walls and
mossy masonry. We can just imagine how *solid* an idea must have been im-
printed by the word *ruins* on an eighteenth-century imagination, and how faintly
its original force must have survived, when we recollect the fashion of erecting
artificial 'follies'. In this connection Dryden's own use of the plural rather than
the singular is interesting, as emphasizing the solid, material reference of the
meaning. Indeed, I believe that to his own fancy, as well as to those of many of
his readers, the phrase was actually an 'accidental' metaphor in which the lady's
face was compared to the 'picturesque' remains of a Gothic abbey.

6

All this suggests a feature, to which attention has not yet been drawn, in the history of Poetic Diction, or rather in the parallel history of that anti-poetic process, which I have ventured to describe as the 'splitting up' of meaning, and
which accompanies the natural decline of language into abstraction. It is this;
that under certain circumstances, poets themselves may assist that process.
Thus, the *first time ruin* was used alone with a blunt and, as it were, purely material, meaning, that use of it may have been original and poetic. The first man
who looked at the ruin of a wall and called it simply a *ruin* may well have had
the true dramatic-poetic sense of the value of *omission*, with its accompanying
phenomenon of *suggestion*. It was this kind of omission, presumably, which
gave to *bode* its dark prophetic significance. Just as the poetry of today, then,
may have been but the normal language of yesterday, so, much that appears in
the light of subsequent development to have been really, by its proper nature, in
the prosaic stream, may yet have been true poetry to the experience of contemporaries. During the eighteenth century itself there may well have been a romance and a flavour clinging to their own favourite use of the word *ruin*—a romance not quite so false and a flavour not quite so insipid as we must think,
whose only understanding of those different minds is derived from a language
which has also changed.

7

Pope made no uncommon use of the word, nor added much to its power. Nor did
anyone else. Nevertheless the word means more than it did before the eighteenth

century had come and gone; for, from now on, it is irradiated with some of the massive quiet of deserted Gothic masonry. And no matter how many times it has been carelessly handled for the purposes of false and facile romanticism, the old magic will always be ready to flash out to a touch of true imagination.

So time passed. Young, it is true, had felt the quality of the word, and there may be other isolated examples. In the second book of the *Night Thoughts* the father is describing the appearance of his dead daughter lying stretched upon her bed:

> Lovely in death the beauteous ruin lay.

It is a definite echo, I think, of the line from *King John*—a dying echo—and with Gray the soul of the word finally runs to seed in the fanciful, allegorical, synthetic dullness of actual personification:

> Ruin seize thee, ruthless King!

Then came Wordsworth, who immediately, in one of his earliest poems, *The Descriptive Sketches*, got a move, as it were, on the word and dislodged it from its sentimental repose. He used it of an avalanche:

> From age to age throughout his lonely bounds
> The crash of ruin fitfully resounds.

And the verb neuter of a waterfall:

> Ruining from the cliffs the deafening load
> Tumbles.

We are back again now with Milton. Wordsworth has gone to the other extreme, and both these uses are a little too near to the word's simplest etymological significance, are not new enough to be very striking; yet doubtless at the time when they were written they had the power to startle. They are a clear enough symptom of that general quickening of perception which found its expression in the Romantic Revival. Hundreds of dead words might be resuscitated by men like Bishop Percy and Sir Walter Scott; it was the task of even more vital spirits to awaken those that were only sleeping.

It is doubtful whether Tennyson or Browning have added much—or perhaps it is too early to say. On the whole, Tennyson's tendency is to abstract the meaning from reality and semi-personify it:

> When the crimson rolling eye
> Glares ruin!

And again:

> The Sea roars Ruin. A fearful night!

Note the capital letter. And yet, in *Lucretius*, there is that one magnificent example of the verb neuter:

> A void was made in Nature; all her bonds
> Crack'd; and I saw the flaring atom-streams
> And torrents of her myriad universe,
> Ruining along the illimitable inane . . .

8

Here, then is the modern word *ruin*—a piece of many lost minds—waiting, like all the other words in the dictionary, to be kindled into life by a living one; and nothing more is necessary than to surround it with other words (the right ones) from the same museum. Is this being done at all in contemporary verse? There is one line at least, written by a modern poet, which may be quoted. Some time ago, when I had finished reading a volume of verse by Mr. E. L. Davison, two passages remained to haunt me. Both of them contained the word *ruin*, and it was, as a matter of fact, this coincidence which first interested me in the word's poetic history. The first is from a poem called *The Sunken City*:

> . . . the climbing tentacles
> Of some sleep-swimming octopus
> Disturb a ruined temple's bells
> And set the deep sea clamorous.

Thus, the very choice of subject suggests that the poet's imagination is one which is attracted by the somewhat dangerous beauty of 'ruin'. So we find. Take these two lines from a love-sonnet in the same volume:

> I stood before thee, calling twice or thrice
> The ruin of thy soft, bewildering name.

In a way this line seems to be a summing up of all previous poetic uses of the word, and then a step beyond them: 'ruin' showers noiselessly over it in a kind of dream waterfall of pangs.

In this chapter, I have taken only one English word, and one no richer in itself than a thousand others. Yet it serves well enough to show how the man of today, overburdened with self-consciousness, lonely, insulated from Reality by his shadowy, abstract thoughts, and ever on the verge of the awful maelstrom of his own fantastic dreams, has among his other compensations these lovely ancestral words, embalming the souls of many poets dead and gone and the souls of many common men. If he is a poet, he may rise for a moment on Shakespeare's shoulders—if he is a lover, then, certainly, there are no more philtres, but he has his four magical black squiggles, wherein the past is bottled, like an Arabian Genie, in the dark. Let him only find the secret, and there, lying on the page, their printed silence will be green with moss; it will crumble slowly even while it whispers with the thunder of primeval avalanches. 'Le mot', murmured Victor Hugo . . . 'tantôt comme un passant mystérieux de l'âme, tantôt comme un polype noir de l'océan pensê. . . .'

Verse and Prose

I

At the opposite pole to the wide sense in which I have been using the phrase 'poetic diction', stands the narrowest one, according to which it signifies 'language which can be used in verse but not in prose'. This artificial identification of the words *poetry* and *poetic* with metrical form is certainly of long standing in popular use; but it has rarely been supported by those who have written on the subject.[1] As *Verse* is an excellent word for metrical writing of all kinds, whether poetic or unpoetic, and *Prose* for un-metrical writing, in this book the formal literary distinction is drawn between *verse* and *prose*; whereas that between *poetry, poetic* on the one hand and *prosaic* on the other is a spiritual one, not confined to literature. The meanings which I attach to these latter words should already be fairly clear from the foregoing chapters. I will, however, add four definite examples:

(i) On the roof
Of an itinerant vehicle I sate
With vulgar men about me . . .

is *verse*, and at the same time *prosaic*.

(ii) The crows and choughs that wing the midway air

1. Hegel, in his *Philosophy of Fine Art*, makes a notable exception.

Show scarce so gross as beetles; half way down
Hangs one that gathers samphire, dreadful trade!
Methinks he seems no bigger than his head.

is *verse* and at the same time *poetry*.

(iii) I told the butcher to leave two and a half pounds of best topside.

is *prose* and at the same time *prosaic*.

(iv) Behold now this vast city, a city of refuge . . .

is *prose* and at the same time *poetry* or *poetic*.

But if those writers who have seriously set out to discuss and define poetry have very rarely made metre their criterion, yet, *for historical reasons*, most of the poetry with which they have actually had to deal has, in fact, been in metrical form; and it is this, in all probability, which has given rise to the terminological confusion.

All literatures are, in their infancy, metrical, that is to say, based on a more or less regularly recurring rhythm. Thus, unless we wish to indulge all sorts of fanciful and highly 'logomorphic' notions,[2] we are obliged to assume that the earliest verse-rhythms were 'given' by Nature in the same way as the earliest 'meaning'. And this is comprehensible enough. Nature herself is perpetually rhythmic. Just as the myths still live on a ghostly life as fables after they have died as real meaning, so the old rhythmic human consciousness of nature (it should rather be called a *participation* than a consciousness) lives on as the tradition of metrical form. We can only understand the origin of metre by going back to the ages when men were conscious, not merely in their heads, but in the beating of their hearts and the pulsing of their blood—when thinking was not merely *of* Nature, but was Nature herself.

It is only at a later stage that prose (= not-verse) comes naturally into being out of the growth of that rational principle which, with its sense-bound, abstract thoughts, divorces man's consciousness from the life of Nature. In our language, for example, it is only during the last three centuries that there has grown up any considerable body of prose, on which the critic could work. Consequently, the derivation from *prose* (= not-verse) of the adjective *prosaic* (= not-poetic) is not accidental. On the contrary, it is a record of certain historical facts. And yet we are wrong if we deduce from it the apparently logical conclusion that not-verse = not-poetry. Why? The question can only be answered historically, and in connection with other questions, such as that which has just been discussed, of the responsibility of individuals for poetic values.

2. E.g., that, before the invention of writing, metrical form was deliberately adopted as an aid to memory.

2

The time at which the prose form (or lack of form) first begins to be used as a vehicle for imaginative writing in any particular language would indeed call for a full treatment in the poet's history of language which I envisaged above. Such a history would no doubt consider to what extent it tended to coincide with that period of a balance, as it were, between the two principles, which seems to make a language ripe for the appearance of its great poet—the period when Italy produces her Dante, England her Shakespeare. I do not myself feel competent to carry this inquiry further than to point out that in this country—though Malory had written poetic prose a century before—it was, in fact, shortly before the time of Shakespeare that serious experiments were first made with prose as an imaginative medium.

Certainly it could be shown, without difficulty, and from many different sides, how the rise of prose, whatever else it may signify, is a necessary event in the biography of a language developing along the lines traced out above. For instance, the increasing fixity of word-order has already been referred to, and this is obviously a factor which encourages the prose form for all kinds of writing. In such a line as Shelley's:

The wise want power: the powerful goodness want

we can feel only too acutely the kind of syntactical stiffness which tempts a modern poet to write in prose. Moreover the late Sir Walter Raleigh did well to point out, apropos of Wordsworth's theory of poetic diction, that some of the flattest passages in that poet's own work are due to his having observed the *prose choice* of words (in accordance with his theory) without at the same time keeping to the natural *prose order*. The meaning of these phrases, the 'prose choice of words' and the 'prose order', implying, as they do, that there is also a poetic choice of words and a poetic order, can be better considered in the next chapter. Meanwhile one may again recall Coleridge's definition of poetry as 'the best words in the best order'.

It is evident without further examples that *ceteris paribus*, where a rigidly regular metrical framework has to be applied to a language in which grammar is itself growing strict concerning the order in which words may be placed, it must become harder and harder for verse and poetry to keep house together. Nor is it without significance that we, today, should be more disgusted by 'inversions' of the kind quoted above, and consequently more afraid of them, than our immediate ancestors; as a glance at a contemporary verse with prove beyond dispute.

Thus, if we chose to confine our prophetic gaze to language and its 'progress', we should certainly behold Poetry giving poor Verse a bill of divorce and flying at some distant date into the arms of prose. A study of Chinese literature, in which word-order, as has been pointed out, is already rigidly determinate and of paramount denotative importance, might possibly throw a more comforting light on this prospect—comforting, that is, to those whose ears delight especially in the rhythms and music of verse.[3] But, in any case, if we try to alter the focus of our vision and look upon the art of poetry as a whole, we shall find plenty of contradictory evidence. Such an attempt I cannot very well make, since it is my object to confine this book to that area of Poetry which is related to the intrinsic nature of language. Thus, I ignore altogether such questions as dramatic or architectonic values, quality of personal emotion, etc.; even the element of rhythm can only be discussed in so far as it is found to be inseparable from the use of speech; and I can hardly touch upon the nature of *music*.

When the individual's part in the making of poetry has reached a point at which poetry becomes an 'art', an entirely new set of forces begins to break through the shell of language proper, forces which tend to increase rather than diminish with the further passing of time. These forces are, as we saw, imparted by the individual poet himself; and one of the moulds into which they flow is the *music* of poetry. Music (if one can use a fraction here) may comprise perhaps as much as half the *meaning* of a modern lyric. But here I merely wish to point to it as one of the factors which counterbalance the tendency towards the prose form which has just been traced. Music may be distinguished from rhythm by the increasing aesthetic value of *sound*, as against mere *time*, and, unlike rhythm, it is not an instinctive element in early speech. As the Aryan languages develop, the *quantitative* values, which gave a rhythm to some extent inherent in the language itself, decay, while *accent*, which is much more *a determination of the material part of language by the speaker's own peculiar meaning*, arises in their stead. Now the decay of the quantitative values leaves us with prose, but, on the other hand, the rise of accent brings us—music. Alliteration and assonance are discovered—both practically unknown[4] to the ancients—and if these are musical devices not wholly peculiar to verse, but open also to poetic prose, yet in rhyme we are face to face with the development, at a comparatively late date, of an entirely new system of versification.

The significance of rhyme to the history and making of poetry I consider to be outside the scope of this book; but the mere fact that such a form has come into being, *since* poetry was an art, may well remind us how much, how very much, is possible to the human imagination, once it has begun to drink, with fuller consciousness, from the primal source of meaning. It would be pure fantasy to attempt to prescribe in advance what uses man himself shall henceforth make of the material element in language.

3. As far, however, as analogies with our own tongue are concerned, it must be remembered that the language of China has apparently remained almost unchanged throughout the whole known period of her history; so that its evolution from a looser, more flexional, form is no more than a hypothesis, albeit a highly convincing one.

4. Deliberate onomatopoeia can safely be distinguished from pure alliteration and assonance, whose end is music before imitation.

from *History in English Words*

Imagination

Art • Fiction • Creative • Genius • Romantic • Fancy • Imagination • Dream

Early Christianity, with its delighted recognition of the soul's reality, its awful consciousness of inner depths unplumbed, had produced, as we saw, many words describing human emotions by their *effects*, and especially by their effects on the soul's relation to the Divine. In the sixteenth and seventeenth centuries, with the increase of self-consciousness among the leisured classes, a more sympathetic, 'introspective'[1] attitude to the emotions grew up, and this we traced to its development in the romantic *sensibility* of the seventeenth and eighteenth centuries. How did it fare, then, with this tender nursling in the years that followed? Was it crushed and dissected into a neatly labelled little corpse, or was it suffered to grow up unchecked, uneducated, into the middle-aged and well-fed *sentimentalism* of our Victorian ancestors? Fortunately it avoided both these fates. Carefully tended by small groups of earnest men, now in this academy and now in that, it had escaped the dissection of Nature because it had learned not to draw its nourishment from Nature and the God of Nature, but from man himself. And on this diet it had thrived and waxed until it was a veritable young giant, able to stand up and confront nature as her equal. But we must retrace our steps a little.

Attentive readers of Jane Austen's novels will have noticed the slightly unfamiliar way in which she employs the two words *romantic* and *picturesque*. A closer examination reveals the fact that in her time they still bore traces of their origin. These adjectives are taken from the arts, *romantic* meaning in the first instance 'like the old Romances', and *picturesque* 'like a picture' or 'reminding one of a picture'. They are thus members of a quite considerable group of words and phrases, *attitude, comic, dramatic, lyrical, melodramatic, point of view,* and

---

1. 1820; but *introspection* was given its modern meaning by Dryden.

33

the like, in which terms taken in the first place from the arts are subsequently applied to life. Nowadays we sometimes go farther and use the name of a particular artist, speaking, for instance, of a *Turneresque* sunset, a *Praxitelean* shape; or we call to our aid a writer's fictitious creatures, as in '*Falstaffian* morality', 'the *Pickwickian* sense', . . . Such a figure of speech looks at first sight like any other kind of imagery, and we perhaps imagine it in use since the beginnings of art. In point of fact, however, it is probable that it was not known before the time of the Renaissance, when men's notions of art changed so suddenly, when, indeed, their very consciousness of it as a separate, unrelated activity, something which can be distinguished in thought from a 'craft', a 'trade', or a religious ceremony, seems to have first sprung into being. Moreover, the ancient word *art* used to include in its purview not only these meanings, but also most of those which we now group under the heading *science*. In the Middle Ages the Seven Liberal Arts[2]—*Grammar, Logic, Rhetoric, Arithmetic, Geometry, Music*, and *Astronomy*—were contrasted with the 'servile' or 'mechanical' arts—that is, handicrafts involving manual labour. And thus, though *art* in this wide sense is old, *artist* first occurs in Sir Philip Sidney's *Apologie for Poetry*. *Artisan* appeared at about the same time, and was not then, as now, confined to mechanical and manual labourers.

> O, what a world of profit and delight

wrote the poet, Marlowe,

> Is promis'd to the studious artisan.

In the light of two or three familiar words let us try and trace the development, from Sidney's time onwards, of some of our modern notions of 'art', and in particular of poetry. Criticism—the branch of literature or journalism with which our daily and weekly reviews make us so familiar—does not date very far back into the past. Its parents were the medieval arts of grammar and philology, which, among the commentators on classical texts, had already sometimes blossomed into the rudiments of aesthetic. The actual words *critic* and *critical*, however, have been traced no farther back than Shakespeare; *critic* in its aesthetic sense is first found in Bacon; and *criticism* and *criticize* are neither of them earlier than the seventeenth century. Based for the most part on Aristotle's *Poetics*, serious criticism began to take shape in England at the Renaissance. From Elizabethan critical essays, such as Sidney's *Apologie for Poetry*, we can get an idea of the light in which poetry and the other arts had begun to be viewed at that time. To Sidney, for example, the distinguishing mark of poetry was, not metre, but a certain 'feigning'. The first philosophers and historians,

2. Hence the titles of our University Degrees—*Bachelor of Arts, Master of Arts*, . . .

he affirmed, were also poets, not indeed because of what we should magnificently call their 'creative imagination', but simply because they 'invented' certain fictitious persons and events. We should not now regard this as a virtue in
an historian. Sidney, however, points out the derivation of *poetry* from the
Greek 'poiein', 'to make'[3] and shows how this distinguishes it from all the
other arts and sciences, which in the last analysis merely 'follow Nature', while
only the poet,

> disdaining to be tied to any such subjection, lifted with the vigour of his own in-
> vention, doth growth in effect another nature, in making things either better than
> Nature bringeth forth, or, quite anew, forms such as never were in Nature, as the
> Heroes, Demigods, Cyclops, Chimeras, Furies, and such like: so as he goeth hand
> in hand with Nature, not enclosed within the narrow warrant of her gifts, but
> freely ranging only within the Zodiac of his own wit.

And Sidney adds that this fact is not to be made light of merely because the
works of Nature are 'essential' while the poet's are only 'in imitation or fiction'.
The poet has contemplated the 'Ideas' behind Nature, and it is those which he
'delivers forth, as he hath imagined them'. With ten or twenty new novels appearing on the bookstalls every week it is not so easy for us to realize the dignity
and glory which were once felt to distinguish this great human achievement of
fiction—that is, of 'making' or 'making up' (from the Latin 'fingere', to 'form'
or 'make') purely imaginary forms, instead of merely copying Nature.

Now the presence of a made-up element, especially when it comprised
supernatural beings such as giants and fairies, was held to be one of the distinguishing marks of a *romance*. The old medieval romances, as their name suggests, had been nursed to life in that curious period of contact between Roman
and Celtic myth which also gave us such words as *fairy* and *sorcery*. They were
so called because they were written or recited in the *romance* vernacular instead
of in literary Latin, and they seem to have developed out of an increasing tendency among the medieval bards to embroider, on their own responsibility, the
traditional accounts of historical and mythical events. This tendency, wherever
it had hitherto been detected among the western Aryans, had been strenuously
opposed in the interests of learning and morality. It was one of the reasons why
Plato decided to expel poets from his Republic, and it is remarkable that the earlier uses of a word like *fable* in twelfth- and thirteenth-century French and
fourteenth-century English should have been all condemnatory. Now by the
time the Renaissance dawned on England this word had come to be applied, in
one instance at least, not merely to the embroidery, but to the garment itself, so

3. Poets were regularly called *makers* in the fourteenth and fifteenth centuries. 'I know not',
says Sidney, 'whether by luck or wisdom we Englishmen have met with the Greeks in calling him a
"maker".'

that, for example, the whole prodigious fabric of classical mythology might be implicit in the disparaging phrase 'fables of poets'. And after the Revival of Learning, when the most able men began to have a very different feeling towards the myths of Greece and Rome, such a phrase became the very opposite of disparaging. *Fiction* and *romance* were gradually recognized as a legitimate and noble expression of the human spirit.

Gradually: to Sidney, poetry was still, after Aristotle's definition, 'an art of imitation'; only poets must 'to imitate, borrow nothing of what is, hath been, or shall be, but range . . . into the divine consideration of what may be and should be'. And during the seventeenth century all art continued to be regarded as imitation, of which, however, there were two kinds—the imitation of other arts and the imitation of Nature herself. The second kind, by analogy from picture-dealing, was called *original*, and the faculty which achieved it was named *invention* (Latin, 'invenire', 'to find'), a word implying that something had been found in Nature which had not *yet* been imitated by man. Early in the eighteenth century the substantive *originality* was formed from *original*, and an increasing importance began to be attached to the element of novelty in experiences of all kinds, Addison placing it on a level with greatness and beauty as a source of pleasure to the imagination.

At the same time another word appeared in the vocabulary of aesthetic criticism. An Elizabethan critic had already pointed out that, if poets could indeed spin their poetry entirely out of themselves, they were as '*creating* gods', and Dryden soon used the same verb of Shakespeare, because, in Caliban, he had *invented* 'a person not in Nature'. So also Addison:

> this Talent, of affecting the Imagination . . . has something in it like Creation: It bestows a kind of Existence, and draws up to the Reader's View several Objects which are not to be found in Being. It makes Additions to Nature, and gives greater Variety to God's Works.

This word, too, with its derivative *creative*, is used far too often and too lightly[4] now to allow us to easily perceive its importance. 'Creare' was one of those old Latin words which had been impregnated through the Septuagint and the Vulgate with Hebraic and Christian associations; its constant use in ecclesiastical Latin had saturated it with the special meaning of *creating*, in divine fashion, out of nothing, as opposed to the merely human *making*, which signified the rearrangement of matter already created, or the imitation of 'creatures'. The application of such a word to human activities seems to mark a pronounced change in our attitude towards ourselves, and it is not surprising that, in the

4. London emporiums even advertise themselves in chatty essays entitled *The Creative Aspect of a Store*.

course of its career, the new use should have met with some opposition on the grounds of blasphemy.

Once established, however, the conception evidently reacted on other terms embodying theories of art, such, for example, as *original* and *originality* (already mentioned), *art, artist, genius, imagination, inspiration, poesy, poetry*, and others. The meaning which *inspiration* possessed up to the seventeenth or eighteenth centuries carries us right back to the old mythical outlook in Greece and elsewhere, when poets and prophets were understood to be the direct mouthpieces of superior beings—such as the Muses, who inspired or 'breathed into' them the divine afflatus. Through Plato and Aristotle this conception came to England at the Renaissance and lasted as an element of aesthetic theory well on into the eighteenth century, if it can be said to have died out altogether even now. But, like so many other words, this one began in the seventeenth century to suffer that process which we have called 'internalization'. Hobbes poured etymologically apposite scorn on the senseless convention 'by which a man, enabled to speak wisely from the principles of Nature and his own meditation, loves rather to be thought to speak by inspiration, like a Bagpipe'. And we may suppose that from about this time *inspiration*, like some of the 'character' words which we traced in a previous chapter, began to lose its old literal meaning and to acquire its modern and metaphorical one. Like *instinct*, it was now felt, whatever its real nature, to be something arising from within the human being rather than something instilled from without.

Such a revised notion of the immediate source of human activities inevitably concentrated attention on the individual artist—a fact which may perhaps be reflected in the use from the seventeenth century onwards of the word *genius* to describe not merely the 'creative' faculty, but its possessor. For we can speak now of such and such a man being 'a *genius*'. This little word, on which a whole chapter might be written, comes from the Latin 'genius'[5] (from 'gign-o', 'to bring into being', a stem appearing also in *ingenious, engine*, . . .), which in Roman mythology meant a person's tutelary spirit, or special angel attending him everywhere and influencing his thoughts and actions. Its early meaning in English was much the same as that of *talent*,[6] which, of course, takes its meaning from the New Testament parable. That is to say, *genius* signified an ability implanted in a man by God at his birth. But from about the seventeenth century this meaning began to ferment and expand in the most extraordinary way; it was distinguished from, and even opposed to, *talent*, and in the following century its

5. *Demon* is the Greek name for the same being, its present infernal associations having been merely imported by the hostility and superstition of early Christianity. Socrates, for instance, attributed all his wisdom to his 'daimonion', and *genius* must undoubtedly have been affected by this word through the assiduous translation of Greek philosophy in Latin.

6. A Greek monetary unit.

force and suggestiveness were much enhanced by the use which was made of it to translate the Arabic 'Djinn', a powerful supernatural being. Although nowadays we generally distinguish this particular sense by the spelling *Genie*, the temporary fusion of meanings certainly deepened the strength and mystery of the older word, and may even have procreated the later Byronic tradition of mighty, lonely *poets* with open necks and long hair and a plethora of mistresses and daguerreotypes.

Before, however, these words could acquire the potent meanings which they bear today, they had to run the gauntlet of the Age of Reason, with its hatred of all that savours of enthusiasm and fanaticism. And it was out of the ridicule and distrust which they encountered at its hands that the important new epithet *romantic*, together with some obsolete terms like *romancy, romancical, romantical*, . . . was born. With its meaning of 'like the old romances' (and therefore barbarous, fantastic), *romantic* was one of those adjectives, like *enthusiastic, extravagant, Gothic*, by which the later seventeenth, and the eighteenth century expressed their disapproval of everything which did not bear the stamp of reason and polite society. It was soon applied to people whose heads were stuffed out with the ballooning extravagancies of the old romances, just as *enthusiastic* was employed to describe superstitious people who believed themselves distended with a special variety of divine inspiration. Above all, it had the sense of fabulous, unreal, unnatural. 'Can anything,' asked Bishop South, 'be imagined more profane and impious, absurd, and indeed romantic?' But at the beginning of the eighteenth century this meaning developed a little farther. *Romantic* was now used of places, or aspects of Nature, of the kind among which the old Romances had been set. It was noticed that 'romantic' people displayed a preference for wild landscapes and ruined castles, and would even 'fancy' these things, where more rational people could see nothing more exciting than a tumbledown barn and a dirty ditch. And it is this particular shade of meaning, together with a strong suggestion of absurdity and unreality, which the word seems still to have conveyed to Jane Austen, who preferred to use *picturesque* in contexts where we should now employ *romantic* in its approving or non-committal sense.

Had one of her heroines, however, succeeded in emerging from that endless round of incredibly dull activities which she contrives to make so incredibly interesting, and had this enterprising young woman then attempted to breast the intellectual currents of the age, she would have been startled to find that that sarcastic consciousness of a war between sense and sensibility, which was her creator's inspiration, was a spent stream flowing from the remote past. For while echoes of the original thinking of men like Bacon, Hobbes, and Locke continued to rumble and reverberate on the disparaging implications carried by a word like *romantic*, a new note that already become audible beneath them as long as the beginning of the century. It was an undertone of reluctant approval. These 'romantic' notions might be absurd, but they were at least pleasant. 'We do not care for seeing through the falsehood', wrote Addison, 'and willingly give ourselves up to so agreeable an imposture.'

It was the second half of the eighteenth century that this aesthetic[7] vocabulary—*genius, original, romantic, . . .*—whose meanings had up to the present developed largely by the English, began to make a stir on the Continent. The words were talked of in France; they were taken up by the critics, poets, and philosophers of Germany; and after much handling by men like Kant, Hegel, Schelling, Goethe, and others, the further and partly popularized meanings which they thus acquired were, in a sense, again inserted into their English forms by one or two Englishmen who, towards the close of the century, felt a strong affinity between their own impulses and the *Sturm und Drang* which had been agitating Germany. The most influential of these was Samuel Taylor Coleridge, and just before the turn of the century there burst, with his help, upon England that strange explosion which received, naturally enough, the name of the Romantic Movement. At first it took the form of a sort of cult of the Middle Ages. *Ballad* is another word which added several cubits to its stature by travelling in France and Germany, where it also gave birth to the musical *ballade*; and we find medieval words like *bard, foray, gramarye* (and its Scotch derivative, *glamour*), and *raid*, revived by Walter Scott after having fallen out of use for two or three hundred years. *Derring-do*—another of these revivals—is interesting because it originates in a mistake made by Spenser about Chaucer. He had described how Troilus was second to nobody in 'derring do that longeth to a knight'—that is to say, ' in daring to do that which belongs to a knight'—or, in Cornish idiom, 'that which a knight "belongs to do' ". It is easy to see the nature of Spenser's error. The mysterious substantive *derring-do* (desperate courage), which he created and used several times, is not found again until Scott's *Ivanhoe*.

Very soon the Romantic Movement was resuscitating the Elizabethan world as well as the 'Gothic'—a word, by the way, which now, for the first time in its history, began to connote approval. It was Coleridge himself who invented the word *Elizabethan*, and his inspiring lectures on Shakespeare must be very largely responsible for that renewed and deepened interest in the great dramatist in which Germany once more set us the example. It is also noteworthy that the word *fitful*, which Shakespeare had probably coined in the famous line from *Macbeth*, was never used again until the close of the eighteenth century; and another word which expired when the Elizabethan spirit expired in Milton, to be resurrected in the nineteenth century, is *faery*, with that spelling, and with the

7. To the beginning of this period in Germany we owe the word *aesthetic*, which we take from the German philosopher Baumgarten's use of 'aesthetik' to describe a 'criticism of taste' considered as part of a complete philosophy. Needless to say, the word chosen (Greek 'aisthētos', 'perceived by the senses') bears a relation to the nature of Baumgarten's theory.

meaning, not so much of an individual sprite as of a magic realm or state of being—almost 'the whole supernatural element in romance'.

This supernatural element—as we saw in the history of the words *creative* and *genius*—is connected very intimately indeed with the origin of the Romantic Movement. And we shall see the connection even more clearly in the semantic development of two more words—the last to be examined in this book—*fancy* and *imagination*. The various Greek words which the Latin 'imago' was used to translate acquired their special meanings among the Stoics, where, as we saw in Chapter VI, that teasing sense of a contrast, a lack of connection, between the 'objective' and 'subjective' worlds appears first to have developed. One of these words was 'phantasia', from which we have taken indirectly the divergent forms *fantasy, phantasy,* and *fancy*. In the first century A.D. the Greek 'phantasia' was predominantly used, so we are told, 'in cases where, carried away by enthusiasm and passion, you think you see what you describe, and you place it before the eyes of your hearers'.[8] 'Phantasia' and 'imagination' were in use among the Schoolmen, and *fantasy* and *imagination* are both found in Chaucer in the sense of 'a mental image or reflection', or more particularly 'an image of something which either has no real existence or does not yet exist'. After the Renaissance Shakespeare suddenly transfigured one of the two words in one of those extraordinary passages which make us feel that genius is indeed something more than earthly:

> And as imagination bodies forth
> The forms of things unknown, the poet's pen
> Turns them to shapes and gives to airy nothing
> A local habitation and a name.

In such a passage we seem to behold him standing up, a figure of colossal stature, gazing at us over the heads of the intervening generations. He transcends the flight of time and the laborious building up of meanings, and, picking up a part of the outlook of an age which is to succeed his by nearly two hundred years, gives it momentary expression before he lets it drop again. That mystical conception which the word embodies in these lines—a conception which would make imagination the interpreter and part creator of a whole unseen world—is not found again until the Romantic Movement has begun.

And then it had to be reached slowly. Seventy years after Shakespeare wrote we find the philosopher, Henry More, cautiously distinguishing from other kinds of imagination 'that Imagination which is most free, such as we use in Romantick Inventions'. 'Imagining', wrote Dryden, 'is in itself the very height and life of poetry'; and in 1712 Addison published in the *Spectator* his papers

---

8. Longinus, *On the Sublime*, a treatise which exerted a remarkable influence on English criticism from the time of Dryden onwards.

on 'The Pleasures of the Imagination', in which he used the two words *fancy* and *imagination* synonymously, describing in one of the essays how, because of the faculty of which they are the names,

> our Souls are at present delightfully lost and bewildered in a pleasing Delusion, and we walk about like the inchanted Hero of a Romance, who sees beautiful Castles, Woods, and Meadows; and at the same time hears the warbling of Birds, and the purling of Streams; but upon the finishing of some secret Spell, the fantastic Scene breaks up, and the disconsolate Knight finds himself on a barren Health, or in a solitary Desart.

The tendency among critics to use this sort of imagery, or words suggestive of it, when writing of the *fancy* and the *imagination*, rapidly increased. Dryden had already distinguished the 'fairy' way of writing, and from Addison's time we constantly hear writers and their art referred to in terms of *fairyland, enchantments, magic, spells, wands, . . .* Shakespeare, we are told by one writer, is 'a more powerful magician than his own Prospero'. 'The world is worn out to us,' wrote Young. 'Where are its formerly sweet delusions, its airy castles, and glittering spires?' And five years later he assured us that 'the pen of an origin writer, like Armida's wand, out of a barren waste calls a blooming spring'.

But as the Romantic impulse grew older and crystallized into a philosophy—when the child which had germinated, as feeling, among the ignorant many who spoke the Romance languages, after passing through its Elizabethan adolescence, achieved self-conscious maturity, as thought, among the learned few who were familiar with the complicated literary languages of modern Europe—the need was felt for some way of distinguishing what were merely 'sweet delusions' from the more perdurable productions of the Romantic spirit. And this Coleridge achieved by his famous distinction between *fancy* and *imagination. Fancy,* since his day, has meant rather the power of inventing illustrative imagery—the playful adornment, as it were, of Nature; but *imagination* is the power of creating from within forms which themselves become a part of Nature—'Forms', as Shelly put it,

> more real than living man,
> Nurslings of immortality.

The next step in the meaning of this word was really taken on the day upon which Coleridge, with his head full of ancient witchery, was introduced to another poet with his heart full of mountains. Under their joint influence we can behold that despised habit of looking at life through the spectacles of the old Romances, the mysterious faculty of superimposing on Nature of magical colour or mood created in the observer by the *fictions* of genius or the myths of bygone ages, expanding until it includes the contemplation of Nature impassioned by the any effluence arising from within—it may be emotion or it may be the individual memory. It was the philosophy of the Lake School that the perception of Nature—that is to say of all in Nature that is not purely mechanical—depends upon what is brought to it by the observer. Deep must call unto deep. To a creation apprehended as automatic by the senses and the reason, only *imagination* could

> Add the gleam,
> The light that never was on sea or land;

for imagination was 'essentially vital, even as all objects (*as* objects) are essentially fixed and dead'.[9]

Imagination was, in fact, *organic*; and the application of this adjective to the inner world has not been traced farther back than Coleridge, who, in his lectures on Shakespeare's plays, emphasized the mistake of confounding 'mechanical regularity with organic form'. But perhaps the most brilliant, even epigrammatic, expression which has ever been given to the everlasting war between the unconscious, because creative, vital principle and the conscious, because destructive, calculating principle, is contained in four lines from a little poem of Wordsworth's called *The Tables Turned*:

> Sweet is the lore which nature brings:
>   Our meddling intellect
> Mis-shapes the beauteous forms of things—
>   We murder to dissect.

And so it is in the philosophy and poetry of Romanticism that we first feel a true understanding, not indeed of the process itself, but of the results of that process, which has been traced in this book under the name of 'internalization'. Slowly the divers of the Romantic expedition brought up to the surface of consciousness that vast new cosmos which had so long been blindly forming in the depths. It was a cosmos in which the spirit and spontaneity of life had moved out of Nature and into man. The magic of Persia, the Muses of Greece, the witches and fairies and charms and enchantments of Romance—all these had been locked safely in man's bosom, there to sleep until the trump of Romanticism sounded its call to imagination to give back their teeming life to Nature. 'O Lady', wrote Coleridge in that most heartrending of all poems, wherein, like the disconsolate knight awaking on the barren heath, he reports the decay in himself of this very power:

> O Lady! we receive but what we give,
> And in our life alone does nature live:

9. Coleridge: *Biographia Literaria*.

Ours is her wedding-garment, ours her shroud!
And would we aught behold, of higher worth,
Than that inanimate cold world allowed
To the poor loveless, ever-anxious crowd,
Ah! from the soul itself must issue forth
A light, a glory, a fair luminous cloud
Enveloping the Earth—
And from the soul itself must there be sent
A sweet and potent voice, of its own birth,
Of all sweet sounds the life and element.

And this re-animation of Nature was possible because the imagination was felt as *creative* in the full religious sense of the word. It had itself assisted in creating the natural forms which the senses were now contemplating. It had moved upon the face of the waters. For it was 'the repetition in the finite mind of the eternal act of creation'—the Word made human.

In tracing the semantic history of important words like these, we must not forget that nine-tenths of the words comprising the vocabulary of a civilized nation are never used by more than at most one-tenth of the population; while of the remaining tithe nine-tenths of those who use them are commonly aware of about one-tenth of their meanings. Nevertheless it is just by following those meanings to the high-water mark which they have reached in a few eager minds that we can observe what may fairly be called changes in the general consciousness. It is true that the new meanings must filter through a graduated hierarchy of imaginative literature, literary journalism, reviews, sermons, journalism, popular novels, advertisements, radio, and cinema captions before what is left of them reaches the general public; but the amount that *is* left, and the spell which is accordingly exerted on the many, depends on how far they have first been carried by the few. A hundred and fifty or more years ago, when mountains were still 'horrid', the foundations of the present economic structure of Switzerland were being quietly laid by the dreams of a few Lake poets and their brother Romantics. And incidentally the extraordinary load of meaning often borne by the word *dream* itself, in phrases like *dreamland, my dreams, the land of my dreams,* ... is no doubt traceable ultimately to the use of this word by the great Romantics. When Shelley wrote:

Through the cold mass
Of marble and of colour his[10] dreams pass . . .

and

He hath awakened from the dream of life . . .

10. I.e. man's; the allusion is, of course, to plastic and visual art.

he was also, we might say, writing the greater part of a good many twentieth-century drawing-room ballads.

Others today are fascinated by their *dreams*, because they regard them as messengers from that mysterious inner world in which, like the Christians of old, they are beginning to divine depths hiterto unimagined. They feel 'forces' at work there which they are tempted to personify in terms of ancient myth—*Ahriman, Lucifer, Oedipus, Psyche*, and the like. But outside the significant adjective *subconscious*, which has almost certainly come to stay, the effect which such tendencies may have on the English language remains a tale to be told a hundred years hence. The numerous secondary implications unfolding within *dream*, however, its popularity, and its obvious power of suggesting images, must interest us as further symptoms of a now almost universal consciousness of at any rate the existence of such an 'inner' world. In some lines written as a preface to the *Recluse*—the long, unfinished philosophical poem of which the *Prelude* and the *Excursion* were to form parts—Wordsworth has described the holy awe which he, for one, entertained as he realized that he must now set out to explore this world:

> Urania, I shall need
> Thy guidance, or a greater Muse, if such
> Descend to earth or dwell in highest heaven!
> For I must tread on shadowy ground, must sink
> Deep—and, aloft ascending, breathe in worlds
> To which the heaven of heavens is but a veil.
> All strength—all terror, single or in bands,
> That ever was put forth in personal form—
> Jehovah—with his thunder, and the choir
> Of shouting Angels, and the empyreal thrones,
> I pass them unalarmed. Not Chaos, not
> The darkest pit of lowest Erebus,
> Nor aught of blinder vacancy, scooped out
> By help of dreams—can breed such fear and awe
> As fall upon us often when we look
> Into our Minds, into the Mind of Man—
> My haunt, and the main region of my song.

from *The Rediscovery of Meaning*

The Harp and the Camera

The harp has long been employed as the symbol of music in general, and of heavenly music in particular; just as music itself has been employed as the symbol of heaven on earth. As the English poet Walter de la Mare put it:

> When music sounds, all that I was I am
> Ere to this haunt of brooding dust I came—

In Ireland the harp is the national symbol. It is even on their postage stamps. I remember, when I was young, a popular song that began: "Just a little bit of heaven fell from out the sky one day / And dropped into the ocean not so many miles away." Years later I came to suspect a grain of substance underlying the sentimental drivel. If you travel to Scotland and then go on to Ireland, you see first the Scottish mountains and then the Irish mountains; and they are very much alike in many ways. In both places it is probably raining, or will be in a minute or two; yet there is a subtle difference between them, the kind of subtlety that really needs a combination of Ruskin and Henry James to put it into words. Perhaps you could put it crudely like this. In the Scottish mountains you feel the mountains are somehow being drawn up into the sky. The earth seems to have been raised up to the sky and to have mingled with it; whereas in Ireland it is the other way round. It is almost as if the mountains were actually a part of the sky that had come down and was mingling with the earth.

There is one kind of harp which most of us never have seen. I have never seen one myself. And that is the aeolian harp or, as I shall call it for short, the wind-harp, since Aeolus was the Greek god of the winds. It sounds a delightful instrument, and I have always meant, but have somehow never managed, to make one. It is simply a series of strings in a box, which you fix up somewhere where the wind will blow through the strings and the strings will sound. A good place is an open window; and that might perhaps remind us that the earliest windows were not the kind we have today with glass in them. They were designed not for letting in the light and keeping out the air, but for letting in both of them together. In fact the word "window" is a corruption of "wind-eye."

The wind-harp has been much more written about than it has been seen or heard. It had a very special fascination for the Romantics. The German poet Eduard Mörike speaks of *"einer luftgeborenen Muse geheimnissvolles Saitenspiel"* the secret string-melody of an air-born muse" (today perhaps it would be safer to say "wind-born"), and describes how, when the wind grows more violent, the harp gives out a kind of human cry. The wind makes a sound of its own, but in the harp's strings it echoes or imitates itself, with a would-be personal sound that reproduces the cosmic, impersonal sound of the wind itself. William Wordsworth begins his long poem, *The Prelude*, by speaking of "aeolian visitations"; and in a later passage of the poem where he is describing the crossing of the Alps, although the wind-harp is not mentioned, he probably has it in mind when he speaks of

> a stream
> That flowed into a kindred stream; a gale
> Confederate with the current of the soul. . . .

Many of the great Romantics were as much interested in the theory of poetry as they were in writing poetry. So Wordsworth's "confederate gales" represented to him not just a flight of fancy, but really an avowed part of his theory of the nature of poetry, or rather of his whole aesthetic theory, that is, his whole theory of the relation between man and nature in perception considered especially in the realm of art. Now you find in reading the Romantics that sometimes their theory of poetry is embodied in the poetry itself. That is the case with Coleridge's poem *The Aeolian Harp*, where you find these often quoted lines:

> And what if all of animated nature
> Be but organic Harps diversely framed,
> That tremble into thought, as o'er them sweeps
> Plastic and vast, one intellectual breeze,
> At once the Soul of each, and God of all?

But more often perhaps the theory is kept apart from the practice and is expressed in prose. There is Shelley, for instance. The wind-harp, as you might expect, made a very strong appeal to his imagination. You find in his early essay "On Christianity" this passage: "There is a Power by which we are surrounded, like the atmosphere in which some motionless lyre is suspended, which visit with its breath our silent chords at will." He is depicting the genesis of poetry. Well, Shelley has his answer in the same early essay, and you remember that it was an attack on Christianity. He tells us that poets are "the passive slaves of some higher and more omnipotent Power. This Power is God." Did he really think that? If we conceive of the genesis of poetry in terms of something like "inspiration," as perhaps we must, we are at once faced with a difficult question. What is the part in it played by the poet himself? That always has been a difficult question and remains one now. Whether we speak, as Shelley does, of the "breath of universal being," or of the unconscious, or the id within the unconscious, or whatever terminology we choose to adopt, we still have an extremely difficult question. And so a few years later, when Shelley came to write his "Defence of Poetry," he felt he had to make his wind-harp a little more complicated. He now put it this way:

> Man is an instrument over which a series of external and internal impressions are driven, like the alternations of an ever-changing wind over an aeolian lyre, which move it by their motion to ever-changing melody. But there is a principle within the human being, and perhaps within all sentient beings, which acts otherwise than in the lyre, and produces not melody alone, but harmony, by an internal adjustment of the sounds or motions thus excited to the impressions which excite them.

So we have now a "principle" which acts otherwise than in the lyre. And one feels he has changed the symbol to something more than an ordinary lyre or harp, something more even than a wind-harp, something more like a kind of magic harp that somehow plays itself by being played on. But then again, does it play itself? Later in the same essay we have him saying it is "those poets who have been harmonized by their own will" who give forth divinest melody, when the breath of universal being sweeps over their frame. That is rather different from the "passive slave" we heard of before. You might think it is rather a queer sort of a passive slave who has to have a will of his own. My idea of a slave— and I am pretty sure it was shared by the author of *Prometheus Unbound*—is someone who is just not allowed to have a will of his own.

The title of this lecture is "The Harp and the Camera"; and while I have been talking about harps, you may have been privately wondering when I am going to come to cameras, and what on earth the two have to do with each other. I must first tell you how they became linked together in my mind. The trick was done for me by one very remarkable man. He was a German Jesuit called Athanasius Kircher, and he lived some three hundred years ago. Kircher was a "polymath" if ever there was one. He studied a variety of subjects including—and these are not the only ones—music, Egyptology, Sinology, botany, magnetism. In the course of his life he had himself let down into the crater of Vesuvius and he is claimed as the founder of geology. But besides his book on music he also wrote one on optics, which is called *Ars Magna Lucis et Umbrae*. I must mention here that I am indebted for my acquaintance with Kircher, and therewith for the germ of this lecture, to M. H. Abrams, the author of that truly admirable book *The Mirror and the Lamp*, in which the notes are almost as excellent as the text. Now Kircher is the first writer to have described the wind-harp. Whether he actually invented it is disputed, and indeed there is an old tradition that it was invented by St. Dunstan. St. Dunstan is also the patron saint of the blind, and whether there is any significance in *that* I shall leave you to ask yourselves at the end of the lecture. Anyway it was during the hundred or so years after Kircher's death that the aeolian harp became a popular tenant's fixture. Quite a lot of people had one as a normal addition to the amenities of the house. Then, towards the end of the eighteenth century, it seems to have died away as a toy and begun a second life as a symbol. It was adopted, as I have said, as a favorite symbol by the Romantics.

But there is another quite different invention, in the development of which the same man, Athanasius Kircher, seems to have taken a leading part; and that is the camera obscura. Moreover it is agreed, I think, that he *was* the actual inventor of yet a third device, and one which occupies a very important place in what I shall later on be calling the "camera sequence." But let us begin with the camera obscura, which Kircher both described and improved, though he probably did not invent it. It is, as I expect you know, something like a box with one single very, very small aperture. One could perhaps think of the aperture as a tiny window. It is either so small as scarcely to deserve the name—just a pinprick, in fact—or else, though not quite so small as a pin-prick, it is still very small and is filled with a particular sort of glass which we now call a lens. Inside the box you fix a mirror, disposed I think at an angle of forty-five degrees; and the result is that, by looking through a larger aperture in the top of the box, you receive a picture in miniature of all that the focused light brings with it through the tiny one.

Reflecting on those two very different ploys of Anthanasius Kircher it struck me that, if the wind-harp can be seen as a kind of emblem of the Romantic Movement, or the Romantic Period if you like, the camera obscura is no less an emblem of the Renaissance. Only in this case it is a good deal more than an emblem; and it is an emblem of a good deal more than the Renaissance. It points us to something that underlay the Renaissance and came to expression not only in the Revival of Learning but also in such other historical movements as on the one hand the Protestant Reformation and on the other the birth of modern science. In other words it is an emblem of that species of Copernican Revolution in the human psyche which was quite as much the cause as it was the consequence of the Copernican Revolution in astronomy. I mean the revolution, formulated rather than initiated by Immanuel Kant, whereby the human mind more or less reversed its conception of its own relation to its environment. It is more than an emblem, because the camera obscura (considered as the original source of the whole camera sequence) was also *instrumental* in actually bringing about the change of which I have spoken. We may better call it a symbol, since the camera sequence as a whole was part of the change which it betokens or symbolizes. You know it has been said that the proper definition of a symbol is that it both represents something other than itself and is also a part of it. Coleridge defined a symbol as "part of the reality it represents." For that reason he held that a historical event may be a symbol of the historical process of which it is a part. It is precisely in that sense that I am claiming the invention of the camera as a symbol of post-Renaissance man.

Let us now have a look at this "camera sequence." In the world in which the camera obscura was invented, in the sixteenth and seventeenth centuries, there was as yet no such thing as photography. There could not have been, since the camera obscura was itself the photographic camera in embryo. Besides therefore being an amusing toy, the camera obscura quickly came to be used for practical purposes, for the production of reduced-size sketches of larger objects or assemblies of objects, and particularly in the business of sketching landscapes. There on the screen you had the complex three-dimensional real world, in which we walk about on legs, conveniently reduced to a little two-dimensional image which the pencil had only to trace. In other words, this convenient device effected, almost of its own accord, a result which many great painters had been trying very hard for a large number of years to learn how to bring about, and in which they were just beginning to succeed. There you had given to you a picture drawn very accurately *in perspective*. Now if it is true that the painters had been trying for a number of years to bring about the use of perspective—to discover what it was—it is also true that, in terms of the whole history of the art of painting, that number is really a very small one. In fact, the gradual and very late discovery of the secret of perspective seems to me to be a truly remarkable phenomenon. I ask you to consider, in support of that contention, the following five facts. There had been for centuries past many great and skillful painters passionately interested in the technique of their art. Secondly, geometry was a study highly advanced among the Greeks. Thirdly, the Greeks were perfectly well able to apply their discoveries in geometry to the practice of art—to architecture for instance—for if you read about the principles on which the building of the Parthenon was conducted you will find most elaborate geometrical principles embodied in it. Fourthly, Euclid himself actually wrote a work on optics. Euclid, the founder of geometry, wrote a work on optics, although that work is lost. And lastly, the Greek theory of art, whether of sculpture or poetry or painting, was a theory of *imitation*, imitation of nature. Now, keeping all that in mind, recall that nevertheless European painters only began to interest themselves in the comparatively simple rules of perspective in perhaps the fourteenth or fifteenth century A.D.; in perspective, which is the kingpin, one could say, of the whole craft of representing three dimensions in two! When it did happen, not only were they interested but they were wildly excited. There is a story somewhere, I believe it is in Vasari, of an Italian painter who walked about the streets, and I believe also woke up his wife at night, constantly repeating, *"Che dolce cosa é questa perspettiva!"* "What a lovely thing this perspective is!" Leonardo's reflections led him to the conclusion that you should make your picture look like a natural scene reflected in a large mirror. And naturally, when the camera obscura came and he heard of it, he soon went on to it.

It seems so obvious; and yet apparently something had to happen, something quite out of the experience of the Greeks, and of the Egyptians, who were also no mean geometricians, to make it appear even possible, let alone obvious, to imitate nature by that simple trick. And now when it did come at last after all those years, here was a simple mechanical device that brought the fruit of years of technical study and experiment by great painters within the reach of every Tom, Dick, and Harry. All he needed was a pencil and a hand steady enough to trace accurately. The art of imitating had been reduced to the technique of copying. The next step in the camera sequence was to do away with even the pencil and the steady hand. For the camera obscura led to the invention of the daguerreotype and so to that of the photograph. And then the advent of the photograph did something which could hardly have been anticipated by those who had invented it, though it may well be that it would not have worried them if it had. It all took a little time, but one thing that the photograph did was to kill stone dead (well not quite stone dead, for the wound has only proved mortal in our own time) just that leading principle of aesthetic theory, that principle of art, which had held sway at least from the time of Aristotle down to the eighteenth century, the theory that the function of the artist is to imitate nature. The imitation of nature, now that it was being done by applying the sweet rules of perspective, had become altogether too easy; so easy that you could make a little gimmick that would do it all for you.

The camera sequence is not altogether simple to narrate. It betrays a certain leapfrogging element. Long before photography was invented, while it was still in embryo as the camera obscura, the next step, which properly *succeeds* photography, had already been taken. It had been taken in fact by Athanasius Kircher himself. For it is generally agreed that Kircher *was* the inventor of what used to be called the "magic lantern." Perhaps it still is. That particular toy does not receive pictures into itself but, with the help of artificial light inside it, it projects (repeat, *projects*) them back onto the world outside itself, normally onto a blank screen, or a blank wall, or some kind of *tabula rasa*. But even if the wall is not blank, provided the artificial light is bright enough, the picture will be projected and it will either mix with or obliterate for the spectator whatever is actually on the wall. Hastening now to a conclusion, the next step was of course to run a lot of these projected pictures together; it was the step from still to motion, from the magic lantern to the movie. And the last step of all followed quickly; from the movie to television. Only here at last do we reach the toy in which

Marshall McLuhan's Herr Gutenberg and his successors probably *have* had as big a hand as Kircher himself and his successors. Only in the technique of television does the art of printing enter the long camera sequence that began with Kircher's camera obscura and his magic lantern.

Let us contemplate for a moment the enormous contrast between the camera and the wind-harp, taken as typifying the process of perception. The process of perception is the means by which what is there outside of us—what is going on "out there"—becomes our own experience. The harp's medium is air, on which of course sound is borne to us, and air is something that is itself both inside and outside of us. Apart from its use in perception, it is entering and leaving us all day and all night from the day we are born until the moment we cease to breathe. In order that we may perceive by means of it, it has to enter quite a long way into the body before, within the labyrinth of the ear, it is converted into sensations of sound. The word "inspiration," as doctors use it, means taking physical air—oxygen—into our lungs. But the same word in common parlance always suggests taking something else in along with the oxygen. The sounding harp in fact may be taken as the emblem of *inspiration*. By contrast the camera's medium is light. And light does not enter into the body at all. It is stopped short at the surface of the eye; and you know how often the eye has been compared to a mirror. From that point on, what happens is so to speak our own affair. But as to what actually *does* happen, to give us the experience of seeing, whether there are produced replicas, or internal reproductions, or what you will, of the world outside us—that is something that has been argued about almost since argument began. It is very much easier to shut our eyes than it is to shut our ears. What exactly *is* it that is there when our eyes are open but is no longer there when they are shut? With the different attempts at answering that question you could fill a line or two of a dictionary; you would need as much simply for the different names that have been given to what *is* there. *Forms, phantoms, idols, simulacra, effigies, films*, are some of them. In Lucretius alone you find a whole mine of different synonyms for this mysterious panorama that the eye delivers to us. But they all mean something like, or some part of, what the word *image* means. And *image* is perhaps the word most commonly employed. The camera then can fairly been seen as an emblem, or perhaps this time one should rather say caricature, of *imagination*.

The Italian word *camera* means a room or chamber; and the camera is of course, a hollow box or little dark room. Unlike the camera the harp has no inside, it does not first of all receive into itself stimuli from without and then respond to them. The wind-harp becomes what it is by itself becoming an "inside" for the environing air, by becoming a modulated voice for it to speak with. If the eyes are shut and there is no other guide, it is very difficult to tell where any particular sound comes from, presumably because the air and its contents are all around us. Well, light and its contents are also all around us. But our eyes are so made that they leave us in no doubt where those contents are placed, and how they are disposed. The two sorts of arrangement are very different and that difference is really all we mean by the word "perspective." Light comes to us impartially from all directions and you might think that our point of view out into it would diverge from the eye in lines going out in all directions into space, at least in all directions open to it. Actually the opposite occurs. If we see in perspective, as we normally do, we have to make those lines converge to one particular point, which is usually called the *"vanishing point."* The farther off from us and from each other things are in space, the nearer they must be in our picture to the vanishing point and therefore to each other. Now that is not the way we *think* about space; it is the way we see it. We vaguely fancy there is a difference between "view" and "point of view"; but in fact there is none. The eye, seeing in perspective, is *projecting* its own point of view, its punctiliar nothingness as I would like to call it, into what geometricians call the plane at infinity but the ordinary man has to imagine as something like the inside of a vast hollow shell. By doing so, the eye converts that hollow sphere into a tableau that reduces depth to surface and flattens three dimensions into only two. That is the *immediate* experience so faithfully recorded by the camera. If there were no such immediate experience, photographs would not be "lifelike." That is also why the camera is a *caricature* of imagination, although it is a true emblem of perspective. Imagination is living, perspective only "lifelike." It used to be said that the camera cannot lie. But in fact it always does lie. Just because it looks only in that immediate way, the camera looks always *at* and never *into* what it sees. I suspect that Medusa did very much the same.

Well, then along come the magic lantern and the movie, and they project all over again that very projection of punctiliar nothingness, that very "film" which the camera itself produced by projection in the first place. Perhaps it is not surprising that "project" and "projection" have become such very loaded words. What a history they have behind them! A student of the history of words and their meanings is apt to acquire a rather profound scepticism concerning the shared mental horizon of his contemporaries. He notices that when poets use metaphors, they at least know they are doing so. But nobody else seems to know it, although they are not only speaking but also thinking in metaphors all the time. I recall very well, when I was writing my early book, *History in English Words*, being astonished at the ubiquitous appearance of the *clock* as a metaphor shortly after it had been invented. It turned up everywhere where anybody was trying to describe the way things work in nature. Then the clocks stopped—but the metaphor went on. The student of words and their meanings and the history of them asks himself uneasily: This Newton-Kant-Laplace universe, in which the nineteenth century found itself so much at home, was it after all much more than metaphorical clockwork? But unfortunately he cannot stop there. Coming a little nearer to our own time he finds the psychology of the unconscious, in which the first half of the twentieth century felt so much at home. Strange how squarely it seems to be based on an image of "repression," which is much the same as *com*pression! Was it after all just the steam-engine in disguise? We no longer live in the age of the steam-engine. We live in the age of $E = mc^2$, the atomic age. We have discovered, or have told ourselves, that matter does not produce energy but that matter is energy; and we bestow our eager attention on the smallest possible detached unit of matter, expecting to find there the ultimate, still source of all energy. Yes, and we also live in the age of existentialism.

So it is that, in the age of the movie, the student of words who is unfashionable enough to examine their history as well as their current use, is not perhaps so impressed as some others are by the universal practice of projection not only in movie houses and on the television screen, but also, as a concealed metaphor, in the ingenious fancies of men. Is projection itself being projected? He finds, for instance, scientists and philosophers joining hands to assure us that the familiar world around us is a projection of our own mental apparatus onto a kind of wall of imperceptible realities, not perhaps a blank wall, but it might just as well be blank for all the resemblance it bears to anything we do actually see or hear. Or again, when he turns to the psychologists, he finds projections (or perhaps they might almost be called projectiles) in the form of neuroses, fantasies, mother-images, father-fixations, feelings of guilt, and various parts of the body including its secreta and excreta, flying to and fro among them so thick and fast that he has to duck to avoid them. Or again, when the psychologists join hands with the anthropologists, he sees a whole cloud of these projectiles flying off in the same direction and landing on the same target—namely, the mind of that luckless repository, primitive man. One thing at least is made very clear from what all these informative people are fond of telling us about primitive man and that is that, whatever else he was doing, he was always projecting his insides onto something or other. It was his principal occupation. He must presumably have had one or two other things to do as well, but that was what he majored in. The eighteenth century, you know, used to talk of a "ruling passion"; but there is also the ruling metaphor. Perhaps for reading the signs of the times, it is a good deal more important. Let us assume for a moment that it is, and ask ourselves how much of all this stuff would ever have been heard of if Kircher had never invented his magic lantern? Was he, while inventing it, engaged at the same time in inventing for example the anthropological theory of animism? We might even go on to ask (except that the question is one that is never raised in humane academic circles) how much of it all is true?

After all, it is we who actually have *got* the magic lantern and the camera; it is we who have *got* perspective, both in pictures and in photographs, together with the habit of vision which they have raised and fostered. Could it be ourselves who are doing the projecting, when we talk of primitive man in that confident way? *Was* he a magic lantern? Was he even a camera obscura? Are we so sure that he even *had* any inside to speak of? The punctiliar sort that *projects*? Now I personally am quite sure that he had not. Moreover I am firmly persuaded that we shall never get anywhere with our anthropological attempts at reconstructing the mind of primitive man until we make up our minds to throw away all this projection business. If we *must* think in metaphor (and we must), why not try beginning again on the assumption that primitive man was not a camera obscura but an aeolian harp? Surely it is only by this route that we can hope to understand the origin of myths and of thinking at all. Leslie Fiedler, writing on the myth, noted a distinction between two elements we can detect in it. He called them respectively "archetype" and "signature," the signature being that part of a narrative myth which has been contributed by an individual mind or minds. That is a useful distinction, but its usefulness in the long run will depend upon what we are prepared to mean by the word "archetype." It will depend on our accepting the central truth which no one who writes today on the subject does appear to accept, though I should have thought it had been made clear enough more than half a century ago by Rudolf Steiner; the truth that it was not man who made the myths but the myths, or the archetypal substance they reveal, which made man. We shall have to come, I am sure, to think of the archetypal element in myth in terms of the wind that breathed through the harp-strings of individual brains and nerves and fluids, rather as the blood still today pervades and sustains them. Then, when we have started off on the right foot instead of the wrong one, we may come fruitfully on to the problem Shelley had to deal with from a rather different point of view, the problem of the wind-harp that is nevertheless played on by a performer. Then we shall come properly equipped to the problem of that "principle within the human being," as Shelley called it, which acts otherwise than in the lyre and produces not melody alone but harmony. We shall approach in the right way the problem of beings (to quote Shelley again) "harmonized by their own will."

Did that enthusiasm of the Romantics for the wind-harp signify that they had come to see the history of the Western mind as a kind of war between the harp and the camera—that they foresaw the camera civilization that was coming upon us? If so, they were true prophets, because it certainly has come. The camera up to date has won that war. We live in a camera civilization. Our entertainment is camera entertainment. Our holidays are camera holidays. We make them so by paying more attention to the camera we brought with us than to the waterfall we are pointing it at. Our science is almost entirely a camera science. One thinks of the photographs of electrons on screens and in cloud-chambers and so forth. Our philosophers—it is no longer possible even to argue with most of them, because you cannot argue about an axiom, and it is already becoming self-evident to camera man that only camera words have any meaning. Even our poetry has become, for the most part, camera poetry. So much of it consists of those pointedly paradoxical *surface* contrasts between words and between random thoughts and feelings, arranged in the complicated perspective of the poet's own often rather meager personality. Where, one asks, has the music gone? Where has the wind gone that sweeps the music into being, the *hagion pneuma*, the *ruach elohim*? It really does feel as though the camera had won hands down and smashed the harp to pieces.

Perhaps it is just this defeat which the guitar-loving hippies have somehow got wind of. But I do not myself believe that the way out of defeat lies in substituting the harp for the camera, except of course as an aid to historical imagination. For I do not believe that the root from which the camera sequence originally sprang is an unmitigated evil. I even believe it was a necessity. But then neither do I believe that the existence of separate, autonomous human spirits is an unmitigated evil. I traced the camera sequence from a beginning only about as far back as the seventeenth century. But its root is much older than that. It began, I would say, as soon as signature was added to and interwoven with archetype in the structure and substance of myth. That is the same as saying that it began as soon as poetry began to exist within myth—at first within, and then alongside of it. And that again is to say it is something that lies within our destiny. Is not this a truth which the most penetrating minds among the Romantics themselves came to realize? It is interesting to note that, whereas in Shelley we found only that rather perplexed transition from a wind-harp to a harpist's harp, Coleridge—who lived so much longer and had more time to think out a full theory of poetry—does not omit the camera obscura from the imagery he chooses. In the *Biographia Literaria*, by way of comment on Milton's wonderful description of the banyan tree in *Paradise Lost*, he writes:

> This is creation rather than painting, or if painting, yet such and with such co-presence of the whole picture flashed at once upon the eye, as the sun paints in a camera obscura.

Coleridge, you see, converts it from a caricature into a true emblem of imagination. How? By placing the sun, instead of the punctiliar nothingness, at that vanishing point which, as he well knew, was really the point of projection from within the eye of the beholder. After all, however it may have been for primitive man, we cannot in our time get away from projection altogether. "The mind of man is not an aeolian harp." That is another sentence from *Biographia Literaria*, reneging rather sharply, it would seem, from the point of view expressed in the author's youthful poem I quoted to begin with. The mind is at least not wholly an aeolian harp. For us there must be projection, and the question for the twentieth century is whether it is to be a projection of nothingness or a projection of the sun-spirit, the spirit of light. Is not this why, in the same book, we find Coleridge quoting that sentence from Plotinus: "The eye could never have beheld the sun if it were not itself of the same nature as the sun"; the sentence which also meant so much to Goethe, and which he rephrased in the form: "If the eye were not of the same nature as the light, it could never behold the light."

If then the story of the harp and the camera is to continue instead of ending with a whimper, it will have to be by way of a true marriage between the one and the other. Is it fanciful, I wonder, to think of a sort of mini-harp stretched across the window of the eye—an Apollo's harp if you will—as perhaps not a bad image for the joy of looking with imagination? That "joy," as will be well-known here, was precisely the thing which C. S. Lewis spent most of his life discovering more about, discovering in particular that it is by no means the same thing as pleasure or happiness or contentment. In a literary climate, which has already become all camera and no harp, all signature and no archetype, we ought not to forget that little group, if group is the right word, which has some-times been referred to as "Oxford Christians," and sometimes as "Romantic theologians," and with which this college has, thanks to the devotion and energy of Dr. Kilby, established a very special connection. For they may perhaps have contributed their mite to the continuation of the story. The German poet and thinker Novalis, you know, specifically compared with an aeolian harp the *Märchen* or adult fairy tale that modern variant of the myth, in which signature may mingle fruitfully with archetype, but without swamping it altogether. The passage where he does so was selected by George MacDonald as the motto to his own *Märchen, Phantastes*, which played (as he has told us) such a crucial part in the literary and spiritual development of C. S. Lewis. Besides giving us *Märchen* of their own, both Lewis and Tolkien, and their comrade in arms Charles Williams, thought deeply and wrote well on the place of myth and *Märchen* in our modern consciousness. One way or another, they were all three concerned with the problem of imagination; and there is perhaps no piece of writing that deals more gently and genially with the place of imagination in the literature of the future than Tolkien's essay "On Fairy-Stories" in the volume *Essays Presented to Charles Williams*. At least that is so, if I am right in sug-gesting (as I have been trying to suggest by my own rather devious route) that the ultimate question, to which imagination holds the key, is the question of how we can learn to sign our own names to what we create, whether as myth or in other ways, but so nevertheless that what we sign as our own will also be the name of Another—the name I would venture to say, without venturing to pro-nounce it, of the Author and the Lord of the archetypes themselves.

Poetic Diction and Legal Fiction

The house of poetry contains many mansions. These mansions are so diverse in their qualities and in their effect on the indweller and some of them are so distant from others that the inhabitants of one mansion have sometimes been heard to deny that another is part of the same building at all. For instance, Edgar Allan Poe said that there is no such thing as a long poem, and the difference between a long narrative poem and a short lyric is admittedly rather baffling, seeming almost to be one of kind. What I have to say here touches mainly lyric poetry, and will interest those who love to dwell with recurring delight on special felicities of expression more than those to whom poetry means taking their *Iliad* or their *Faerie Queene* a thousand lines at a time and enjoying the story. It is highly specialized. Think for a moment of poems as of pieces of fabric, large tapestries, or minute embroideries as the case may be. What I have to say does not concern the whole form of even one of the embroideries, but only the texture itself, the nature of the process at any given point, as the fabric comes into being, the movements which the shuttle or the needle must have made. It is still more specialized than this; for in examining the texture of poetry one of the most important elements (a mansion to itself) is rhythm, sound, music; and all this is of necessity excluded. I am fully aware that this involves the corollary that the kind of poetry I am talking about may also be written in prose; but that is a difficulty which is chronic to the subject. I wish, however, to treat of that element in poetry which is best called "meaning" pure and simple. Not the meaning of poetry, nor the meaning of any poem as a whole, but just meaning. If this sounds like an essay in microscopy, or if it be objected that what I am talking about is not poetic diction, but etymology or philosophy or even genetic psychology, I can only reply that whatever it ought to be called, it is to some people, extraordinary interesting, and that if, in all good faith, I have given it a wrong address, it is still to me the roomiest, the most commodious, and the most exciting of all the mansions which I rightly or wrongly include in the plan and elevation of the great house.

The language of poetry has always been in a high degree figurative; it is always illustrating or expressing what it wishes to put before us by comparing that with something else. Sometimes the comparison is open and avowed, as when Shelley compares the skylark to a poet, to a high-born maiden, and to a rose embowered in its own green leaves; when Keats tells us that a summer's day is:

> like the passage of an angel's tear
> That falls through the clear ether silently.

Or when Burns writes simply: "My love is like a red red rose." And then we call it a "simile." Sometimes it is concealed in the form of a bare statement, as when Shelley says of the west wind, not that it is *like*, but that it *is* "the breath of Autumn's being," calls upon it to "make him its lyre," and says of himself that *his* leaves are falling. This is known as "metaphor." Sometimes the element of comparison drops still farther out of sight. Instead of saying that A is like B or that A is B, the poet simply talks about B, without making any overt reference to A at all. You know, however, that he intends A all the time, or, better say that you know he intends *an* A; for you may not have a very clear idea of what A is and even if you have got an idea, somebody else may have a different one. This is generally called "symbolism."

I do not say that these particular methods of expression are an absolute *sine quo non* of poetic diction. They are not. Poetry may also take the form of simple and literal statement. But figurative expression is found everywhere; its roots descend very deep, as we shall see, into the nature, not only of poetry, but of language itself. If you took away from the stream of European poetry every passage of a metaphorical nature, you would reduce it to a very thin trickle indeed, pure though the remainder beverage might be to the taste. Perhaps our English poetry would suffer the heaviest damage of all. Aristotle, when treating of diction in his *Poetics*, provides the right expression by calling the element of metaphor πολὺ μέγιστον—far the most important.

It may be noticed that I am now using the word "metaphor" in a slightly different and wider sense than when I placed it in the midst between simile on the one hand and symbol on the other. I am now using it, and shall use it frequently throughout this article, to cover the whole gamut of figurative language including simile and symbol. I do not think this need confuse us. Strict metaphor occurs about the middle of the gamut and expresses the essential nature of such language more perfectly perhaps than either of the extremes. In something the same way Goethe found that the leaf of a plant expressed its essential nature as plant, while the blossom and the root could be considered as metamorphoses of the leaf. Here I want to try and consider a little more closely what the essential nature of figurative language is and how that nature is most clearly apparent in the figure called metaphor.

But first of all let us return to the "gamut" and take some examples. This time let us move along it in the reverse direction, beginning from symbolism.

> Does the road wind uphill all the way?
>   Yes, to the very end.
> Will the day's journey take the whole long day?
>   From morn to night, my friend.

> But is there for the night a resting-place?
>   A roof for when the slow, dark hours begin.
> May not the darkness hide it from my face?
>   You cannot miss that inn.

> Shall I meet other wayfarers at night?
>   Those who have gone before.

Then must I knock or call when just in sight?
    They will not keep you waiting at that door.

Shall I find comfort, travel-sore and weak?
    Of labour you shall find the sum.
Will there be beds for me and all who seek?
    Yea, beds for all who come.

As I have already suggested, the ordinary way of characterizing this kind of language would be to say that the poet says one thing and means another. Is this true? Is it fair to say that Christina Rossetti says B but that she *really means* A? I do not think this is a question which can be answered with a simple "yes" or "no." In fact the difficult and elusive relation between A and B is the heart of my matter. For the time being let me hazard, as a rather hedging sort of answer, that the truer it is to say "yes," the worse is the poem, the truer it is to say "no," the better is the poem. We feel that B, which is actually said, ought to be necessary, even inevitable in some way. It ought to be in some sense the best, if not the only, way of expressing A satisfactorily. The mind should dwell on it as well as on A and thus the two should be somehow inevitably fused together into one simple meaning. But if A is too obvious and could be equally or almost as well expressed by other and more direct means, then the mind jumps straight to A, remains focused on it, and loses interest in B, which shrinks to a kind of dry and hollow husk. I think this is a fault of Christina Rossetti's poem. We know just what A is. A = "The good life is an effort" plus "All men are mortal." Consequently it detaches itself from B, like a soul leaving a body, and the road and the inn and the beds are not a real road and inn and beds, they look faintly heraldic—or as if portrayed in lacquer. They are not even poetically real. We never get a fair chance to accord to their existence that willing suspension of disbelief which we are told constitutes "poetic faith." Let us try another:

'Is there anybody there?' said the Traveller,
    Knocking on the moonlit door;
And his horse in the silence champed the grasses
    Of the forest's ferny floor:
And a bird flew up out of the turret,
    Above the Traveller's head:
And he smote upon the door again a second time:
    'Is there anybody there?' he said.
But no one descended to the Traveller:
    No head from the leaf-fringed sill
Leaned over and looked into his grey eyes,
    Where he stood perplexed and still.

But only a host of phantom listeners
    That dwelt in the lone house then
Stood listening in the quiet of the moonlight
    To that voice from the world of men:
Stood thronging the faint moonbeams on the dark stair,
    That goes down to the empty hall,
Hearkening in an air stirred and shaken
    By the lonely Traveller's call.
And he felt in his heart their strangeness,
    Their stillness answering his cry,
While his horse moved, cropping the dark turf,
    'Neath the starred and leafy sky;
For he suddenly smote on the door, even
    Louder, and lifted his head:—
'Tell them I came, and no one answered,
    That I kept my word', he said.
Never the least stir made the listeners,
    Though every word he spake
Fell echoing through the shadowiness of the still house
    From the one man left awake:
Ay, they heard his foot upon the stirrup
    And the sound of iron on stone,
And how the silence surged softly backward,
    When the plunging hoofs were gone.

This poem seems to me to possess as symbolism most of the virtures which I miss in Christina Rossetti's. First it obviously *is* a symbol. There *is* an A and a good solid one, though we do not know what it is, because we cannot put it into a separate container of words. But that is just the point. A has not got (perhaps I should say, it has not *yet* got) a separate existence in our apprehension; so it makes itself felt by modifying and enriching the meaning of B—it hides itself in B, hides itself in language which still *could* on the face of it be heard and interpreted as though no A came into the question at all.

I must here remark that merely making A obscure is not in itself a recipe for writing good symbolical poetry. William Blake at his worst, and, I fancy, many modern poets who write or intend to write symbolically, go astray here. They are so anxious to avoid the error of intending too obvious an A, so anxious to avoid a mere old-fashioned simile, that we end by being mystified or disgusted by the impossibility of getting any sort of feeling at all of what they are talking about, or why. Why are they talking about B at all? we ask ourselves. If they are doing it simply for the sake of B, it is pure drivel. On the other hand, if they intend an A, what evidence is there of it? We do not mind A being intangible, because it is still only half born from the poet's unconscious, but you cannot make poetry by cunningly removing all the clues which, if left, would discover the staleness of your meaning. In other words, if you set out to say one thing and mean another, you must really mean another, and that other must be worth meaning.

It will be observed that when we started from the simile and moved towards the symbol, the criterion or yard-stick by which we measured our progress was the element of *comparison*—paramount in the simile and very nearly vanished out of sight in the symbol. When, on the other hand, we move backwards, starting from the symbol, we find ourselves with another yard-stick, viz., the fact of saying one thing and meaning another. The poet says B but he means A. He hides A in B. B is the normal everyday meaning which the words so to speak "ought" to have on the face of them, and A is what the poet *really* has to say to us, and which he can only say through or alongside of, or by modifying, these normal everyday meanings. A is his own new, original, or poetic meaning. If I were writing this article in Greek or German, my public would no doubt be severely restricted, but there would be this advantage to me—that I could run the six words "say-one-thing-and-mean-another" together and use the resulting conglomerate as a noun throughout the rest of it. I cannot do this, but I will make bold to borrow another German word instead. The word *Tarnung* was, I believe, extensively used under the heel of the Nazi tyranny in Germany for the precautionary practice of hiding one meaning in another, the allusion being to the *Tarnhelm* of the Nibelungs. I shall give it an English form and call it "tarning." When I say "tarning," therefore, the reader is asked to substitute mentally the concept of saying one thing and meaning another, in the sense in which I have just been trying to expound it. We have already seen that the more A lives as a modification or enrichment of B, the better is the tarning.

Now let us proceed to the next step in our backward progress from symbol to simile. We come to the metaphor. And here we find both the best and the most numerous examples of tarning. Almost any poem, almost any passage of really vivid prose which you pick up is sure to contain them in abundance. I will choose an example (the source of which he does not disclose) given by Dr. Hugh Blair, the eighteenth-century writer on style.

> Those persons who gain the hearts of most people, who are chosen as the companions of their softer hours, and their reliefs from anxiety and care, are seldom persons of shining qualities or strong virtues: it is rather *the soft green* of the soul on which we rest our eyes, that are fatigued with beholding more glaring objects.

Consider how the ordinary literal meaning of the word "green" blends with the ineffable psychic quality which it is the writer's object to convey! How much weaker it would be, had he written: "It is rather persons whose souls we find restful, as the eye finds green fields restful, etc." Put it that way and nearly all the tarning, and with it half the poetry, is lost. The passage reminds me of this from Andrew Marvell's *Garden*:

> The Mind, that Ocean where each kind
> Does straight its own resemblance find;
> Yet it creates, transcending these,
> Far other Worlds, and other Seas;
> Annihilating all that's made
> To a green Thought in a green Shade.

What a lot of tarning can be done with the word "green"!

We see that any striking and original use of even a single word tends to be metaphorical and shows us the process of tarning at work. On the whole, I think it is true to say that the fewer the words containing the metaphor, the more the expression is in the strict sense a "trope" rather than a metaphor—the more tarning we shall feel. For the long and elaborate metaphor is already almost a simile—a simile with the word "like" missed out. We must, however, remember that the tarning may not have actually occurred in the particular place where we find it. People copy one another and the metaphor may be a cliché or, if not a cliché, part of our common heritage of speech. Thus, when Tennyson writes:

> When the happy Yes
> Falters from her lips,
> Pass and blush the news
> Over glowing ships.

we feel that the peculiarly effective use of the word "blush" throughout this lyric is a tarning of his own. It actually goes on in us as we read. When, on the other hand, Arnold writes in the *Scholar Gypsy*:

> O Life unlike to ours!
> Who fluctuate idly without term or scope

or:

> Light half-believers of our casual creeds
> Who never deeply felt, nor clearly willed,
> Whose insight never has borne fruit indeeds

though none of this writing can be described as cliché, yet we feel that the metaphorical element in "fluctuate" and in "borne fruit" is the product of a tarning that happened before Arnold was born. So, too, in the passage I first quoted the "*shining* qualities" and the "*softer* hours" are metaphors of the kind we are all using every day, almost without thinking of them as metaphors. We all speak of *clear* heads, of *brilliant* wit, of *seeing* somebody's meaning, of so-and-so being the *pick of the bunch*, and so on: and most of us must use at least, say, a hundred of these dead or half-dead metaphors every day of our lives. In fact, in dealing with metaphor, we soon find ourselves talking, not of poetry, but of language itself. Everywhere in language we seem to find that the process of tarning, or something very like it, either is or has been at work.

We seem to owe all these tropes and metaphors embedded in language to the fact that somebody at some time had the wit to say one thing and mean another, and that somebody else had the wit to tumble to the new meaning, to detect the bouquet of a new wine emanating from the old bottle. We owe them all to tarning, a process which we find prolifically at work wherever there is poetry—from the symbol, where it shouts at us and is all too easily mishandled, to the simile, where we already hear the first faint stirrings of its presence, inasmuch as the B image even here is modified, enriched, or colored by the A image with which it is this time overtly compared.

> Then fly our greetings, fly our speech and smiles!
> —As some grave Tyrian trader, from the sea,
> Descried at sunrise an emerging prow
> Lifting the cool-hair'd creepers stealthily,
> The fringes of a southward-facing brow
>   Among the Aegean isles;
> And saw the merry Grecian coaster come,
> Freighted with amber grapes, and Chian wine,
> Green bursting figs, and tunnies steep'd in brine;
> And knew the intruders on his ancient home,
> The young light-hearted masters of the waves.

The grave Tyrian trader and the merry Grecian coaster are not the same figures that we should meet in a history book. They have their own life, they take in the imagination a special color from the things with which they are compared— that is, the *Scholar Gypsy* on the one hand and our too modern selves on the other. They are pregnant with the whole of the poem that has gone before.

I said at the beginning that I might be accused of indulging in a kind of aesthetic microscopy. The drawback of the microscope is this, that even if the grain of sand which we see through it does indeed contain a world, mere magnification is not enough to enable us to see that world. Unfortunately the processes which are said to give to the infinitesimal a cosmic character are not merely minute; they are also very rapid. This is certainly true of the process of tarning as it takes place in the mind of the poet and his reader. It is both rapid and delicate and, as the reader may have felt already, it is difficult to take it out and examine it without rushing in where angels fear to tread. But there is another modern invention which may be brought to the aid of the microscope in order to meet this drawback; and that is the slow-motion film. Can we find in any sphere of human life something analogous to a slow-motion picture of the tarning process? I think we can. I have said that tarning can be detected not only in accredited poetry or literature but also in the history of language as a whole. Is there any other human institution in which tarning also happens, and in which it happens on a broader scale and at a more leisure pace? I think there is. I think we shall find such an illustration as we want in the law, notably in the development of law by means of fictions.

We are accustomed to find something crabbed and something comic in legal fictions. When we read in an old pleading an averment that the plaintiff resides in the Island of Minorca, "to wit in the parish of St. Mary le Bow in the Ward of Cheap"—or, in a Note in the *Annual Practice* for 1945, that every man-of-war is deemed to be situated permanently in the parish of Stepney—it sounds funny. But it must be admitted that it is not any funnier *per se* than Shelley's telling us that his leaves are falling or Campion informing us as to his mistress that "there is a garden in her face." It is funny when we take it literally, not particularly funny when we understand what is meant and why it is expressed in that particular way.

There is one kind of metaphor which occurs both in law and in poetry and which is on the whole commoner and less odd-sounding in modern law than it is in modern poetry. This is personification of abstractions:

> Let not Ambition mock their useful toil,
> Their homely joys, and destiny obscure;
> Nor Grandeur hear with a disdainful smile
> The short and simple annals of the poor.

We find this particular usage almost vanished from English poetry by the beginning of the twentieth century. The personification of abstractions and attributes which we find in the more high-flown sort of eighteenth-century poetry or in the occasional allegorical papers which Johnson inserted in the *Rambler* sound stiff and unnatural to us, and a modern poet would hardly bring himself to try and introduce the device at all. On the other hand, the personification of limited companies by which they are enabled to sue and be sued at law, to commit trespasses, and generally to be spoken of as carrying on all sorts of activities which can only *really* be carried on by sentient beings, is as common as dirt and no one ever dreams of laughing at it. But these examples will hardly do for our slow-motion picture. On the contrary, in them the gap between the B meaning and the A meaning is as wide and the prima facie absurdity of the B or surface-meaning is hardly less than in, let us say, Ossian's description of the Hero: "In peace, thou art the Gale of Spring, in war, the Mountain Storm."

The important thing is to see how and why the legal fiction comes into being and what is its positive function in the life of human beings. If you have suffered a wrong at the hands of another human being, the practical question for you, the point at which law really touches your life as a member of society, is, Can you do anything about it? Can you bring the transgressor to book and obtain restitution? In other words, can you bring an action against him, obtain judgment, and get that judgment executed? Now the answer to that question must always depend to some extent, and in the earlier stages of a society governed by law it depends to a very large extent indeed, on the answer to another question. It is not enough simply to show that the transgressor has, in common parlance, broken the law. What you or your advisers have to make up your mind about is something rather different and often much more complicated. You have to ask yourselves, Is there a form of procedure under which I can move against him? If so, is it sufficiently cheap and expeditious for me to be able to adopt it with some hope of success? Where, as in the case of English Common Law down to the middle of the nineteenth century, these forms of procedure, or forms of action as they are more often called, are severely restricted in number, these questions are very serious ones indeed.

While the so-called historical fictions (which are the only ones I am concerned with) have no doubt played a broadly similar part in every known system of law, I think it will be best if I confine myself to England and take a particular example. The forms of action were not the arbitrary inventions of an ingenious legislator. They grew up out of the whole history of English social life, and one of the results of this was a wide difference between those forms of action which had their roots in the feudal system and those which sprang from later and different sources. I think it is true to say that they were different because they were really based on two different ways of looking at human beings in society. You may look at a human being in what I will call the genealogical way, in which case you will conceive of his legal rights and position as being determined by what he *is* rather than by what he may choose to *do*. They will then seem to be determined by the kind of father he had, by the piece of land to which he and his ancestors were attached or which was attached to them, and by its relations to adjoining land attached to other people and their ancestors and descendants. Or alternatively you may look at him in what I will call the personal way, in which case his position will seem to be determined more by the things which he himself has chosen to *do* of his own free will. Maine in his *Ancient Law* calls the first way "Status" and the second way "Contract," and he depicts society as evolving from the first towards the second. Broadly speaking, forms of action having to do with the ownership of land had grown up out of the first way, forms of action having to do with the ownership of personal property out of the second way, of looking at human beings.

Now suppose you had a good claim to the ownership of a piece of land, perhaps with a pleasant house on it, which was in the possession of somebody else who also, but wrongfully, claimed to be the owner. Your proper normal form of action, say, five hundred years ago, was by Writ of Right, a form of action which was very much of the first type and hedged about accordingly with all sorts of ceremonies, difficulties, and delays.

At trahere atque moras tantis licet addere rebus!

One of the drawbacks of this type of action was that it was subject to things called *essoins*. Essoins seem to have corresponded roughly to what we should call "adjournments"; they no doubt grew up procedurally with a view to preventing an unscrupulous plaintiff from taking unfair advantage of the defendant's ill health, absence, or other accidental disability. But they must have been corn in Egypt for a usurping defendant. I am tempted to let Glanville,[1] in his own sedate language and at his own pace, give the reader some idea of their nature and complexity:

> If the Tenant, being summoned, appear not on the first day, but Essoin himself, such Essoin shall, if reasonable, be received; and he may, in this manner, essoin himself three times successively; and since the causes on account of which a person may justly essoin himself are various, let us consider the different kinds of Essoins.
>
> Of Essoins, some arise on account of ill health, others from other sources.

(I will here interpose that, among the essoins arising from other sources were the *de ultra mare* and the *de esse in peregrinatione* and that, if a person cast the essoin *de esse in peregrinatione*, "it must be distinguished whether he went to Jerusalem or to another place. If to the former place, then a year and a day at least is generally allowed him." And with that I will let Glanville proceed again in his own order:)

> Of those Essoins which arise from ill health, one kind is that *ex infirmitate veniendi*, another *ex infirmitate de reseantisa*.

> If the Tenant, being summoned, should on the first day cast the Essoin *de infirmitate veniendi*, it is in the election of his Adversary, being present, either to require from the Essoiner a lawful proof of the truth of the Essoin in question on that very day, or that he should find pledges or bind himself solemnly that at the day appointed he will have his Warrantor of the Essoin . . . and he may thus Essoin himself three times successively. If on the third day, he neither appear nor essoin himself, then let it be ordered that he be forthcoming in person on another day; or that he send a fit Attorney in his place, to gain or lose for him. . . . It may be asked, what will be the consequence if the Tenant appear at the fourth day, what will be

1. Beame's *Translation of Glanville* (London, 1812).

the consequence if the Tenant appear at the fourth day, after having cast three Essoins, and warrant all the Essoins? In that case, he shall prove the truth of each Essoin by his own oath and that of another; and, on the same day, he shall answer to the suit. . . .

If anyone desire to cast the Essoin *de infirmitate de reseantisa*, he may thrice do it. Yet should the Essoiner, on the third day preceding that appointed, at a proper place and before a proper person, present his Essoin. If, on the third Summons the Tenant appear not, the Court should direct that it may be seen whether his indisposition amount to a languor, or not. For this purpose let the following Writ issue, directed to the Sheriff of the County . . . :

"The King to the sheriff, Health. I command you that, without delay, you send 4 lawful men of your County to see if the infirmity of which B. hath essoined himself in my Court, against R., be a languor or not. And, if they perceive that it is a languor, then, that they should put to him a day or one year and one day, from that day of the view, to appear before me or my justices. . . ."

Nor was it forgotten that essoiners themselves may be subject to infirmities and languors:

The principal Essoiner is also at liberty, if so disposed, to essoin himself by another Essoiner. In this case the second Essoiner must state to the Court that the Tenant, having a just cause of Essoin, had been detained, so that he could not appear at the day appointed, neither to lose nor gain, and that therefore he had appointed a certain other person to essoin him; and that the Essoiner himself had met with such an impediment, which had prevented his appearance on that day: and this he is prepared to prove according to the practice of the Court. . . .

Having at last succeeded in getting your opponent out of bed and fixing the day for the trial, you still could not be certain that he would not appear in court followed (subject, no doubt, to essoins) by a professional boxer or swordsman, whom you would have to tackle in lieu of calling evidence. And so on. And all this maybe about a claim so clear that you could get it disposed of in five minutes if you could only bring it to the stage of being tried at all!

It would have been a very different matter, so perhaps your counsel would advise you, if only the issue were about *personal* property instead of real property. We could go to a different court with a different form of action. No essoins. No wager of law. No trial by battle. No trial by order. Everything up to date and efficient. What *is* personal property, you might ask. Well, your horse for one thing and your hawk and your clothes and your money—oh! yes, and oddly enough if you were a leaseholder instead of a freeholder and had only a term of years in this precious piece of land, *that* would be personal property too. But can't I get *my* case heard by these people? Don't they understand anything about fee simple? Oh! yes, they understand it all right; in fact they often have to decide the point. For instance, if a leaseholder in possession is ousted by a trespasser—by Jove! I've just thought of something! And then if your counsel had a touch of creative genius, he might perhaps evolve the following device. It *was* evolved at all events, by Tudor times or thereabouts and continued in use down to the middle of the nineteenth century.

Remember the situation: You are the rightful owner of a piece of land of which X, who is in possession, wrongfully claims to be the owner. The device was this: you proceeded to inform the court by your pleadings that you, as owner of the land, had recently leased it to a person whose name was John Doe, and John Doe had been ousted from his possession violently, *vi et armis*, by X, the defendant. *You* were not bringing the action, you pretended: John Doe was; but as X might aver in his defense that the blameless Doe had no title, Doe has joined you, his landlord, in the proceedings to prove that you did have a good title at the time when you leased the land to him. By this means you got your case before the court that had jurisdiction to deal with the action known as ejectment, and were able to take advantage of the simpler and more effective procedure. Sometimes the fiction was a little more elaborate. Instead of alleging that X had ejected John Doe, you said that another gentlemen called Richard Roe, or possibly William Stiles, had done so. Richard Roe having subsequently allowed X to take possession now claimed no interest in the proceedings, but he had given X notice that they were pending, so as to give X a chance to defend his title. In this case the first thing X heard of it all was a letter, signed "your loving friend, Richard Roe," telling him what had happened. Needless to say, John Doe and Richard Roe had no existence.

Many thousands of actions of this pattern and using these names must have been brought between the fifteenth and the nineteenth centuries and before long the whole procedure was no doubt so much a matter of course that it was little more than a kind of mathematical formula. There must, however, have been some earlier occasions on which it was a good deal more, and it is upon any one of these—perhaps the first of all—that I want the reader to bend his mind. Picture to yourself the court, with counsel on his feet opening the case. The story of John Doe and Richard Roe is being unfolded. At one point the judge suddenly looks up and looks very hard at counsel, who either winks very slightly or returns a stolid, uncomprehending stare according to his temperament and the intimacy of his acquaintance with the judge out of hours. But counsel knows all the same what has happened. The bench has tumbled to it. The judge has guessed that there is no John Doe, no Richard Roe, no lease, no entry, no ouster. At the same moment, however, the judge has seen the point of the whole fiction, the great advantage in the speedy administration of justice (for the real issue—the validity of X's title and yours—will be heard fairly and in full) and in the extended jurisdiction of his own court. He decides to accord to the pleadings that willing suspension of disbelief which hundreds of years later made Mr. Bumble say that the law was a "hass." The case proceeds. Place this picture before your mind's eye and there I think you will have a slow-motion picture of "tarning."

Has new law been made? It is much the same as asking whether new language has been made when a metaphor disappears into a "meaning." At all events, we begin to understand more fully what Maitland meant, when he wrote of English law that "substantive law has at first the look of being gradually secreted in the interstices of procedure." This is particularly true of an unwritten system like the English Common Law, where the law itself lay hidden in the unconscious, until it was expressed in a judgment, and where rights themselves depended on the existence of remedies. Consider that very important fiction, which is very much alive and flourishing all round us today—the fiction on which the law of trusteeship is based. Anyone who is a trustee will know how absurdly remote from reality is the B interpretation of his position, according to which he is the "owner" of the trust property. Yet this fiction, which permeates the whole of our jurisprudence, which most certainly is law, and not merely procedure, was introduced in the first place by devices strictly procedural, devices and circumstances which had their origin in that same contrast between the genealogical and the personal conceptions of society which gave us John Doe and Richard Roe.

Moreover, this fictitious ownership, which we can trusteeship, has been strong enough to have other fictions erected on it. By the Common Law the personal property of a married woman became her husband's as soon as she married. But by a particularly ingenious piece of tarning the equity judges expressed in the form of law, and in doing so no doubt partly created, a more modern view of the rights of married women. They followed the Common Law doctrine that the husband *owned* everything but, as to property which someone had given to the wife with the intention that she should have it for her own separate use, the courts of equity began in the eighteenth century to say that the husband did indeed own this, but he owned it as *trustee* for his wife; and they would prevent him from dealing with it in any other way.

In the same way a metaphor may be strong enough to support a metaphor, as when Shelley bids the west wind "Make me thy lyre even as the forest is." If Shelley is not a lyre, neither is the forest; yet he illustrates the one fiction with the other. Nor is there anything grotesque or strained in this magnificent line. It is only when we begin to ponder and analyze it that we see how daring it is.

The long analogy which I have been drawing may be expressed more briefly in the formula:

metaphor : language : meaning :: legal fiction : law : social life.

It has no particular significance if poetry is to be regarded *only* as either a pleasurable way of diverting our leisure hours or a convenient vehicle for the propagation of doctrine. For it must be conceded that there is all the difference in the world between the propagation of a doctrine and the creation of a meaning. The doctrine is already formulated and, if we choose to espress it by tarning, that is simply a matter of technique or political strategy. The creation of meaning is a very different matter. I hope I may have succeeded in showing in the earlier part of this article that metaphor is something more than a piece of the technique of one of the fine arts. It is πολὺ μέγιστον not merely in the diction of poetry but in the nature and growth of language itself. So far we have only considered in this connection those ubiquitous figures of speech which are, or used to be, called "tropes," as when we speak of our lives *fluctuating*, of our insight *bearing fruit* in deeds, of *seeing the point*, and so on. But if we proceed to study language with a more definitely historical bias, and look into the etymologies and derivations of words, then the vast majority even of those meanings which we normally regard as "literal" are seen to have originated either in metaphors or in something like them. Such words as *spirit, sad, humor, perceive, attend, express, understand*, and so on immediately spring to the mind as examples. Indeed the difficulty here would rather be to find words that are *not* examples. There is no doubt that they were once metaphorical. The question which a good many people have asked themselves, a little uneasily, is, Are they *still* metaphors? And, if not, when—and still more *how*—precisely, did they cease to be so?

What is essential to the nature and growth of language is clearly essential to the nature and growth of our thought, or rather of our consciousness as a whole. In what way then is metaphor or tarning essential to that nature and that growth? Here we begin to tread on metaphysical ground and here I think the analogy of legal fictions can really help us by placing our feet on one or two firmer tufts in the quaking bog. It can help us to realize in firmer outlines certain concepts which, like all those relating to the nature of thought itself, are tenuous, elusive, and difficult of expression.

Students of history will have observed that rebellions and agitations arising out of dissatisfaction with the law tend, at any rate in the earlier stages of society, to demand, not so much a reform of the law as its *publication*. People complain that they do not know what the law is. They want to know what it is, because otherwise they cannot be sure that it will be the same tomorrow as it is today. In fact it is the very essence of a law that it should apply to every case. It follows that the forms of action must be limited in number, and they must not change from day to day. If there is a different law for every case that arises, then what is being administered is simply not law at all but the arbitrary (though not necessarily unjust) decisions of those who govern us. But that is exactly what the word "law" *means*—something which is *not* such a series of arbitrary decisions or events, something which will be *the same* for the next case as it was for the last. This is where the difficulty arises; for it is the nature of life itself (certainly of human life) never to repeat itself exactly. Phenomena exactly repeated are not life, they are mechanism. Life varies, law is of its nature unvarying. Yet at the same time it is the function of law to serve, to express and indeed partly to *make* the social life of the community. That is the paradox, the diurnal solution of which constitutes the process called society. One solution is legislation, the other is fiction. Legislation is drastic, *a priori*, and necessary. Fiction is flexible, empirical, and also necessary. "Without the Fiction of Adoption," says Maine in his *Ancient Law*, "it is difficult to understand how Society would ever have escaped from its swaddling-clothes."

In the paradoxical relation of law to social life I think we have a useful picture of the paradoxical relation of language to consciousness. Formal logic is not much studied nowadays, but that does not alter the fact that logic is essential to the very existence of language and the forms of proposition and syllogism underlie all expression. Now logic presupposes first and foremost that the same word means the same thing in one sentence as it does in another. Humpty Dumpty may speak of making his words "mean" what he chooses, and if somebody made a noise never heard before or since he might possibly manage to convey some sort of vague sympathetic impression of the state of his feelings. Yet repetition is inherent in the very meaning of the word "meaning." To say a word "means" something implies that it means that same something more than once.

Here then is the paradox again. The logical use of language presupposes the meanings of the words it employs and presupposes them constant. I think it will be found to be a corollary of this, that the logical use of language can never add any meaning to it. The conclusion of a syllogism is implicit already in the premises, that is, in the *meanings* of the *words* employed; and all the syllogism can do is to make that meaning clearer to us and remove any misconception or confusion. But life is not constant. Every man, certainly every original man, has something new to say, something new to mean. Yet if he wants to express that meaning (and it may be that it is only when he tries to express it, that he knows what he means) he must use language—a vehicle which presupposes that he must either mean what was meant before or talk nonsense!

If therefore he would say anything really new, if that which was hitherto unconscious is to become conscious, he must resort to tarning. He must talk what is nonsense on the face of it, but in such a way that the recipient may have the new meaning suggested to him. That is the true importance of metaphor. I imagine that is why Aristotle, in calling metaphor "the most important," gives as a reason that "it alone does not mean borrowing from someone else." In terms of mixed law and logic we might perhaps say that the metaphorical proposition contains a judgment, but a judgment pronounced with a wink at the court. Bacon put it more clearly in the *Advancement of Learning* when he said:

Those whose conceits are seated in popular opinions need only but to prove or dispute; but those whose conceits are beyond popular opinions have a double labour; the one *to make themselves conceived*, and the other to prove and demonstrate. So that it is necessity with them to have recourse to similitudes and translations to express themselves.

If we consider Bacon's position in the history of thought, it will not surprise us that the problem should have presented itself to him so clearly. Himself a lawyer, was he not attempting to do for science the very thing which Maitland tells us those old legal fictions were contrived for, that is, "to get modern results out of medieval premisses"?

At all events there is a sentence in the *Novum Organum* which provides one of the most striking illustrations of tarning that it would be possible to imagine. It is a double illustration: first, there was an attempt at deliberate and fully conscious meaning-making, which failed: Bacon tried to inject new meaning into a word by *saying* precisely what he wanted it to mean. But we have seen that what is said precisely cannot convey new meaning. But, since his meaning *was* really new, there had at some point in the process to be a piece of actual tarning. There was—and it succeeded. He did in fact inject new meaning into another word— not by saying, but by just meaning it!

> Licet enim in natura nihil vere existat praeter corpora individua edentia actus puros individuos ex lege; in doctrinis tamen, illa ipsa lex, ejusque inquisitio et inventio atque explicatio, pro fundamento est tam ad sciendum quam ad operandum. Eam autem legem ejusque paragraphos *formarum* nomine intelligimus; praesertim cum hoc vocabulum invaluerit, et familiariter occurrat.[2]

The "forms" of which Bacon here speaks were none other than the Platonic ideas, in which Bacon did not very much believe. What he did believe in was that system of abstract causes or uniformity which we have long since been accustomed to express by the phrase "the laws of nature," but for which there was then no name, because the meaning was a new one. He therefore tried deliberately by way of a *simile* to put this new meaning into the old word *"forma"*; but he failed, inasmuch as the new meaning never came into general use. Yet at the same time, more unconsciously, and by way of *metaphor*, he was putting the new meaning into the word *"lex"* itself—that curious meaning which it now bears in the expression "the laws of nature." This is one of those pregnant metaphors

2. 'Although it is true that in nature nothing exists beyond separate bodies producing separate motions according to law; still for the *study* of nature that very law and its investigation discovery and exposition are the essential thing, for the purpose both of science and of practice. Now it is that law and its clauses which we understand by the term "forms"—principally because this word is a familiar one and has become generally accepted.' *Novum Organum*, ii. 2.

which pass into the language, so that much of our subsequent thinking is based on them. To realize that after all they *are* metaphors, and to ask what that entails, opens up avenues of inquiry which are beyond the province of this article. Certainly, they may be misleading, as well as illuminating. Long after Bacon's time, two great men—a lawyer who was concerned with the nature of law and a poet who was concerned with the nature of Nature—felt bound to draw attention to this very metaphor.

"When an atheist," wrote Austin, "speaks of *laws* governing the irrational world, the metaphorical application is suggested by an analogy still more slender and remote. . . . He means that the uniformity of succession and co-existence resembles the uniformity of conduct produced by an imperative rule. If, to draw the analogy closer, he ascribes these laws to an author, he personifies a verbal abstraction and makes it play the legislator. He attributes the uniformity of succession and co-existence to *laws* set by *nature*: meaning by nature, the world itself; or perhaps that very uniformity which he imputes to nature's commands."[3]

The introduction of the atheist into this passage does not, I think, weaken its force as an illustration, for whatever the strength of Bacon's religious faith, it is quite plain that the "laws" of which he speaks in the *Novum Organum* have very little to do with the "commands" of any being other than nature itself.

"Long indeed," says Coleridge in *The Friend*, "will man strive to satisfy the inward querist with the phrase, laws of nature. But though the individual may rest content with the seeming metaphor, the race cannot. If a law of nature be a mere generalization, it is included . . . as an act of the mind. But if it be other and more, and yet manifestable only in and to an intelligent spirit, it must in act and substance be itself spiritual; for things utterly heterogeneous can have no intercommunion."

Perhaps we may supplement the last sentence by saying that an *apparent* intercommunion between things utterly heterogeneous is the true mark of metaphor and may be significant of spiritual substance. If this is so, and if the aptness of a metaphor to mislead varies inversely with the extent to which it continues to be felt and understood *as* a metaphor and is not taken in a confused way semi-literally, then the contemplation by the mind of legal fictions may really be a rather useful exercise. For these are devices of expression, of which the practical expediency can easily be understood, and whose metaphorical nature is not so easily forgotten as they pass into general use.

There is not much that is more important for human beings than their relations with each other, and it is these which laws are designed to express. The

3. *Jurisprudence* (1869), i. 213.

making and application of law are thus fundamental human activities, but what is more important for my purpose is that they bear the same relation to naked thinking as traveling does to map-reading or practice to theory. It is not by accident that such key-words as *judgment* and *cause* have two distinct meanings; the practical task of fixing personal responsibility must surely have been the soil from which, as the centuries passed, the abstract notion of cause and effect was laboriously raised. Accordingly it would be strange indeed if the study of jurisprudence were not well adapted to throw light on the mind and its workings.

That study was formerly regarded as an essential element in a liberal education. It was a distinguished Italian jurist, Giovanni Battista Vico, who at the turn of the seventeenth and eighteenth centuries became interested in the figurative element in language and evolved therefrom a theory of the evolution of human consciousness from an instinctive "poetic" wisdom *(sapienza poetica)* to the modern mode of analytical thought.

It is perhaps a pity that this respectful attitude to legal studies has long since been abandoned; a pity both on general grounds and because the vast change in man's idea of himself wrought by the new notions of evolution and development, and by the comparatively recent birth of historical imagination, have opened up rich new fields of speculation both in language and in law. A better and more widely diffused knowledge of the latter could hardly fail to be beneficial in far-reaching ways at a time when the whole theory of human society is in the melting-pot. For instance, a deeper, more sympathetic understanding of the long, slow movement of the human mind from the feudal, or genealogical, way of regarding human relationships towards what I have called the "personal" way would do no harm.

But I have been mainly concerned here with the subject of fictions. Properly understood, are they not a telling illustration of the fact that knowledge—the fullest possible awareness—of the nature of law is the true way of escape from its shackles? "ἐλῶ λὰρ διὰ νόμον νόμῳ ἀπέθανον," 'I, by the law, died unto the law,' wrote St. Paul; and the *nature* of law, as law, is the same, whether it be moral, or logical, or municipal. If it be important for men to get a deep feeling for this process of liberation in general, it is equally important, for special reasons, that they should better comprehend the particular problem of the part played by metaphor in the operation and development of language. Here too the way to achieve liberation from the "confusion" of thought on which metaphor is based is not by attack or rebellion. The intrinsic nature of language makes all such attitudes puerile. It is not those who, like the optimistic Mr. Stuart Chase,[4] set out to cut away and expose all metaphorical usage who escape the curse of Babel. No. The best way to talk clearly and precisely and to talk sense is to understand as fully as possible the relation between predication and suggestion,

4. *The Tyranny of Words* (London, 1938).

between "saying" and "meaning." For then you will at least know what you are *trying* to do. It is not the freemen of a city who are likeliest to lose their way, and themselves, in its labyrinth of old and mazy streets; it is the simple-minded foreign nihilist making, with his honest-to-god intentions and suitcase, straight for the center, like a sensible man.

Note.—The author expresses his thanks to Mr. de la Mare and to Messrs. Faber & Faber for permission to quote *The Listeners*. Reprinted with permission of The Literary Trustees of Walter de la Mare, and The Society of Authors as their representative.

Selected Short Passages

The Soul of the Past

In the common words we use every day the souls of past races, the thoughts and feelings of individual men stand around us, not dead, but frozen into their attitudes like the courtiers in the garden of the Sleeping Beauty. The more common a word is and the simpler its meaning, the bolder very likely is the original thought which it contains and the more intense the intellectual or poetic effort which went to its making. Thus, the word *quality* is used by most educated people every day of their lives, yet in order that we should have this simple word Plato had to make the tremendous effort (it is one of the most exhausting which man is called on to exert) of turning a vague feeling into a clear thought. He invented the new word 'poiotēs', 'what-ness', as we might say, or 'of-what-kind-ness', and Cicero translated it by the Latin 'qualitas', from 'qualis'. Language becomes a different thing for us altogether if we can make ourselves realize, can even make ourselves feel how every time the word *quality* is used, say upon a label in a shop window, that creative effort made by Plato comes into play again. Nor is the acquisition of such a feeling a waste of time; for once we have made it our own, it circulates like blood through the whole of the literature and life about us. It is the kiss which brings the sleeping courtiers to life.

from *History in English Words*

The English Language

We must not be misled . . . into supposing that English is a language which has given away much. On the contrary, surveying it as a whole, we are struck, above all, by the ease with which it has itself appropriated the linguistic products of others. . . . Its genius seems to have lain not so much in originality as in the snapping up of unconsidered trifles; and where it has excelled all the others languages of Europe, possibly of the world, is in the grace with which it has hitherto digested these particles of foreign matter and turned them into its own life's blood. Historically, the English language is a muddle; actually it is a beautiful, personal, and highly sensitive creature.

from *History in English Words*

The Poet

The farther back language as a whole is traced, the more poetical and animated do its sources appear, until it seems at last to dissolve into a kind of mist of myth. The beneficence or malignance—what may be called the soul-qualities— of natural phenomena, such as clouds or plants or animals, make a more vivid impression at this time than their outer shapes and appearances. Words themselves are felt to be alive and to exert a magical influence. . . . It is only in glimpses that we can perceive this; in a word here and a word there we trace but the final stages of a vast, age-long metamorphosis from the kind of outlook which we loosely describe as 'mythological' to the kind which we may describe equally loosely as 'intellectual thought'. To comprehend the process fully, we must build up the rest of it in the imagination, just as, from seeing a foot of cliff crumble away at Dover, we may set wings to time and call up the immemorial formation of the English Channel.

. . . .

First, the poet was conceived of as being definitely 'possessed' by some foreign being, a god or angel, who gave utterance through his mouth, and gave it only as and when it chose. Then the divine power was said to be 'breathed in' to the poet, by beings such as the Muses, at special times and places, over which he had some measure of control, in that he could go himself to the places and 'invoke' the Muse. Finally this 'breathing in' or *inspiration* took on the more metaphorical sense which it has today—definitely retaining, however, the original suggestion of a diminished *self*-consciousness. Inspiration! It was the only means, we used to be told, by which poetry could be written, and the poet himself hardly knew what it was—a kind of divine wind, perhaps, which blew where it listed and might fill his sails at some odd moment after he had whistled for it all day in vain. So we were told not long ago; but today we are more inclined to think of inspiration as a mood—a mood that may come and go in the course of a morning's work.

. . . .

The very fact that his rhythms have high poetic value should now suggest to us that the poet, while creating anew, is likely to be in a sense restoring something old. And if the most ancient rhythms of verse are but the sound, dying away, of just those 'footsteps of Nature' whose visible print we have observed, with Bacon, in the present possibility of true metaphor, we shall hardly be surprised to hear in the music which such a poet creates, albeit spontaneously, something like an echo of just those rhythms.

from *Poetic Diction*

A Felt Change of Consciousness

Thus, an introspective analysis of my experience obliges me to say that appreciation of poetry involves a 'felt change of consciousness'. The phrase must be taken with some exactness. Appreciation takes place at the actual moment of change. It is not simply that the poet enables me to see with his eyes, and so to apprehend a larger and fuller world. He may indeed do this, as we shall see later; but the actual moment of the pleasure of appreciation depends upon something rarer and more transitory. It depends on the change itself. If I pass a coil of wire between the poles of a magnet, I generate in it an electric current—but I only do so while the coil is positively moving across the lines of force. I may leave the coil at rest between the two poles and in such a position that it is thoroughly permeated by the magnetic field; but in that case no current will flow along the conductor. Current only flows when I am actually bringing the coil in or taking it away again. So it is with the poetic mood, which, like the dreams to which it has so often been compared, is kindled by the passage from one plane of consciousness to another. It lives during that moment of transition and then dies, and if it is to be repeated, some means must be found of renewing the transition itself.

Poetry, as a possession, as our own souls enriched, is another matter. But when it has entered as deeply as that into our being, we no longer concern ourselves with its *diction*. At this stage the diction has served its end and may be forgotten. For, if ever we go back to linger lovingly over the exquisite phrasing of some fragment of poesy whose essence has long been our own, and of which the spirit has become a part of our every waking moment, if we do this, is it not *for the very reason* that we want to renew the thrill which accompanied the first acquisition of the treasure? As our lips murmur the well-known—or it may be the long-forgotten—words, we are trying, whether deliberately or no, to cast ourselves back into the frame of mind which was ours before we had learnt the lesson. Why? Because we know instinctively that, if we are to feel pleasure, we must have change. Everlasting day can no more freshen the earth with dew than everlasting night, but the change from night to day and from day back again to night.

from *Poetic Diction*

Poetic Imagination

There is a certain kind of nocturnal dream, in which we dream with one part of ourselves, and yet at the same time we know with another part that we are dreaming. The dream continues, and is a real dream (that is, it is not just a waking reverie). And yet we know that we are dreaming; we are there outside the dream, as well as being there within it. I think we may let ourselves be instructed by such dreams in the nature of true vision.

Poets have sometimes been called "visionaries" and sometimes "dreamers"; but they are likely to be poor poets, unless it is *this* kind of dream that we are connoting when we use the word. Poetic imagination is very close to the dreaming of such dreams, and has little to do with reverie. In reverie we lose ourselves (we speak of being "lost in reverie"), we are absorbed; but in imagination we find ourselves in finding vision. The vision is objective (as if it were part of ordinary consciousness); but its very objectivity is as much our own as what we call subjectivity—for it is the content of extraordinary consciousness; and that is what we now mean by "objectivity"; it is what we mean (in terms of the spectrum of consciousness) even by rocks and stones and trees. Imagination is a Western concept, and imagination is potentially extraordinary consciousness—not just the dream stage, but the whole gamut of it—*present with* ordinary consciousness.

I believe moreover that this potential lies at the root of the "tension" that is often spoken of in connection with the use of metaphor. Metaphor involves a tension between two ostensibly incompatible meanings; but it also involves a tension between that part of ourselves which experiences the incompatibles as a mysterious unity and that part which remains well able to appreciate their duality and their incompatibility. Without the former metaphor is nonsense language, but without the latter it is not even language.

from *The Rediscovery of Meaning*

Language and Meaning

I suspect the difficulty is already obvious enough to all who are not deeply habituated to the line of thought I have been trying to advocate. It is that language, by definition (that is to say, by virtue of its very nature *as* language) *does* point beyond itself. When a man talks, we are affected by what he says precisely because we assume that he is talking about *something*—and that that something is *not* simply the effect he hopes his talking is going to have on us. He may want to get at our ganglia, but he will succeed in doing so only as long as we are convinced that he is not talking *about* our ganglia. Thus, when I. A. Richards long ago distinguished the "emotive" language of poetry from the "referential" language of science, and insisted that the semantic function of emotive language is not to make statements but to arouse emotion, he overlooked the fact that emotive language arouses emotion precisely *because* it is taken to refer to something; and to something other than the emotion. For talking about an emotion will neither express nor arouse it; rather the opposite. Lovers do not intend to talk about the emotion of love; they intend to talk qualitatively about each other, and a speaker's intention *is* his meaning; indeed it is another word for it.

This difficulty is, for me, so fatal that I cannot find any more profundity in the proposition that "a poem must not mean, but be" than I could in the proposition, say, that "a satellite must not orbit, but stop still." Alas, it is by virtue of orbiting that it *is* a satellite at all. In the same way, it is by virtue, not of orbiting but of leading, or pointing, or hinting, or referring—what you will, but certainly of relating in *some way*—to what is other than its own syllables that a word is a word at all. Words are only themselves by being more than themselves. Perhaps the same thing is true of human beings.

from *The Rediscovery of Meaning*

The Spirit of Poetry

But without the continued existence of poetry, without a steady influx of new meaning into language, even the knowledge and wisdom which poetry herself has given in the past must wither away into a species of mechanical calculation. Great poetry is the progressive incarnation of life in consciousness. Hence the absolute value of aesthetic pleasure as a criterion; for before we can feel it, we must have become aware in some degree of the actual progress—not merely of its results. Over the perpetual evolution of human consciousness, which is stamping itself upon the transformation of language, the spirit of poetry hovers, for ever unable to alight. It is only when we are lifted above that transformation, so that we behold it as present movement, that our startled souls feel the little pat and the throbbing, feathery warmth, which tell us that she has perched. It is only when we have risen from beholding the creature into beholding creation that our mortality catches for a moment the music of the turning spheres.

from *Poetic Diction*

Philosophy and Meaning

Without ever abandoning his base in language and literature, Barfield over time enlarged his concerns to address ever more specifically the philosophic implications of the evolution of consciousness. He sought to understand what that evolution meant in terms of the nature of reality and the nature of meaning. He has said that all of his writings have been about the evolution of consciousness, but that is a comprehensive term for a broad philosophic position. During his middle and late periods he advanced his concepts of Participation and Polarity and continued to refine his views on Meaning and Imagination. His crowning achievement in this area has long been regarded as being *Saving the Appearances*, which is accordingly the most substantially represented in the selections that follow. Other selections reflect his concern with the history of ideas, with thinking, with materialistic evolution, and with Rudolf Steiner. Bracketed titles of short passages have been supplied by the editor.

from *Saving the Appearances*

The Rainbow

Look at a rainbow. While it lasts, it is, or appears to be, a great arc of many colours occupying a position out there in space. It touches the horizon between that chimney and that tree; a line drawn from the sun behind you and passing through your head would pierce the centre of the circle of which it is part. And now, before it fades, recollect all you have ever been told about the rainbow and its causes, and ask yourself the question *Is it really there*?

You know, from memory, that if there were a hillside three or four miles nearer than the present horizon, the rainbow would come to earth in front of and not behind it; that, if you walked to the place where the rainbow ends, or seems to end, it would certainly not be 'there'. In a word, reflection will assure you that the rainbow is the outcome of the sun, the raindrops and your own vision.

When I ask of an intangible appearance or representation, Is it really there? I usually mean, Is it there independently of my vision? Would it still be there, for instance, if I shut my eyes—if I moved towards or away from it. If this is what you also mean by 'really there', you will be tempted to add that the raindrops and the sun are really there, but the rainbow is not.

Does it follow that, as soon as anybody sees a rainbow, there 'is' one, or, in other words, that there is no difference between an hallucination or a madman's dream of a rainbow (perhaps on a clear day) and an actual rainbow? Certainly not. You were not the only one to see that rainbow. You had a friend with you. (I forbear asking if you both saw 'the same' rainbow, because this is a book about history rather than metaphysics, and these introductory chapters are merely intended to clear away certain misconceptions.) Moreover, through the medium of language, you are well aware that thousands of others have seen rainbows in showery weather; but you have never heard of any sane person claiming to have seen one on a sunless or a cloudless day. Therefore, if a man tells you he sees a rainbow on a cloudless day, then, even if you are convinced that he means what he says, and is not simply lying, you will confidently affirm that the rainbow he sees is 'not there'.

In short, as far as being really there or not is concerned, the practical difference between a dream or hallucination of a rainbow and an actual rainbow is that, although each is a representation of appearance (that is, something which I perceive to be there), the second is a *shared* or collective representation.

Now look at a tree. It is very different from a rainbow. If you approach it, it will still be 'there'. Moreover, in this case, you can do more than look at it. You can hear the noise its leaves make in the wind. You can perhaps smell it. You can certainly touch it. Your senses combine to assure you that it is composed of what is called solid matter. Accord to the tree the same treatment that you accorded to the rainbow. Recollect all you have been told about matter and its ultimate structure and ask yourself if the tree is 'really there'. I am far from affirming dogmatically that the atoms, electrons, nuclei, etc., of which wood, and all matter, is said to be composed, are particular and identifiable objects like drops of rain. But if the 'particles' (as I will here call them for convenience) *are* there, and are all that is there, then, since the 'particles' are no more like the thing I call a tree than the raindrops are like the thing I call a rainbow, it follows, I think, that—just as a rainbow is the outcome of the raindrops and my vision— so, a tree is the outcome of the particles and my vision and my other sense-perceptions. Whatever the particles themselves may be thought to be, the tree, as such, is a representation. And the difference, for me, between a tree and a complete hallucination of a tree is the same as the difference between a rainbow and an hallucination of a rainbow. In other words, a tree which is 'really there' is a collective representation. The fact that a dream tree differs in kind from a real tree, and that it is just silly to try and mix them up, is indeed rather literally a matter of 'common sense'.

This background of particles is of course presumed in the case of raindrops themselves, no less than in that of trees. The relation, *raindrops : rainbow*, is a picture or analogy, not an instance, of the relation, *particles : representation*.

Or again, if anyone likes to press the argument still further and maintain that what is true of the drops must also be true of the particles themselves, and that there is 'no such thing as an extra-mental reality', I shall not quarrel with him, but I shall leave him severely alone; because, as I say, this is not a book about metaphysics, and I have no desire to demonstrate that trees or rainbows—or particles—are not 'really there'—a proposition which perhaps has not much meaning. This book is not being written because the author desires to put forward a theory of perception, but because it seems to him that certain wide consequences flowing from the hastily expanded sciences of the nineteenth and twentieth centuries, and in particular their physics, have not been sufficiently considered in building up the general twentieth-century picture of the nature of the universe and of the history of the earth and man.

A better term than 'particles' would possibly be 'the unrepresented', since anything particular which amounts to a representation will always attract further physical analysis. Moreover, the atoms, protons and electrons of modern physics are now perhaps more generally regarded, not as particles, but as notional models or symbols of an unknown supersensible or subsensible base. All I seek to establish in these opening paragraphs is, that, whatever may be thought about the 'unrepresented' background of our perceptions, the *familiar* world which we see and know around us—the blue sky with white clouds in it, the noise of a waterfall or a motor-bus, the shapes of flowers and their scent, the gesture and utterance of animals and the faces of our friends—the world too, which (apart from the special inquiry of physics) experts of all kinds methodically investigate—is a system of collective representations. The time comes when one must either accept this as the truth about the world or reject the theories of physics as an elaborate delusion. We cannot have it both ways.

Collective Representations

A representation is something I perceive to be there. By premising that the everyday world is a system of collective representations, it may be thought that we blur the distinction between the fancied and the actual or, following the everyday use of language, between the apparently there and the really there. But this is not so. It only seems to be so because of the very great emphasis which—especially in the last three or four hundred years—the Western Mind has come to lay on the ingredient of spatial depth in the total complex of its perception. I shall return to this later.

As to what is meant by 'collective'—any discrepancy between my representations and those of my fellow men raises a presumption of unreality and calls for explanation. If, however, the explanation is satisfactory; if, for instance, it turns out that the discrepancy was due, not to my hallucination, but to their myopia or their dullness, it is likely to be accepted; and then my representation may itself end by becoming collective.

It is, however, not necessary to maintain that collectivity is the *only* test for distinguishing between a representation and a collective representation (though, to creatures for whom insanity is round the corner, it is often likely to be the crucial one).

I am hit violently on the head and, in the same moment, perceive a bright light to be there. Later on I reflect that the light was 'not really there'. Even if I had lived all my life on a desert island where there was no-one to compare notes with, I might do as much. No doubt I should learn by experience to distinguish the first kind of light from the more practicable light of day or the thunderbolt, and should soon give up hitting myself on the head at sunset when I needed light to go on working by. In both cases I perceive light, but the various criteria of difference between them—duration, for instance, and a sharp physical pain, which the one involves and the other does not, are not difficult to apprehend.

What is required, is not to go on stressing the resemblance between collective representations and private representations, but to remember, when we leave the world of everyday for the discipline of any strict inquiry, that *if* the particles, or the unrepresented, are in fact all that is *independently* there, then the world we all accept as real is in fact a system of collective representations.

Perception takes place by means of sense-organs, though the ingredient in it of sensation, experienced as such, varies greatly as between the different senses. In touch I suppose we come nearest to sensation without perception; in sight to perception without sensation. But the two most important things to remember about perception are these: *first*, that we must not confuse the percept with its cause. I do not hear undulating molecules of air; the name of what I hear is *sound*. I do not touch a moving system of waves or of atoms and electrons with relatively vast empty spaces between them; the name of what I touch is *matter*. *Second*, I do not perceive any *thing* with my sense-organs alone, but with a great part of my whole human being. Thus, I may say, loosely, that I 'hear a thrush singing'. But in strict truth all that I ever merely 'hear'—all that I ever hear simply by virtue of having ears—is *sound*. When I 'hear a thrush singing', I am hearing, not with my ears alone, but with all sorts of other things like mental habits, memory, imagination, feeling and (to the extent at least that the act of attention involves it) will. Of a man who merely heard in the first sense, it could meaningfully be said that 'having ears' (i.e. not being deaf) 'he heard not'.

I do not think either of these two maxims depends on any particular theory of the nature of perception. They are true for any theory of perception I ever heard of—with the possible exception of Bishop Berkeley's. They are true, whether we accept the Aristotelian and medieval conception of form and matter, or the Kantian doctrine of the forms of perception, or the theory of specific sense-energy, or the 'primary imagination' of Coleridge, or the phenomenology that underlies Existentialism, or some wholly unphilosophical system of physiology and psychology. On almost any received theory of perception the familiar world—that is, the world which is apprehended, not through instruments and inference, but simply—is for the most part dependent upon the percipient.

Figuration and Thinking

In the conversion of raindrops into a rainbow, or (if you prefer it) the production of a rainbow out of them, the *eye* plays a no less indispensable part than the sunlight—or than the drops themselves. In the same way, for the conversion of the unrepresented into a representation, at least one sentient organism is as much a *sine qua non* as the unrepresented itself; and for the conversion of the unrepresented into representations even remotely resembling our everyday world, at least one nervous system organized about a spinal cord culminating in a brain, is equally indispensable. The rainbow analogy does not imply, nor is it intended to suggest, that the solid globe is as insubstantial as a rainbow. The solid globe is solid. The rainbow is not. Only it is important to know what we mean by solidity. More than that, it is necessary to remember what we meant by solidity in one context, when we go on to use the word or think the thing in another.

It is easy to appreciate that there is no such thing as an unseen rainbow. It is not so easy to grasp that there is no such thing as an unheard noise. Or rather it is easy to grasp, but difficult to keep hold of. And this is still more the case, when we come to the sense of touch. Obvious as it may be to reflection that a system of waves or quanta or discrete particles is no more like solid matter than waves of air are like sound, or raindrops like a rainbow, it is not particularly easy to grasp, and it is almost impossible to keep in mind, that there is no such thing as unfelt solidity.[1] It is much more convenient, when we are listening for example to the geologist, to forget what we learnt about matter from the chemist and the physicist. But it really will not do. We cannot go on for ever having it both ways.

It may be expedient at this point to examine a little further the collective representations and our thinking about them. And it is clearly of little use to begin by asking what they are; since they are everything that is obvious. They are, for instance, the desk I am writing at, the noise of a door being opened downstairs, a Union Jack, an altar in a Church, the smell of coffee, a totem pole, the view from Malvern Hills, and the bit of brain-tissue that is being dissected before a group of students in a hospital laboratory. Some of them we can manipulate, as the lecturer is doing, and as I do when I move the desk. Some of them we cannot.

---

1. 'The thermometer is below freezing point, the pipe is cracked, and no water comes out of the tap. I know nothing about physics of chemistry; but surely I can say that there is solid ice in the pipe!' Certainly you can; and if there was salt in the water, you can say that there is solid, *white* ice in the pipe. I am only pointing out that the solidity you are talking about involves your fancied touch, just as the whiteness involves your fancied glance. Only it is harder to remember.

What is important here is that there are, broadly speaking, three different things that we can do with all of them; or, alternatively, they are related to the mind in three different ways.

First, we can simply contemplate or experience them—as when I simply look at the view, or encounter the smell. The whole impression appears then to be given to me in the representation itself. For I am not, or I am not very often, aware of smelling an unidentified smell and then thinking, 'That is coffee! It appears to me, and appears instantly, that I smell coffee—though, in fact, I can no more merely *smell* 'coffee' than I can merely *hear* 'a thrush singing'. This immediate impression of experience of a familiar world has already been mentioned in Chapter II. It is important to be clear about it. It is plainly the result of an activity of some sort in me, however little I may recollect any such activity.

When a lady complained to Whistler that she did not see the world he painted, he is said to have replied: 'No, ma'am, but don't you wish you could?' Both Whistler and the lady were really referring to that activity—which in Whistler's case was intenser than the lady's. Ought it to be called a 'mental' activity? Whatever it ought to be called, it really is the percipient's own contribution to the representation. It is all *that* in the representation which is not sensation. For, as the organs of sense are required to convert the unrepresented ('particles') into sensations for us, so *something* is required in us to convert sensations into 'things'. It is this something that I mean. And it will avoid confusion if I purposely choose an unfamiliar and little-used word and call it, at the risk of infelicity, *figuration*.

Let me repeat it. On the assumption that the world whose existence is independent of our sensation and perception consists solely of 'particles', two operations are necessary (and whether they are successive or simultaneous is of no consequence), in order to produce the familiar world we know. First, the sense-organs must be related to the particles in such a way as to give rise to sensations; and secondly, those mere sensations must be combined and constructed by the percipient mind into the recognizable and nameable objects we call 'things'. It is this work of construction which will here be called *figuration*.

Now whether or no figuration is a mental activity, that is, a kind of thinking, it is clearly not, or it is not *characteristically*, a thinking *about*. The second thing, therefore, that we can do with the representations is to think about them. Here, as before, we remain unconscious of the intimate relation which they in fact have, as representations, with our own organisms and minds. Or rather, more unconscious than before. For now our very attitude is, to treat them as independent of ourselves; to accept their 'outness' as self-evidently given; and to speculate about or to investigate their relations *with each other*. One could perhaps name this process 'theorizing' or 'theoretical thinking', since it is exactly what is done in most places where science is pursued, whether it be botany, medicine, metallurgy, zoology or any other. But I do not think the term is wide enough. The kind of thing I mean covers other studies as well—a good deal of history, for instance. Nor need it be systematic. There are very few children who do not do a little of it. Moreover, if a common word is chosen, there is the same danger of confusion arising from its occasional use with a less precise intention. Therefore, at the like hazard as before, I propose to call this particular kind of thinking *alpha-thinking*.

Thirdly, we can think about the *nature* of collective representations as such, and therefore about their relation to our own minds. We can think about perceiving and we can think about thinking. We can do, in fact, the kind of thinking which I am trying to do at the moment, and which you will be doing if you think I am right and also if you think I am wrong. This is part of the province of one or two sciences such as physiology and psychology, and of course it is also part of the province of philosophy. It has been called reflection or reflective thinking. But for the same reasons as before, I shall reject the simpler and more elegant term and call it *beta-thinking*.

It should be particularly noted that the distinction here made between alpha-thinking and beta-thinking is not one between two different *kinds* of thinking, such as for instance that which is sometimes made between analytical thinking on the one hand and synthetic or imaginative thinking on the other. It is purely a distinction of subject-matters.

The three operations—*figuration, alpha-thinking* and *beta-thinking*—are clearly distinguishable from one another; but that is not to say that they are divided by impassable barriers at the points where they mutually approach. Indeed the reverse is true. Moreover they may affect each other by reciprocal influence. In the history of the theory of colour, for instance, colour began by being regarded as a primary quality of the coloured object and was later transferred to the status of a 'secondary' quality dependent on the beholder. Here we can detect the interaction of alpha-thinking and beta-thinking; and again in the whole influence which experimental science has exerted on philosophy in the last two or three hundred years. This book, on the other hand, will be more concerned with the interaction between figuration and alpha-thinking.

That the former of these affects, and largely determines, the latter hardly needs saying; since the primary product of figuration is the actual subject-matter of most alpha-thinking. That the converse may sometimes also be true, and further, that the borderline between the one and the other is sometimes quite impossible to determine—this is less obvious. Yet a little serious reflection (that is, a little beta-thinking) makes it apparent enough.

Recall for a moment the familiar jingle from *Sylvie and Bruno*, with its persistent refrain of 'he thought he saw' followed by 'he found it was':

> He thought he saw a Banker's Clerk
> Descending from the bus,

> He looked again, and found it was
> A hippopotamus.
>   etc., etc.

This is of course only a very improbable instance of an experience which, in itself, is quite common, especially with those among our representations (and they form the overwhelming majority) which reach us through the sense of sight alone. When we mistake one representation, that is to say one thing, for another, so that there is a transition from an 'I thought I saw' to an 'I found it was', it is often very difficult indeed to say whether there is first a figuration (based, let us say, on incomplete sensation) and then another and different figuration, producing a different representation; or whether there is one and the same representation, veiled from us at first by some incorrect alpha-thinking, which is subsequently discarded as inapplicable. In the particular case of a puzzled man trying to descry an object spotted far off at sea, it feels more like the latter. Often it feels much more like the former. We have made the mistake before we are aware of having done any thinking at all.

Anyone who wishes to investigate this further should attend carefully to the sort of mistakes we are apt to make on awaking abruptly from deep sleep in a darkened room; especially if it happens to be a strange room. Either way we must conclude that figuration, whether or no it is a kind of thinking, is something which easily and imperceptibly passes over into thinking, and into which thinking easily and imperceptibly passes over. For in both cases there was a representation; otherwise I should not have been deceived. And if the first representation was the result of incorrect thinking, then thinking can do something very much like what figuration does. Alternatively, if it was the result of figuration alone, then the very fact that figuration can 'make a mistake' suggests that it has a good deal in common with thinking.

Original Participation

It is characteristic of our phenomena—indeed it is this, above all, which distinguishes them from those of the past—our participation in them, and therefore also their representational nature, is excluded from our immediate awareness. It is consequently always ignored by our 'common sense' and sometimes denied even in theory. For this reason it will be best to begin the brief series of observations which I want to make upon the history of phenomena—that is, the history of the familiar world—from the present day, and to work backwards from there to the remoter past. Our first step, then, is to trace the last stage of this development, which has led up to the collective representations with which we are familiar to-day.

Participation is the extra-sensory relation between man and the phenomena. It was shown in Chapter III that the existence of phenomena depends on it. Actual participation is therefore as much a fact in our case as in that of primitive man. But we have also seen that we are unaware, whereas the primitive mind is aware of it. This primitive awareness, however, is obviously not the theoretical kind which *we* can still arrive at by beta-thinking. For that presupposes some acquaintance with the findings of modern physics and physiology and can only be applied to the kind of collective representations that go with this. The primitive kind of participation is indeed not theoretical at all, inasmuch as it is given in immediate experience. Let us distinguish it from ours by calling it 'original' participation. It would however be cumbersome to add the epithet every time the word is used and I propose very often to omit it, having first made it plain here and now that by 'participation' I shall mean *original participation*, unless the context otherwise requires.

There is another difference between sophisticated and primitive participation. Hitherto we have spoken of *representations* and of the *unrepresented*; but we have said nothing of any 'represented'. This raises the question whether *representation* was the proper word to use at all, or whether it is merely misleading. If an appearance can properly be called a representation, it will certainly be a representation *of* something. Just as 'the particles', then (the name here chosen for all that is conceived to exist *independently* of consciousness), have also been called the *unrepresented*, so, whatever is *correlative* to the appearances or representations will here be called the *represented*. This is of course a mere name, and gives as yet no clue to the nature of what is meant. I hope that further light will be thrown upon it, gradually, as we proceed. Meanwhile I must use the name, leaving the reader to make up his mind, ambulando, whether it was justified or not.

We have seen that a very large part of the collective representations is found by beta-thinking to have been contributed by the percipient's own activity. Beta-thinking therefore inevitably assumes that a very large part of their correlative, the *represented*, is to be found 'within' ourselves. Consequently if *our* participation, having been first understood and accepted, by beta-thinking, as a fact, should then become a conscious experience, it would have to take the form of conscious (instead of, as now, unconscious) figuration. This is because for us, the represented is conceived as within our percipient selves; and it is only an unrepresented physical base ('particles') which we conceive of as without. Not so for primitives. For them the represented, too, is conceived as outside, so that there is no question of conscious figuration. It may also sometimes be detected within, but it is detected primarily without. The human soul may be one of the 'stopping-places' for *mana*, but what differentiates the primitive mind from ours is, that it conceives itself to be only *one* of those stopping-places and not necessarily the most significant. The essence of *original* participation is that there stands behind the phenomena, *and the other side of them from me*, a represented which is of the same nature as me. Whether it is called 'mana', or by the names of many gods and demons, or God the Father, or the spirit world, it is of the same nature as the perceiving self, inasmuch as it is not mechanical or accidental, but psychic and voluntary.

I have here assumed that what Lévy-Bruhl and Durkheim and their followers say about contemporary primitive man is substantially correct; and it seems to me likely to be so.[1] But whether or not it is correct for contemporary primitive man, it is certainly true of historically early man. All the evidence from etymology and elsewhere goes to show that the further back we penetrate into the past of human consciousness, the more mythical in their nature do the representations become. Moreover there is no evidence to the contrary. I shall say something later on of the testimony borne by etymology. Here it must suffice to affirm categorically that, for the nineteenth-century fantasy of early man first gazing, with his mind *tabula rasa*, at natural phenomena like ours, then seeking to explain them with thoughts like ours, and then by a process of inference 'peopling' them with the 'aery phantoms' of mythology, there just is not any single shred of evidence whatever.

I do not mean, by using the word 'fantasy', to imply contempt. If great scholars like Max Müller and Sir James Frazer, in seeking for the historical origins of myth, made the same mistake as the early anthropologists, it will, I hope, become apparent in the course of this and the ensuing chapters how inevitable it was that they should do so. To-day, on the other hand, partly thanks to their work, any little man, provided he is not hopelessly prejudiced, can convince himself of the contrary. The point is, not to find someone to turn up our noses at, but to grasp the fact that alpha-thinking, when men first began to exercise it, had to be directed upon *that* kind of collective representation (namely the participated kind) and not on collective representations resembling ours, which (as we shall see) are a later product of that very alpha-thinking.

For alpha-thinking, as I have defined it, is a thinking *about* collective representations. But when we think 'about' anything, we must necessarily be aware of ourselves (that is, of the self which is doing the thinking) as sharply and clearly detached from the thing thought about. It follows that alpha-thinking involves *pro tanto* absence of participation. It is in fact the very nature and aim of pure alpha-thinking to exclude participation. When, therefore, it is directed, as

1. Compare, more recently, the last two talks in *The Institutions of Primitive Society* (A series of Broadcast Talks). Blackwell. 1954.

it has to be to start with, on phenomena determined by original participation, then, at first simply by being alpha-thinking, and at a later stage deliberately, it seeks to destroy that participation. The more so because (as we shall also see), participation renders the phenomena less predictable and less calculable.

The history of alpha-thinking accordingly includes the history of science, as the term has hitherto been understood, and reaches its culmination in a system of thought which only interests itself in phenomena to the extent that they can be grasped as independent of consciousness. This culmination appears to have been reached about the close of the nineteenth century. For, along with the recent tendency of physics to implicate the observer again in the phenomena, there goes the tendency of physicists to give up alpha-thinking about phenomena and occupy themselves, as mathematicians, only with the unrepresented.

Systematic alpha-thinking appears to have begun with astronomy. Whether this was because the movements of the heavenly bodies display a regularity which is mostly lacking in sublunary phenomena, and which would be first therefore to attract the attention of minds beginning for the first time to interest themselves in regularity, or whether it was for some other reason, we need not consider. Astronomy is generally regarded as the *doyen* of the sciences, and a glance at its history from Greek times to the present day or thereabouts will afford some insight into the development of that exact thinking about phenomena which is called science and the effect of that development on the collective representations of Western man. I say from Greek times because, although the Egyptians and Chaldeans appear to have kept astronomical records over a very long period, we know nothing of any avowedly *speculative* thought earlier than the Greeks either on this or on any other subject.

That the collective representations to which this speculative thought was applied were of the kind already indicated, i.e. participated, is obvious enough. Apart from speculative thought, it would never have occurred to an ancient Greek to doubt that the heavenly bodies and their spheres were in one way or another representations of divine beings. Such a doubt was, in fact, voiced occasionally—simply because the Greek mind was of such an incorrigibly speculative nature that there was very little that did *not* occur to it—as a purely notional possibility. But the point is that, in the early days of alpha-thinking, any such notion was a secondary speculation, and rather a wild one, about collective representations whose character made the contrary, 'representational', view seem the obvious one.

The systematic alpha-thinking exercised only by the thoughtful few is applied to the phenomena, that is, to collective representations which they share with the many. And we are left in no doubt by Plato's Dialogues, and by the whole language and literature of Greece, what these, in general, were like. There it was the materialist who looked like a Berkeley, and the Greek equivalent of Dr. Johnson would return from speculation to common sense, not by kicking a stone, but by appealing to collective representations made obvious by his upbringing, by the language he spoke and heard spoken all around him, and by the active cults which were his daily matter of fact experience. Even the atoms of Democritus were, of course, not atoms, as the word has been understood in the nineteenth and twentieth centuries. They were imagined as components of mind no less than of matter. In other words they were the only sort of atoms which alpha-thinking about participated phenomena *could* present to itself for the purpose of speculation.

It is in this light that we must approach, if we wish to understand them, not only the speculations of Plato, and Aristotle, for instance, on the nature of the stars and planets, but also the meanings of common words like νοῦς (*nous*) and λόγος (*logos*), and the whole apparatus of language by which they expressed these speculations. If we are content to translate, and to *think*, 'mind' for νοῦς and 'reason' or 'word' for λόγος, we are in continual danger of surreptitiously substituting our own phenomena for those which they were in fact dealing with. It is not only that they speculated on whether the planets were 'visible gods' or only images of the gods, as statues are; on the nature of the Fifth Essence and its relation to the earthly elements; on the Anima Mundi; on whether or not the Aether, which is the substance of the spheres, has a soul, etc. The very meanings of the incidental words with the help of which they did the speculating, implied participation *of some sort*. Whereas the words into which we struggle to translate them imply the reverse. Some examples of these words will be considered in a later chapter, when it will be seen that original participation survived in an attenuated form even into the Middle Ages.

It may remove the risk of misunderstanding if I mention at this early stage that it is no part of the object of this book to advocate a return to original participation.

The Texture of Medieval Thought

Once the fact of participation is granted, the connection between words and things must, we have seen, be admitted to be at any time a very much closer one than the last two or three centuries have assumed. Conscious participation, moreover, will be aware of that connection; and original participation was conscious. It is only if we approach it in this light that we can hope to understand the extreme preoccupation of medieval learning with words—and with grammar, dialectic, rhetoric, logic and all that has to do with words. For words—and particularly nouns—were not then, and could not then be regarded as *mere* words. I was taught in my first class at school to recite aloud with the rest of the class: 'A noun is the name of anything,' and the philosophers, from Plotinus to Aquinas, were wont to treat at the same time of words and things under the inclusive topic of 'names'. Thus, Dionysius in his *De Divinis Nominibus*, and Aquinas in the 13th Quaestio of Part I of the *Summa* ('concerning the names of God') and in the little treatise *De Natura Verbi Intellectus* and elsewhere, are both concerned, not with philology but with epistemology and metaphysics.

In the last two chapters I have said a little of the world as it was for the common man and a little of the world as it was for science immediately before the scientific revolution. Now I am to say a little of the world as it was show forth in philosophy. In all cases the plan of this book as well as the time at my disposal both for study and for writing, have determined that that little must be a very little indeed. I am only too well aware that a whole book, instead of a chapter, would not be too much to give to the philosophy alone of that lost world. Once again, it *is* a lost world—although the whole purpose of this book is to show that its spiritual wealth can be, and indeed, if incalculable disaster is to be avoided, *must* be regained. No good can come of any attempt to hark back to the original participation from which it sprang.

That lost world, then, was a world in which both phenomenon and name were felt as representations. On the one hand 'the word conceived in the mind is representative of the whole of that which is realized in thought' (*Verbum igitur in mente conceptum est repraesentativum omnis ejus quod actu intelligitur*).[1] But on the other hand the phenomenon itself only achieves full reality (*actus*) in the moment of being 'named' by man; that is, when that in nature which it represents is united with that in man which the name represents. Such naming, however, need not involve vocal utterance. For the name or word is not mere sound, or mere ink. For Aquinas, as for Augustine, there are, anterior to the uttered word, the intellect-word, the heart-word and the memory-word (*verbum intellectus, verbum cordis, verbum memoriae*). The human word proceeds from the memory, as the Divine Word proceeds from the Father.[2] Proceeds from it, yet remains one with it. For the world is the thought of God realized through His Word. Thus, the Divine Word is also *forma exemplaris*;[3] the phenomena are its representations; as the human word is the representation of *intellectus in actu*. But, once again, the phenomenon itself only achieves its full reality (*actus*) in being named or thought by man; for thinking in act *is* the thing thought, in act; just as the senses in act, are the things sensed, in act. (*Intellectus in actu est intelligible in actu; sicut sensus in actu est sensible in actu.*[4]) And elsewhere St.

---

1. *Summa Theologica*, 1a, Qu. 34, a. 3.
2. *De Differentia Divini Verbi et Humani* ; De Natura Verbi Intellectus, *etc.*
3. *Summa*, 1a, Qu. 3, a. 8, ad 2.
4. Ibid., 1a, Qu. 12, a. 2. 3.

Thomas expressly ratifies the dictum of Aristotle in his *De Anima*, that 'the soul is in a manner all things': (*Anima est quodammodo omnia*).[5]

It is against a background of thoughts like these, and of the collective representations on which they were based, that we must see the medieval conception of the Seven Liberal Arts, with Grammar at their head, followed immediately by Rhetoric and Dialectic. To learn about the true nature of words was at the same time to learn about the true nature of things. And it was the only way. We may reflect how the meaning of the word *grammar* itself has been polarized, since the scientific revolution, into the study of 'mere' words, on the one hand, and, on the other, into the half-magical *gramarye*, which altered its form to *glamour* and was useful for a season to the poets, before it was debased. One may reflect also on the frequent appearances made by Grammar and the other liberal arts, as persons, in medieval allegory, and how easily and naturally they mingle there with the strange figure of the Goddess Natura—at once so like and so unlike the Persephone of Greek mythology. This might easily lead us into a consideration of allegory itself—a literary form which is so little to our taste, and yet was so popular and all-pervasive in the Middle Ages. Is it not clear that *we* find allegory desiccated precisely because, for us, mere words are themselves desiccated—or rather because, for us, words are 'mere'? For us, the characters in an allegory are 'personified abstractions', but for the man of the Middle Ages Grammar or Rhetoric, Mercy or 'Daunger', were real to begin with, simply *because* they were 'names'. And names could be representations, in much the same solid-feeling way as things were.

For this very reason we are in some danger of confusing their allegory with the 'symbolism' in which we ourselves are again beginning to be interested, or at least of judging them by the same standards. This is an error. Symbolism often expresses itself in language, as so much else does, though it can also express itself through other media. Yet the essence of symbolism is, not that words or names, as such, but that things or events themselves, are apprehended as representations. But this, as we have seen, is the normal way of apprehension for a participating consciousness. *Our* 'symbolical' therefore is an approximation to, or a variant of, *their* 'literal'. Even when they got down to the bedrock of literal, they still experienced that rock as a representation. And so Aquinas, in dealing with the use of language in Holy Scripture, first divides its meaning into *literal* and *spiritual* and then subsumes the *allegorical* (and certain other) interpretations under the heading of *spiritual*. But when he comes to the *sensus parabolicus* (which is our 'symbolical') he includes it in the literal (*sub literali continetur*). When, for example, in the Bible, 'the right arm of God' is spoken of, 'It is not the figure, but the figured which is the literal meaning'.[6] All this will bear some meditation.

5. Ibid., 1a, Qu. 14, a. 1.
6. *Summa*, 1a, Qu. 1, a. 10, ad 3.

Indeed, to understand how the word 'literal' has changed its meaning is to understand the heart of the matter. For our problem is, precisely, to transport ourselves into the interior of minds, for which the *ordinary* way of looking at, and of thinking about, phenomena, was to look at and to think about them as appearances—representations. For which, therefore, knowledge was defined, not as the devising of hypotheses, but as an act of union with the represented behind the representation. And it is only by reconstructing in imagination, and not just in theory, the nature of the representations they confronted that we can hope really to understand the mode of their thinking. If we approach it from this end, instead of, as is usual, by way of our own representations and our own consequent distortions of the then meanings of their terms, then the Scholastic terminology does indeed spring into life for us—form and matter, *actus* and *potentia*, species, essence, existence, the active and the passive intelligence, and the rest. We must forget all about our 'laws of nature', those interposed, spectral hypotheses, before we can understand the 'forms' of medieval scholasticism. For the forms determined the appearances, not as laws do, but rather as a soul determines a body; and indeed the animal and human soul was defined as the 'form' of the body. We must forget all about causality, as we understand it, if we want to understand how the form was also *causa exemplaris*. But there is not anything to forget, for we have not even a transmuted survival, of that *actus: potentia* polarity, which was the very life-blood of Scholastic thought, central in its heart and manifest, through its capillaries, at all points of its surface organism. Being is potential existence; existence actualizes being. Yet, in the universe, *actus* precedes *potentia*; for out of potentiality a subject cannot be brought except by a being that is actual. The being of God is wholly actual, and is at the same time His existence; but, for creatures, it is only their *existence* which actualizes—actualizes not their own being, but the being of God, which they participate. Everywhere around us we must see creatures in a state of *potentia* being raised to *actus*: and yet, behind the appearances, the *actus* is already there. What is the intellectual soul but the potentiality of determining the species of things? And what are the phenomena themselves? *Actually* the likeness or representations of all sorts of 'species'—but *potentially* (that is, in the condition described as *in potentia*) immaterial in the soul itself.[7] Phenomena and mind in perpetual interplay, with 'species' hovering somewhere between them as the moment in which the one becomes the other—*Anima enim quasi transformata est in rem per speciem.*[8]

'Knowledge', for such a consciousness, was conceived of as the perfection or completion of the 'naming' process of thought. In ordinary thinking or speaking, as in perception, the participation was a half-conscious process. But knowledge was an actual union with the represented behind the representation.

7. Ibid., 1a, Qu. 79, a 4, ad 4.
8. Aquinas, *De Natura Verbi Intellectus.*

'The knowledge of things that are, *is* the things' (*Cognitio eorum, quae sunt, ea, quae sunt, est*) wrote John Scotus Erigena in the ninth century, quoting Dionysius. 'Nothing', wrote Aquinas, 'is known except truth—which is the same as being' (*nihil enim scitur nisi verum, quod cum ente convertitur*).[9] Or, as a mean between *potentia* and *actus*, it was the process of actualization of the soul's potentiality to become what it contemplated, and thus, a stage on its journey back to God. God's own knowledge was alike the case of all things and identical with His substance, and man participated in the being of God. Indeed, it was only by virtue of that participation that he could claim to *have* any being.

Now, participation, as an actual *experience*, is only to be won for our islanded consciousness of to-day by special exertion. It is a matter, not of theorizing, but of 'imagination' in the genial or creative sense of the word, and therefore our first glimpse of it is commonly an aesthetic experience of some sort, derived from poetry or painting. And yet this experience, so foreign to our habit, is one which we positively must acquire and apply before we can hope to understand the thought of any philosopher earlier than the scientific revolution. Without it we shall not really understand what they mean when they use the commonest terms—species and genus, form and matter, subject and accident, cause and effect. Instead, we shall clumsily substitute a meaning of our own. In the work of Thomas Aquinas, in particular, the word *participate* or *participation* occurs almost on every page, and a whole book could be written—indeed one has been written[10]—on the uses he makes of it. It is not a technical term of philosophy, and he is no more concerned to define it than a modern philosopher would be to define some such common tool of his thought as, say, the word *compare*. Only in one passage, from the whole of his voluminous works, according to M. Geiger, did he feel it necessary to indicate its meaning, and this he did principally by illustrating it. Thus, after telling us that the species participates the genus, and the accident the subject, that matter participates form and effect participates cause, he gives us a glimpse of what all these participations signify to him, by adding: 'Suppose we say that air participates the light of the sun, because it does not receive it in that clarity in which it is in the sun.'[11]

At one end of the scale the subject participates its predicate; at the other end, a formal or hierarchical participation *per similitudinem* was the foundation of the whole structure of the universe; for all creatures were in a greater or lesser degree images or representations, or 'names' of God, and their likeness or unlikeness did not merely measure, but *was* the nearer or more distant emanation of his Being and Goodness in them. It was a spiritual structure, and much of it lay beyond the world of appearance altogether. Angels, for example, are not simply the subject of a separate work, or a separate chapter of the *Summa*, but

9. *Summa*, Ia, Qu. I, a I, 2.
10. L.-B. Geiger, *La Participation dans la Philosophie de S. Thomas d'Aquin*. Paris, 1942.
11. *De Hebdomadibus*, cap. 2.

occur everywhere in it and are as likely to be referred to in a purely epistemo-logical, as in a cosmological, context.

It will be well to point out here that, if I have concentrated on one particular medieval philosopher, rather than attempted a conspectus of the whole field of medieval philosophy or theories of knowledge, it is because that is the method which a history of consciousness, as distinct from a history of ideas, must adopt. It must attempt to penetrate into the very texture and activity of thought, rather than to collate conclusions. It is concerned, semantically, with the way in which words are used rather than with the product of discourse. Expressed in terms of logic, its business is more with the proposition than with the syllogism and more with the term than with the proposition. Therefore it must particularize. It must choose some one, or at best a few points, for its penetration. It is a question of making the best choice, and to me the best choice seemed to be the language and thought of Thomas Aquinas. I could probably have found more sensational illustrations of participation in, for example, Erigena or Albertus. For the Ara-bians, participation—with a particular intellectual emphasis—was so complete as practically to exclude individual human identity. I should, I think, have found fewer illustrations among the Nominalists, but they can fairly be regarded as forerunners of the scientific revolution, in whom the decline of participation cast its shadow before. Moreover, in the mind of Aquinas, with his enormous er-udition, the whole corpus of medieval thought is in a manner recapitulated; and he is as sober as he is profound.

Before and After the Scientific Revolution

For medieval man, then, the universe was a kind of theophany, in which he par-ticipated at different levels, in being, in thinking, in speaking or naming, and in knowing. And then—the evolutionary change began. Not, of course, at any given moment, but with anticipations, localized delays, individual differences. But no beginning is instantaneous—otherwise the very word 'begin' would be unnecessary and indeed meaningless. We need not pay too much attention to those historians who cautiously refuse to detect any process in history, because it is difficult to divide into periods, or because the periods are difficult to date precisely. The same objections apply to the process of growth from child to man. We should rather remind them that, if there is no process, there is in fact no such thing as history at all, so that they themselves must be regarded as mere chroniclers and antiquarians—a limitation which I cannot fancy they would relish. Moreover, the mental image, which they transfer to history, or a formless process determined by the chance impact of events, is itself . . . a product of the idolatry of the age of literalness.

However this may be, and whatever chronological limits we choose to assign to it, a change there certainly was. Professor Butterfield has commented well on it:

> through changes in the habitual use of words, certain things in the natural philosophy of Aristotle had now acquired a coarsened meaning or were actually misunderstood. It may not be easy to say why such a thing should have happened, but men unconsciously betray the fact that a certain Aristotelian thesis simply has no meaning for them any longer—they just cannot think of the stars and heavenly bodies as things without weight even when the books tell them to do so. Francis Bacon seems unable to say anything except that it is obvious that these heavenly bodies have weight, like any other kind of matter which we meet in our experience. Bacon says, furthermore, that he is unable to imagine the planets as nailed to crystalline spheres; and the whole idea only seems more absurd to him if the spheres in question are supposed to be made of that liquid, aethereal kind of substance which Aristotle had in mind. Between the idea of a stone aspiring to reach its natural place at the *centre of* the universe—*and rushing* more fervently as it came nearer home—and the idea of a stone accelerating its descent under the constant force of gravity, there is an intellectual transition which involves a change in men's feeling for matter.[1]

We have see that this change in men's feelings for matter is merely one aspect of a much deeper and more fundamental change. And the change in men's feeling for the nature of words and of thought was no whit less marked. Thus, the polarity of *actus* and *potentia* had carried perhaps half the weight of the philosophical thought of the Western mind through all the centuries that elapsed between Aristotle and Aquinas. A medieval philosopher would not have put the argument as I was obliged to do, when I said [earlier] that there is 'no such thing' as unfelt solidity, just as there is no such thing as an unseen rainbow. He would have said that both the unseen rainbow and the unfelt matter are *in potentia*. Yet this polarity, taken for granted for more than a thousand years by some of the acutest intellects the world has ever known—this polarity has become, for Bacon, a 'frigida distinctio'—mere words! Again, in the *Novum Organum* he tells men bluntly that they ought not to think of 'forms' any more. The are really more like 'laws'.

> It may be that nothing really exists except individual bodies, which produce real motion according to law; in science it is just that law, and the inquiry, discovery and explanation of it, which are the fundamental requisite both for the knowledge and

1. *Origins of Modern Science*, p. 104.

for the control of Nature. And it is that law and its 'clauses', which *I* mean when I use (chiefly because of its currently prevalence and familiarity) the word 'forms'.[2]

Causa exemplairs is gone, in other words, and mechanical causality and the idols are already in sight.

If, with the help of some time-machine working in reverse, a man of the Middle Ages could be suddenly transported into the skin of a man of the twentieth century, seeing through our eyes and with our 'figuration' the objects we see, I think he would feel like a child who looks for the first time at a photograph through the ingenious magic of a stereoscope. 'Oh!' he would say, 'look how they *stand out!*' We must not forget that in his time perspective had not yet been discovered, nor underrate the significance of this. True, it is no more than a device for pictorially representing depth, and separateness, in space. But how comes it that the device had never been discovered before—or, if discovered, never adopted? There were plenty of skilled artists, and they would certainly have hit upon it soon enough if depth in space had characterized the collective representations they wish to reproduce, as it characterizes ours. They did not need it. Before the scientific revolution the world was more like a garment men wore about them than a stage on which they moved. In such a world the convention of perspective was unnecessary. To such a world other conventions of visual reproduction, such as the nimbus and the halo, were as appropriate as to ours they are not. It was as if the observers were themselves *in* the picture. Compared with us, they felt themselves and the objects around them and the worlds that expressed those objects, immersed together in something like a clear lake of— what shall we say?—of 'meaning', if you choose. It seems the most adequate word. Aquinas's *verbum intellectus* was *tanquam speculum, in quo res cernitur*[3]—'like a mirror in which the object is discerned'.

It happened that, at a time when I was studying the *De Natura Verbi Intellectus*, with that peculiar mixture of perplexity and delight which Thomas's sentences arouse, when his thinking is at its intensest and tersest, I had the good fortune to receive from a friend the gift of a volume of his own poems. It seemed to me then, and it still seems to me now, that in one of them he has managed, without setting out to do so, to convey more vividly than I could ever hope to do, the qualitative difference between a participating outlook on the world, and our own. I therefore conclude my chapter with it.

REFLECTION

When hill, tree, cloud, those shadowy forms
Ascending heaven are seen,

2. *Novum Organum*, II, 2. Author's translation.
3. *De Natura Verbi Intellectus.*

Their mindless beauty I from far
Admire, a gulf between;

Yet in the untroubled river when
Their true ideas I find,
That river, joined in trance with me,
Becomes my second mind.[4]

The Development of Meaning

In the course of this book many scattered references have been made to words
and language. It is desirable that some attempt should now be made to draw the
threads together.

When we are disputing about the proper meaning to be attached to a particular
word in a sentence, etymology is of little use. Only children run to the dictionary
to settle an argument. But if we would consider the *nature* of meaning, and the relation between thought and things, we cannot profitably dispense with etymology. It is long since men gave up the notion that the variety of natural species and
the secrets of their relation to each other can be understood apart from their history; but many thinkers still seek to confine the science of language, as the Lin-
naeans once confined botany, within a sort of network of timeless abstractions.
Method, for them, is another name for classification; but that is a blind alley.

Now etymology depicts the process of language in time. And it is a com-
monplace of the subject that, whatever word we hit on, if we trace its meaning
far enough back, we find it apparently expressive of some tangible, or at all
events, perceptible object or some physical activity. *Understanding* once meant
'standing under', and abstractions like *concept* and *hypothesis* merely disguise,
in the garb of a dead language, a similarly humble origin. Even *right* and *wrong*
are said to have once meant 'straight' and 'sour'.

In much more recent times we can observe the evolution of a great deal of the
emotional and psychological meaning in contemporary words out of an astro-
logical, chemical, or physiological past. Many people are aware, without turning to a dictionary, of what *disposition, influence, melancholy*, etc. used to
mean, and I have already referred . . . to the fact that similar changes are *still
going on* in the case of such words as *heart* and *blood*. It would be in line with

4. George Rostrevor Hamilton. *The Carved Stone*. Heinemann. 1952.

the general process of etymological change if, in future, the meaning of *heart* should become purely emotional, some other word such as *cardium* being appropriated to the physical organ.

Here and there, it is true, we may observe a change in the opposite direction; and it is certainly striking that the most abstract of all abstract terms—*relation* —should have become capable of signifying a solid, three-dimension aunt or cousin. But these are the rare exceptions. Throughout the recorded history of language the movement of meaning has been from concrete to abstract.

I am here using the word 'abstract' in its broadest, and admittedly vague, sense, to cover everything in the familiar world we talk about, which is not, actually or theoretically, accessible to the senses; everything which a nineteenth-century logician would have termed an 'attribute'; and which some twentieth-century philosophers classify as a mere part of speech. In this sense *melancholy* and *a kind heart* may be as much abstractions as *concept* and *hypothesis*—it depends how we think of them. How we ought to think of them may be disputed, and indeed I am engaged in disputing it. But it is enough for my present purpose that nearly everybody to-day thinks of them as divorced from the 'appearances' of nature which are accessible to the senses—in a way which nearly everybody before the scientific revolution did not.

Systematic reflection on the *history* of language hardly began before the second half of the nineteenth century, when idolatry, as we have seen, was already near its culminating point; and when it had already, as described in Chapter IX, distorted the picture which men formed of the remote past. It was against this background, therefore, that the philologists of the nineteenth century sought to account for that unmistakable, semantic progress from concrete to abstract—or from 'outer' to 'inner'—to which I have just referred. In those circumstances, their answer to the problem was—metaphor. Before speech was invented, they said, primitive man lived in a world, except for details, very much like ours. His next step was to invent simple words for the simple things he saw about him— trees and animals, the sun and the moon, and so forth. And then, when his reason had evolved, and he found he needed words in which to express his inner life, he used these simple words again, but this time as metaphors. Herbert Spencer and Max Müller went further than this and added that, later on, men made the mistake of taking their own metaphors literally; and that this was the origin of mythology. Mythology, said Müller, is 'a disease of language'. Of course, as time went on (they said), the metaphors 'faded'. We no longer call up any mental image of 'standing beneath', when we use the word *understand*, or of a physical 'pressing out', when we speak of *expressing* a sentiment or an idea. The progress was assumed to be from the metaphor, through the trope (which is a kind of moribund metaphor—as when we speak of following the *thread* of an argument), to the ordinary straightforward 'meaning'. But, whatever meanings its words might bear to-day, language was considered historically as a tissue of faded or dead metaphors.

Now there is no doubt that in the last few centuries the meanings of quite a number of the words with which we endeavour to express psychological facts or opinions *have* come into being in just this way—by deliberate transference from the outer world to the inner. *Emotions* is probably an example. But it is equally certain that the great majority have not. If we look into them, we find that they point us back, not to metaphor, but to participation; whether, like *disposition, influence*, and many others, through astrology, or whether, like *temper* and *humour*, through the old physiology, or whether, without being traceably connected with any particular system of thought, in one way or another they stem from a time before that exclusive disjunction between outer and inner, which the term 'metaphor' pre-supposes. Such is the case with many of the oldest words in the language—like *heart* and *blood*, to which I have already referred. Moreover, many much more recent words, to which a simple metaphorical origin may be hastily attributed, will be found on closer examination to betray similar birth-marks. *Depression*, for instance, would seem at first sight to be in the same class as *emotion*. But the evidence collected by the Oxford Dictionary suggests that its psychological significance did not, in fact, originate in a spatial metaphor (such as we use, when we speak of being 'on top of the world'), but as a literal discription of the state of the 'vital spirits'.

Many years ago, in a book called *Poetic Diction*, I drew attention to another fatal objection to this theory that words which to-day have a mental or emotional content acquired that content originally as a metaphorical extension of their meaning. It is this. If we find language growing more and more metaphorical, the further back we go into the past, what possible justification can there be for assuming a still earlier time when it was not metaphorical at all? Thus, Max Müller postulated a 'metaphorical period', during which the progress from literal to metaphorical meanings must have taken place. But, what is this but a purely arbitrary surmise? And is it not highly improbable? Why was such an assumption found necessary? Simply in order to make the evidence presented by the history of language fit in somehow or other with that 'evolution of idols'. . . .

It would take a very long time to trace all the influences exerted by preconceptions of this nature on the theories which men have formed about the origin and development of language, and even on lexicography itself. They are most easily detected by the train of inconsistencies they have left in their wake. Take, for instance, the old philological teaching of the building up of inflected and complex words from simple 'roots' of speech. Some languages, among which Hebrew is probably an outstanding example, are clearly formed about a relatively small number of consonant-groups consisting of three or even two letters each. Here is the bare fact. But what we make of it is all too likely to depend on the preconceptions with which we approach it. If we have preconceived a world in which the earliest speakers were surrounded by idols in all respects like our own, we shall treat these consonant-groups practically as 'words', and shall attribute to them meanings which were wide because they were generalized from particulars. This is what the philologists did; and it is particularly interesting to watch Max Müller relating this 'root' concept, as it was presented in his time, to his theory of a 'metaphorical period', to which I have already referred. He invented a distinction between *radical* metaphor and *poetical* metaphor.

> I call it a radical metaphor when a root which means to shine is applied to form the names, not only of the fire or the sun, but of the spring of the year, the morning light, the brightness of thought, or the joyous outburst of hymns of praise. Ancient languages are brimful of such metaphors, and under the microscope of the etymologist almost every word discloses traces of its first metaphorical conception.
>
> From this we must distinguish *poetical* metaphor, namely, when a noun or verb, ready made and assigned to one definite object or action, is transferred poetically to another object or action. For instance, when the rays of the sun are called the hands or fingers of the sun.[1]

The assumption is, that men had on their lips the roots and in their minds the meanings, very much as we have words and their meanings to-day, and then proceeded to 'apply' them to a varied selection of phenomena. But, as was pointed out in the book already referred to,[2] this assumption is inconsistent in two respects with all that we know of primitive languages. Among very primitive and otherwise almost wordless peoples very short words are exactly what we do *not* find. Anthropologists tell us, instead, of the 'holophrase' or long, rambling conglomeration of sound and meaning. Words grow longer, not shorter, the nearer we get to the end of our backward journey towards the origin of speech. Secondly, a word meaning 'to shine' in general, as distinct from any particular kind of shining, is the very thing which a primitive mind is incapable of grasping. Indeed, much simpler generalizations, such as 'tree'—as distinct from a coconut-tree or a gum-tree—are equally beyond it. If, therefore, in any language the roots were there from the beginning, then, whatever else they were, they cannot have been words devised by men for the purpose of expressing general ideas.

I do not believe, then, that there is any such thing as a 'radical metaphor'. But I believe that reflection on the working of metaphor may nevertheless be a good approach to reflection on the nature of roots. For it is the peculiarity of metaphorical language that, at first sight, it does often resemble very closely the language of participation; though upon closer examination its existence is seen to depend precisely on the *absence* of participation.[3] It is at all events important to have made some such examination before we approach the wider question of the nature and origin of language.

1. *Science of Language*, p. 451.
2. *Poetic Diction*, 2nd Edition, Faber 1952.
3. Cf. p. 127.

The Origin of Language

We have seen that, in the older doctrine of invented and applied 'roots of speech, as pointing to the origin of language, and in the more recent one of 'metaphor' as the principal instrument of the growth of meaning, we are saddled with two notions, which are both of them inconsistent with the testimony of language itself. If, on the other hand, we approach the history of meaning free from all assumptions based on biological theories of evolution; if we take our stand simply on a faithful study of the *nature* of language, then we shall not be seduced into any such arbitrary surmises. Instead, we shall be obliged to admit that 'metaphor' is a misleading concept to apply to any but the later and more sophisticated stages of language. For all the evidence points rather to that sort of 'polarization' of an ancient unity into an outer and an inner meaning. . . . In other words, it points to the source of language in original participation—and, in doing so, indicates the direction in which we must look for a true understanding of those mysterious 'roots'. It is there, too, that we may hope in the end to espy the historical function of the word in determining the relation between thought and things.

We have seen that the difference between what I have called 'original' participation and the participation which can be grasped to-day in beta-thinking is, above all, a difference of direction. In the former, the represented is felt to be on the other side of the phenomena from the perceiving self. At the same time, it is to be linked with, or related to, that self otherwise than through the senses. The self, so far as there yet is one, is still aware that it and the phenomena derive from the same supersensible source. This kind of consciousness, then, is the subjective aspect of that coming-into-being, *pari passu*, of man and of his phenomena. . . . Objectively, we could only describe the earlier stages of this process as a time when man—not only as a body, but also as a soul—was a part of nature in a way which we to-day, of course, find it difficult to conceive. Subjectively, he could not yet 'call his soul his own'. The farther back we penetrate, the more indistinguishable would his acts and utterances become from processes taking place in what has since become 'outer' nature.

It is conditions such as these which we must strive to realize in imagination, if we would hope to understand the 'root' element in language. Speech did not arise as the attempt of man to imitate, to master or to explain 'nature'; for speech and nature came into being along with one another. Strictly speaking, only idolators can raise the question of the 'origin of language'. For anyone else to do so is like asking for the origin of origin. Roots are the echo of nature herself sounding in man. Or rather, they are the echo of what once sounded and fashioned in both of them at the same time. And therefore it is, that they have always fascinated those adventurous souls—such as Fabre d'Olivet, Court de Gébelin or, in our own time, Herman Beckh, A. D. Wadler and others—who have sought to explore that difficult and perplexing territory—devastated as it has been by ensuing millennia of cultural divergence and etymological accidents—the relation between the sounds of language and its meanings.

The split between sound and meaning—for their relation in any modern language is no more than vestigial—is one aspect of the ever-widening gulf between outer and inner, phenomenon and name, thing and thought, with which this book is concerned. We have seen how that polarization into man: nature, which was the means to man's self-consciousness, was exaggerated by the scientific revolution into an exclusive disjunction. It was still a polarity, so long as *some* image-consciousness, *some* participation survived. We have seen also, in the preceding chapter, how the disjunction was deliberately purposed by the Jewish nation. I believe it will some day be realized that their mission was at the same time to prepare humanity against the day when it should be complete— that is, our own time.

The Hebrew language, through which (as we have seen) the inwardness of the Divine Name was later revealed, is at the same time, according to some opinions, that one among the ancient languages in which the roots preserve most clearly (though still dimly enough) the old unity of sound and meaning. If we try to think of these roots as 'words', then we must think of words with a potential rather than an actual meaning. Certainly those who have any feeling for sound-symbolism, and who wish to develop it, will be well advised to ponder them. They may find, in the consonantal element in language, vestiges of those forces which brought into being the external structure of nature, including the body of man; and, in the original vowel-sounds, the expression of that inner life of feeling and memory which constitutes his soul. It is the two together which have made possible, by first physically and then verbally embodying it, his personal intelligence.

The objective of this book is, however, a limited one, namely, to demonstrate on general grounds the necessity of smashing the idols. It cannot, therefore, attempt to investigate in detail what sort of knowledge may result from doing so, and it would be quite beyond its scope to carry this difficult subject any further. Suffice it to say that the Semitic languages seem to point us back to the old unity of man and nature, through the shapes of their sounds. We feel those shapes not only as sounds, but also, in a manner, as *gestures* of the speech-organs—and it is not so difficult to realize that these gestures were once gestures made with the whole body—once—when the body itself was not detached from the rest of nature after the solid manner of to-day, when the body itself was spoken even while it was speaking.

In an Aryan language, such as Greek, on the other hand, where natural and mythological significances so easily meet and mingle, we can feel more easily the nature of *phenomenal*—that is, imaginal—participation. The Aryan tongues point to the same ancient unity as the Semitic—but they do so through the quality of their *meaning*. Among the speakers of both types of language, a few centuries before the Christian era, a last faint echo of that unity appeared in the form of tradition and doctrine.

In the *Sefer Yezirah*, for instance, whose authorship was traditionally assigned to Abraham, and which was perhaps first committed to writing about B.C. 600, the account of creation given in the Book of Genesis is expanded, and related in considerable detail to the sounds and signs of a language at once divine and human. And the influence of the Jewish doctrine of the Word of God, which was at the same time the source of the phenomenal world and the incarnation of wisdom in man, is still clearly apparent in the Book of Proverbs and in the apocryphal *Ecclesiasticus* and *Wisdom of Solomon*. In the world of Greek thought the development in a similar direction, and particularly by the Stoic sect, of the *logos* of the Greek philosophers is better known; and it is an old story how the two streams met in Alexandria and united in a form which is probably best exemplified in the writings of Philo Judaeus.

All things came into being through the Word. This teaching of the creative Word, this last testimony to a creation which was not a mere creation of idols, and to an evolution which was not a mere evolution of idols, is one which Christian thought, thanks to the opening verses of St. John's Gospel, has never been able entirely to ignore, though it has by now come near to doing so. But the significance of this must be deferred to a later chapter.

Symptoms of Iconoclasm

We have seen that the theory of metaphor, as the means by which language originally acquired its 'inner' meanings, is incorrect. But it is important to remember how it arose. It arose because there *is* a close relation between language as it is used by a participating consciousness and language as it is used, at a later stage, metaphorically or symbolically. When we use language metaphorically, we bring it about of our own free will that an appearance means something other than itself, and, usually, that a manifest 'means' an unmanifest. We start with an idol, and we ourselves turn the idol into a representation. We use the phenomenon as a 'name' for what is not phenomenal. And this, it will be remembered, is just what is characteristic of participation. Symbolism . . . is made possible by the elimination of participation. But . . . in certain circumstances this may give rise to a new kind of participation—one which could no longer be described as 'original'.

What then has occurred? If we rapidly review the whole historical development of 'the word', we must say that, as soon as unconscious or subconscious organic processes have been sufficiently polarized to give rise to phenomena on the one side and consciousness on the other, *memory* is made possible. As consciousness develops into self-consciousness, the remembered phenomena become detached or liberated from their originals and so, as images, are in some measure at man's disposal. The more thoroughly participation has been eliminated, the more they are at the disposal of his imagination to employ as it chooses. If it chooses to impart its own meaning, it is doing, *pro tanto*, with the remembered phenomena what their Creator once did with the phenomena themselves. Thus there *is* a real analogy between metaphorical usage and original participation; but it is one which can only be acknowledged at this high, or even prophetic, level. It can only be acknowledged if the crude conception of an evolution of idols, which has dominated the last two centuries, is finally abandoned, or at all events is enlightened by one more in line with the old teaching of the Logos. There is a valid analogy *if*, but only if, we admit that, in the course of the earth's history, something like a Divine Word has been gradually clothing itself with the humanity it first gradually created—so that what was first spoken by God may eventually be respoken by man.

This granted, we can see how language, in the course of its history, has indeed mediated the transformation of phenomena into idols. But we can also see how, by reason of this very fact, *within* man the phenomena have gradually ceased to operate as compulsive natural processes and have become, instead, mere memory-images available for his own creative 'speech'—using 'speech' now in the wide sense of Aquinas's 'word'.

We should expect, accordingly, that, with the progressive decrease of participation throughout the Graeco-Roman, or Aristotelian age, we should find a growing awareness—however faint—of this capacity of man for creative speech. And we should expect to find a marked increase in that awareness after the scientific revolution. It is what we do find. Let us take, for example, the Romantic theory of the 'creative imagination' and glance briefly at its previous history. Premonitory hints of an attribution of 'creative' power to man as artist or poet, appear as early as the first Christian century, with Dio Chrysostom. A century later Philostratus maintained of the works of Pheidias and Praxiteles, that:

> Imagination made them, and she is a better artist than imitation; for where the one carves only what she has seen, the other carves what she has not seen.

By the third century Plotinus is maintaining that:

> If anyone disparages the arts on the ground that they imitate nature, we must remind him that natural objects are themselves only imitations, and that the arts do not simply imitate what they see but reascend to those principles (λόγοι) from which nature herself is derived.

For Scaliger in the sixteenth century (who was closely followed by Sidney in his *Apologie for Poesie*) the poet is one who 'maketh a new Nature and so maketh himself as it were a new God'.[1]

Coleridge's doctrine of the primary and secondary imagination, when it came, and the whole Romantic stress in England and Germany on the 'creative' function of art and poetry was, then, by no means a wholly new adventure in thought. It was rather that the whole attitude to nature, which it implied, had been rendered acceptable to a much wider circle by the rapidly increasing idolatry of the seventeenth and eighteenth centuries. Something very much like it had already been thought by a few. It became almost a popular movement in a world beginning at last to hunger for iconoclasm.

We have already had occasion to note the close relation between the apprehension of images and the making of them. As long as nature herself continued to be apprehended as image, it sufficed for the artist to imitate Nature. Inevitably, the life or spirit in the object lived on in his imitation, if it was a faithful one. For at the same time it could not help being more than an imitation, inasmuch as the artist himself participated the being of the object. But the imitation of an *idol* is a purely technical process; which (as was quickly discovered) is better done by photography. To-day an artist cannot rely on the life inherent in the object he imitates, any more than a poet can rely on the life inherent in the words he uses. He has to draw the life forth from within himself.

It is for the same reason that an ever-increasing importance came to be attached to the *invented* image and men become more and more dissatisfied with imitations of nature both in the practice and in the theory of art. It is easy to see how it came to be held that 'the truest poetry is the most feigning'. For there is no doubt about where the life in an invented or fictitious image comes from. There can be no 'pathetic fallacy' there. What is peculiar to the Romantic Movement—as, indeed, its very name recalls—is the further reaction of this enthusiasm for fictitious and *fabulous* representations on the phenomena—on Nature herself. This is also what took the Romantic conception of art, properly understood, a step beyond the Neo-platonic theory referred to above. The Neo-platonic theory holds that man the artist is, in some measure, a creator.

1. This important little piece of history will be found most effectively summarized at the beginning of Bk. III of Professor C. S. Lewis's *English Literature in the Sixteenth Century*. Clarendon Press, 1954.

The Romantic conception agrees—but goes further and returns him, in this capacity, to Nature herself.

With what result? It is no longer simply that the arts 're-ascend to those principles from which nature herself is derived'. The 'principles' themselves have changed their venue. For we are told by the Romantic theory that we must no longer look for the nature-spirits—for the Goddess Natura—on the farther side of the appearances; we must look for them *within ourselves*.

> Unbewusst der Freuden, die sie schenket,
> Nie entzückt von ihrer Herrlichkeit,
> Nie gewahr des Geistes, der sie lenket,
> Sel'ger nie durch meine Seligkeit,
>
> Fühllos selbst für ihres Künstlers Ehre,
> Gleich dem toten Schlag der Pendeluhr,
> Dient sie knechtisch dem Gesetz der Schwere,
> Die entgötterte Natur.[2]

Pan has shut up shop. But he has not retired from business; he has merely gone indoors. Or, in the well-known words of Coleridge:

> We receive but what we give
> And in our life alone does Nature live.[3]

It is again beyond the scope of this book to trace in detail the way in which the origin of the Romantic response to nature is exemplified in that association between Coleridge and Wordsworth which gave rise to the *Lyrical Ballads*. It was the dejected author of the *Ancient Mariner* who grasped the theory; but it was Wordsworth who actually *wrote* the nature-poetry.

If nature is indeed 'dis-godded', and yet we again begin to experience her, as Wordsworth did—and as millions have done since his time—no longer as dead but as alive; if there is no 'represented' on the far side of the appearances, and yet we begin to experience them once more *as* appearances, as representations—the question arises, of *what* are they representations? It was no doubt the difficulty of answering this question which led Wordsworth to relapse occasionally into that nostalgic hankering after *original* participation, which is called pantheism—and from which Coleridge was rendered immune by his acquaintance with Kantian

---

2. From Schiller's *Die Götter Griechenlands*: 'Unconscious of the joy she bestows, never transported by her own glory, never aware of the spirit that directs her, never blest through my blessedness, without feeling even for the honour of her artist—as with the dead stroke of a clock's pendulum she—disgodded Nature—slavishly obeys the law of gravity.'

3. *Ode to Dejection*.

philosophy. We shall find somewhat the same contrast, in this respect, between Goethe and Schiller.

It is because of its failure to answer this question that the true, one might say the tremendous, impulse underlying the Romantic movement has never grown to maturity; and, after adolescence, the alternative to maturity is puerility. There is only one answer to the question. Henceforth, if nature is to be experienced as representation, she will be experienced as representation of—Man. But what is Man? Herein lies the direst possibility inherent in idolatry. It can empty of spirit—it has very nearly succeeded in doing so—not only nature, but also Man himself. For among all the other idols is his own body. And it is part of the creed of idolatry that, when we speak of Man, we mean only the body of this or that man, or at most his finite personality, which we are driven more and more to think an attribute of his body.

Thus it is, that the great change which the evolution of consciousness has brought about and the great lessons which men had begun to learn have all been wrenched awry. We had come at last to the point of realizing that art can no longer be content with imitating the collective representations, now that these are themselves turning into idols. But, instead of setting out to smash the idols, we have tamely concluded that nothing can now be art which in any way reminds us of nature—and even that practically anything may be art, which does not. We have learned that art can represent nothing but Man himself, and we have interpreted that as meaning that art exists for the purpose of enabling Mr. Smith to 'express his personality'. And all because we have not learnt—though our very physics shouts it at us—that nature herself is the representation of Man.

Hence the riot of private and personal symbolisms into which both art and poetry have degenerated. If I know that nature herself is the system of my representations, I cannot do otherwise than adopt a humbler and more responsible attitude to the representations of art and the metaphors of poetry. For in the case of nature there is no danger of my fancying that she exists to express my personality. I know in that case that what is meant, when I say she is my representation, is, that I stand, whether I like it or not, in—(I do not love the expression, but I can find no defter one in English) a 'directionally creator' relation to her. But I know also that what so stands is not my poor temporal personality, but the Divine Name in the unfathomable depths behind it. And if I strive to produce a work of art, I cannot then do otherwise than strive humbly to create more nearly as *that* creates, and not as my idiosyncrasy wills.

After all, there is warrant for it. At the beginning of the first chapter I pointed to the phenomenon of the rainbow, because it is especially easy there to realize the extent to which it is 'our' creation. But we know equally well that it is not only the colours and curve of the rainbow which proceed from the eye; it is not only 'Iris' who has gone indoors; we know that light—*as light* (whatever we may think about the particles)—proceeds from the same source. Now for the

Impressionist painters, this became a real experience. They really painted nature in the light of the eye, as no other painters had done before them. They were striving to realize in consciousness the normally unconscious activity of 'figuration' itself. They did not imitate; they expressed 'themselves'—inasmuch as they painted nature as the representation of Man. They will serve as a reminder—though they are not the only one—that the rejection of original participation may mean, not the destruction but the liberation of images.

Final Participation

I referred [earlier] to symbolism as something in which we to-day are again becoming interested. There is no respect in which the imaginative literature and drama of to-day differs more strikingly from that of even fifty years ago. In those days there was an Ibsen, there was a Maeterlinck, but nobody really understood what they were up to and everyone was dubious and uncomfortable. Whereas to-day every other writer strives to imply some sort of symbolized content and, even if he does not, it is obligingly done for him by confident critics who have read their Freud and their Jung. It would be an interesting experiment to resuscitate a habitual reader of, say, the *Times Literary Supplement* in the 'nineties, to set him down before the second half of the *New Statesman* in the 1950's, and to see what he made of it.

In mentioning Freud and Jung I have, of course, touched on the most startling phenomenon of all. The unaccountable rapidity with which a literal-minded generation developed a sympathetic response to the psycho-analytical gnosis of dream-imagery, and accepted the (one would have thought) fantastic idea of an immaterial realm of 'the unconscious', is another sign . . . that the development of man's consciousness is an evolutionary as well as a dialectical process. Who could possibly have foreseen it in the year of the Great Exhibition? Who could have failed to deny the possibility of such a change, if it had been foretold to him? Possibly the greatest, possibly the only lasting, value of psycho-analysis lies in its clinical aspect. It may or may not be so. But for the historian of consciousness the most significant thing will always be the way it 'caught on'; the number of its technical terms—and still more the characters out of Greek mythology—which had become household words even before the death of its founder. Pan, it seems, has not only not retired from business; he has not only gone indoors; he has hardly shut the door, before we begin to hear him moving about inside.

Yet here again, as far as any extra-clinical value is concerned, the historian of the future will observe the fatally blighting influence of the conventional idolatry. It never seems to have even occurred to Freud that an individual man's 'unconscious mind' could be anything but a 'somewhat' lodged inside the box of his bones. Representation, as a principle, is accepted by him as a matter of course; inasmuch as a great variety of dream-imagery is interpreted as symbolizing particular physical functions. From the perception that physical functions and organs are *themselves* representations, he is, however, cut off by all the assumptions of idolatry. Again, we have watched with interest Jung developing his concept of a 'collective unconscious' of humanity as a whole, a concept which is inherently repugnant to the foundation of idolatry on which he had to build it. Yet, because of that very idolatry, the traditional myths and the archetypes which he tells us are the representations of the collective unconscious, are assumed by him to be, and always to have been, neatly insulated from the world of nature with which, according to their own account, they were mingled or united.

The psychological interpretation of mythology is, it is true, a long way nearer to an understanding of participation than the old 'personified causes' of Tylor and Frazer and Lemprière's Classical Dictionary. But it is still a long way off. In the last resort, when it actually comes up against the nature-content of the myths, it still relies on the old anthropological assumption of 'projection'. I believe it will seem very strange to the historian of the future, that a literal-minded generation began to accept the actuality of a 'collective unconscious' before it could even admit the possibility of a 'collective conscious'—in the shape of the phenomenal world.

I do not, however, think it can be very long now before this, too, is accepted; since it not only opens up possibilities of new knowledge of which the need is being increasingly felt, but also removes many inconsistencies in the contemporary picture of the world, which cannot fail to be noticed more and more as time passes. Idolatry carries in it the seeds of its own destruction. The reader will, for instance, recall the dilemma of 'pre-history'. . . . We have chosen to form a picture, based very largely on modern physical science, of a phenomenal earth existing for millions of years before the appearance of consciousness. The same physical science tells us that the phenomenal world is correlative to consciousness. The phenomena attributed to these millions of years are therefore, in fact, abstract models or 'idols of the study'. We may compromise by calling them 'possible phenomena', implying thereby that that was how the world would have looked, sounded, smelt and felt, *if* there had been someone like ourselves present. But if the only phenomena we know are collective representations, and what is represented is the collective unconscious, the awkward fact remains that it is highly fanciful, if not absurd, to think of any unperceived process in terms of potential phenomena, unless we also assume an unconscious, ready to light up into actual phenomena at any moment of the process.

This of course applies not only to pre-history, but to all the imperceptible process assumed in our picture of the contemporary world—the goings-on, for instance, at the bottom of the sea. But in the case of pre-history, we have further to remember that it does not suffice to accept the reality of a collective unconscious *now*. We have to accept that an unconscious, available to be represented, is at least coeval with any process describable in terms of phenomena. The employment of 'models' for the purpose of thinking may be very well; for the purposes of exposition it may even be essential—as long as we know what we are doing and do not turn the models into idols. And we shall know what we are doing with pre-history, when we have firmly grasped the fact that the phenomenal world arises from the relation between a conscious and an unconscious and that evolution is the story of the changes that relation has undergone and is undergoing.

But it is not only for the study of pre-history that it is all-important for us to realize this truth, that the phenomena are collective representations of what can *now* properly be called 'man's' unconscious. It is vital for the future of the sciences, especially those at the other end of the scale from the technological ones—those, in short, for which 'dash-board-knowledge' is not enough. When, for instance, we are dealing with living organisms, our whole approach, our whole possibility of grasping *process* as such, is hamstrung by the lack of just such a concept of the potentially phenomenal and the actual phenomenal.

With the help of the Arabian schoolmen the Aristotelian concept of 'potential' existence was gradually drained away into the mere notional 'possibility' of being—into *contingent* being. Thus, the word *potentialis* (itself a translation of the vigorous Greek word from which we take our 'dynamic' and 'dynamite') had been changed to *possibilis* before Aquinas wrote, though his *possibilis* still meant more than our 'possible'. Since the scientific revolution, to ask whether a thing 'is' or 'is not' is, for science, to ask whether it is or is not a phenomenon—either experienced or extrapolated. Francis Bacon, it will be remembered, found the distinction between *actus* and *potentia* 'frigida distinctio'; and so it had to be, while the phenomena were becoming, and will be as long as they remain, idols. But to-day, it is no longer open to anyone who regards the unconscious as more than a fiction to contend that the concept of the potentially phenomenal, that is, of potential existence, is too difficult for human minds to grasp.

Even so, merely grasping the concept will not take mankind very far. Beta-thinking can go thus far. It can convince itself that, just as for original participation potential existence was something quite different from not-being, so, for the kind of participation at which we have arrived to-day, the potentially phenomenal is not the same as nothing. Let us call the man-centered participation with which the opening chapters of this book were concerned *final participation*. Beta-thinking, then, can convince itself of the *fact* of final participation. It can convince itself that we participate the phenomena with the unconscious part of ourselves. But that has no epistemological significance. It can only have that to the extent that final participation is consciously experienced. Perhaps (if we may already start using the old terminology which we have just taken out of the refrigerator) we may say that final participation must itself be raised from potentiality to act.

Are there any signs of such a development taking place? We have seen, in the Romantic movement, and elsewhere, symptoms of a kind of instinctive impulse towards iconoclasm. Are there any signs up to now of a *systematic* approach to final participation? And what does such an approach involve?

It was pointed out . . . that participation as an actual experience is only to be won to-day by special exertion; that it is a matter, not of theorizing, but of imagination in the genial or creative sense. A systematic approach towards final participation may therefore be expected to be an attempt to use imagination systematically. This was the foundation of Goethe's scientific work. In his book on the *Metamorphosis of Plants* and the associated writings descriptive of his method, as well as in the rest of his scientific work, there is the germ of a systematic investigation of phenomena by way of participation. For his *Urpflanze* and *Urphänomen* are nothing more or less than potential phenomena perceived and studied as such. They are processes grasped directly and not, as hitherto since the scientific revolution, hypotheses *inferred from* actual phenomena.

I have here used both the word 'scientific' and the word 'perceived' advisedly, though in such a context both of them run counter to all the assumptions of the received idolatry. It is a common objection that Goethe's method ought not to be called 'scientific', because it was not purely empirical; but that objection obviously cannot be raised here without begging the whole argument of this book. As to 'perceived'—we have seen that the major part of any perceived phenomenon consists of our own 'figuration'. Therefore, as imagination reaches the point of enhancing figuration itself, hitherto unperceived parts of the whole field of the phenomenon necessarily become perceptible. Moreover, this conscious participation enhances perception not only of present phenomena but also of the memory-images derived from them. All this Goethe could not prevail on his contemporaries to admit. Idolatry was too all-powerful and there were then no premonitory signs, as there are to-day, of its collapse. No one, for instance, had heard of 'the unconscious'.

For a student of the evolution of consciousness, it is particularly interesting that a man with the precise make-up of Goethe should have appeared at that precise moment in the history of the West. By the middle of the eighteenth century, when he was born, original participation had virtually faded out, and Goethe himself was a thoroughly modern man. Yet he showed from his earliest childhood and retained all through his life an almost atavistically strong remainder of it. It breathes through his poetry as the peculiar Goethean attitude to Nature, who is felt as a living being, almost as a personality, certainly as a 'thou' rather than as an 'it' or an 'I'. It is almost as if the Gods had purposely retained this sense in Goethe as a sort of seed-corn out of which the beginnings of final participation could peep, for the first time, on the world of science. Perhaps it was an instinctive understanding of this which made him so determined to keep clear of beta-thinking.

> Mein Kind, ich hab'es klug gemacht,
> Ich hab' nie über das Denken gedacht.[1]

For beta-thinking leads to final, by way of the inexorable elimination of all original, participation. Consequently Goethe was able to develop an elementary technique, but unable, or unwilling, to erect a metaphysic, of final participation. The contrast in this respect between him and Schiller, who knew his Kant and stood firm in the idolatry of his contemporaries—especially as it appeared in a certain conversation[2] between the two on the subject of the *Urphänomen*—is illuminating and is in a manner, as I said, analogous to the contrast between Wordsworth and Coleridge. There is, so far as I know, more of the historical *theory* of participation in Schiller's poem *Die Götter Griechenlands* (from which I have already quoted . . .) than in anything Goethe ever wrote. Yet Schiller could not admit the practical possibility of final participation at all. He told Goethe that his *Urphänomen* was no more than an idea, a hypothesis; and the poem itself, after a magnificent account of the retreat of the Gods from nature into man, has nothing more significant or prophetic to conclude with than the rather trite:

> Was unsterblich im Gesang soll leben
> Muss im Leben untergehen.[3]

The significance of Goethe in the history of science will be appreciated, as time passes, in the measure that idolatry is overcome. His theory of colour, for instance, will always be heterodox as long as the phenomenon of light is simply identified with the unrepresented 'particles'. But that significance, however great it may ultimately appear, grows pale before the significance of Rudolf Steiner (1861–1925) who, in the early part of his life, studied and developed the method of Goethe. Unlike Goethe, however, Steiner did not avoid beta-thinking. At the same time that he was editing Goethe's scientific works in Weimar, he was writing his book *The Philosophy of Spiritual Activity*, in which the

1. I have managed things cleverly, my boy: I have never thought about thinking.' *Zahme Xenien*, vi.
2. *Naturwissenschaftliche Schriften (Kürschner-Ausgabe)*. Vol. i, p. 109; Appendices to the *Metamorphosenlehre (Glückliches Ereignis)*.
3. 'What is to live immortal in song must go under in life.'

metaphysic of final participation is fully and lucidly set forth. Educated on 'the modern side' (as we should then have said) at school and university, he was thoroughly at home with the idols and never relied on any relic of original participation there may have been in his composition to overcome them. It is in his work and that of his followers that the reader should look for further signs of a development towards final participation in the field of science.

If a single example is sought, let it be the research now going on in the domain of cancer. Cancer is a process of generation, and once we admit the concept of the potentially phenomenal, we must see that generation is not a transition from not-being to being, but a transition from potential to phenomenal existence. Steiner's method, based on perception of the potentially phenomenal, was to diagnose a pre-cancerous condition of the blood, a condition not yet detectable by physical symptoms, and thus to take the disease at a stage where it answers better to treatment. This is another way of saying that the method involves investigation of a part of the field of the whole phenomenon named *blood* which, for a non-participating consciousness, is excluded from it, not by empirical proof but rather . . . by definition. He sought to apply the same method to the discovery of remedies, and The Society for Cancer Research founded by his followers is patiently continuing this difficult work at Arlesheim in Switzerland. At the moment in which I am writing, however, more people are probably acquainted with the 'Bio-dynamic' method in Agriculture than with the particular example I have chosen.

The mind of Rudolf Steiner was of course not only applied to the scientific sphere, and it was perhaps not even the most important part of his work. He is, for instance, far more illuminating and, I would say, reliable on the subject of language and its origin than Fabre d'Olivet and the others I mentioned [earlier]. To say that he advocated, and practised, 'the systematic use of imagination' is to place so much emphasis on the mere beginning of what he taught and did, that it is rather like saying that Dante wrote a poem about a greyhound. Steiner showed that imagination, and the final participation it leads to, involve, unlike hypothetical thinking, the whole man—thought, feeling, will, and character—and his own revelations were clearly drawn from those further stages of participation—Inspiration and Intuition—to which the systematic use of imagination may lead. Although the object with which this book was originally conceived was none other than to try and remove one of the principal obstacles to contemporary appreciation of precisely this man's teaching—the study and use of which I believe to be crucial for the future of mankind—I shall here say no more of it. This is a study in idolatry, not a study of Rudolf Steiner.[4]

4. All the published works of Rudolf Steiner are obtainable in London, either in English translation or in the original German, from: Rudolf Steiner Book Shop, 35 Park Road, N.W.1. or Rudolf Steiner Book Centre, 54 Bloomsbury St., W.C.1.

Saving the Appearances

It may be well, before proceeding further, to restate very briefly what this book has so far endeavoured to establish. It has been sought to show firstly, that the evolution of nature is correlative to the evolution of consciousness; and, secondly, that the evolution of consciousness hitherto can best be understood as a more or less continuous progress from a vague but immediate awareness of the 'meaning' of phenomena towards an increasing preoccupation with the phenomena themselves. The earlier awareness involved experiencing the phenomena as representations; the latter preoccupation involves experiencing them, non-representationally, as objects in their own right, existing independently of human consciousness. This latter experience, in its extreme form, I have called *idolatry*.

Idolatry is an ugly and emphatic word and it was deliberately chosen to emphasize certain ugly features, and still more certain ugly possibilities, inherent in the present situation. Not much has been said of the benefits—not only material ones—which have been conferred on mankind by this 'idolatry' and nothing, as yet, of the supreme benefit, which will be dealt with in the final chapters. As to the former, most people are so well aware of these benefits, and they have been so often and so fully emphasized by others, that I have thought it unnecessary to draw attention to them. But I will mention two at this point. In the first place together with the ability to experience phenomena as objects independent of human consciousness, there has grown up our enormously improved power of grasping them in exact and quantitative detail. (Indeed, it was by shifting our attention to this detail that we gained that ability.) With this has come the progressive elimination of those errors and confusions in which alpha-thinking is inevitably entangled while, in its initial stages, it is still overshadowed by participation; that is, the vague but immediate awareness of 'meaning' already referred to. And with this again, has come the power of effective manipulation on which our civilization, with its many works of mercy, is based. Surgery, for example, presupposes an acquaintance with the human anatomy exact in the same mode that our knowledge of a machine is exact.

Yet these practical considerations are not the only ones. Along with his idolatry, and because of it, modern man has found the possibility of an entirely new and very charming emotional relation to nature. The devoted love which thousands of naturalists, for example, have felt for some aspect of nature to which they have been drawn, is not in spite of, it is actually *dependent* on their experience of the 'appearances' as substantially independent of themselves. The whole joy of it depends on its being an 'I–it' relation—oblivious, or contemptuous, of the teleological approach which dominated Aristotle and the Middle Ages. The happy bird-watcher does not say: 'Let's go and see what we can learn about ourselves from nature'. He says: 'Let's go and see what nature is doing, bless her!' Without idolatry there would have been no Gilbert White, no Richard Jefferies, no W. H. Hudson, no Lorenz. Nor is this emotional relation confined to the naturalists, professional and amateur. They are merely the most striking example. The possibility of a selfless and attentive love for birds, animals, flowers, clouds, rocks, water, permeates the whole modern mind, its science, its art, its poetry and its daily life. It is something which only a fool would be in a hurry to sacrifice.

On the other hand, precisely if we are *not* fools, our very love of natural phenomena 'for their own sake' will be enough to prevent us from hastily turning a blind eye on any new light which can be shed, from any direction whatsoever, on their true nature. Above all will this be the case, if we feel them to be in danger. And if the appearances are, as I have sought to establish, correlative to human consciousness and if human consciousness does not remain unchanged but evolves, then the future of the appearances, that is, of nature herself, must indeed depend on the direction which that evolution takes.

Now in considering future possibilities there are, it has been suggested, two opposing tendencies to be taken into consideration. On the one hand, a further development in the direction, and on the basis, of idolatry; involving in the end the elimination of those last vestiges of original participation, which . . . survive in our language and therefore in our collective representations. On the other hand, there is the impulse, rudimentary as yet, of the human imagination to substitute for original participation, a different kind of participation, which I have called 'final'. This, we saw, is based on the acceptance (mainly impulsive so far, but occasionally explicit) of the fact that man himself now stands in a 'directionally creator relation'[1] to the appearances. It would seem that the appearances are in danger from both quarters, and that they will require 'saving', in a rather different sense of the term from that used of old by Simplicius.

The plain fact is, that all the unity and coherence of nature depends on participation of one kind or the other. If therefore man succeeds in eliminating all original participation, without substituting any other, he will have done nothing less than to eliminate all meaning and all coherence from the cosmos. We have seen that here and there he is already beginning an attempt to eliminate meaning—that is, a valid relation to nature—from his language, and therewith striking a blow at the very roots of his collective representations. Less sensationally, but far more effectively and over a much wider area, his science, with the progressive disappearance of original participation, is losing its grip on any principle of unity pervading nature as a whole and the knowledge of nature. The

1. Cf. p. 132.

hypothesis of chance has already crept from the theory of evolution into the theory of the physical foundation of the earth itself; but, more serious perhaps than that, is the rapidly increasing 'fragmentation of science' which occasionally attracts the attention of the British Association. There is no 'science of sciences'; no unity of knowledge. There is only an accelerating increase in that pigeonholed knowledge by individuals of more and more about less and less, which, if persisted in indefinitely, can only lead mankind to a sort of 'idiocy' (in the original sense of the word)—a state of affairs, in which fewer and fewer representations will be collective, and more and more will be private, with the result that there will in the end be no means of communication between one intelligence and another.

The second danger arises from final participation itself. Imagination is not, as some poets have thought, simply synonymous with good. It may be either good or evil. As long as art remained primarily mimetic, the evil which imagination could do was limited by nature. Again, as long as it was treated as an amusement, the evil which it could do was limited in scope. But in an age when the connection between imagination and figuration is beginning to be dimly realized, when the fact of the directionally creator relation is beginning to break through into consciousness, both the good and the evil latent in the working of imagination begin to appear unlimited. We have seen in the Romantic movement an instance of the way in which the making of images may react on the collective representations. It is a fairly rudimentary instance, but even so it has already gone beyond the dreams and responses of a leisured few. The economic and social structure of Switzerland, for example, is noticeably affected by its tourist industry, and that is due only in part to increased facilities of travel. It is due not less to the fact that (whatever may be said about their 'particles') the *mountains* which twentieth-century man sees are not the mountains which eighteenth-century man saw.

It may be objected that this is a very small matter, and that it will be a long time before the imagination of man substantially alters those appearances of nature with which his figuration supplies him. But then I am taking the long view. Even so, we need not be too confident. Even if the pace of change remained the same, one who is really sensitive to A (for example) the difference between the medieval collective representations and our own will be aware that, without travelling any greater distance than we have come since the fourteenth century, we could very well move forward into a chaotically empty or a fantastically hideous world. But the pace of change has *not* remained the same. It has accelerated and is accelerating.

We should remember this, when appraising the aberrations of the formally representational arts. Of course, in so far as these are due to affectation, they are of no importance. But in so far as they are genuine, they are genuine because the artist has in some way or other experienced the world he represents. And in so far as they are appreciated, they are appreciated by those who are themselves willing to make a move towards seeing the world in that way, and, ultimately therefore, seeing that kind of world. We should remember this, when we see pictures of a dog with six legs emerging from a vegetable marrow or a woman with a motor-bicycle substituted for her left breast.

The systematic use of imagination, then, will be requisite in the future, not only for the increase of knowledge, but also for saving the appearances from chaos and inanity. Nor need it involve any relinquishment of the ability which we have won to experience and love nature as objective and independent of ourselves. Indeed, it cannot involve that. For any such relinquishment would mean that what was taking place was not an approach towards final participation (which is the proper goal of imagination) but an attempt to revert to original participation (which is the goal of pantheism, of mediumism and of much so-called occultism). To be *able* to experience the representations as idols, and then to be able also to perform the act of figuration consciously, so as to experience them as participated; that is imagination.

The extremity of idolatry towards which we are moving renders the attainment of this dual relation to nature a necessity for both art and science. The attempt to unite the voluntary creativity demanded by the one with the passive receptivity demanded by the other is the significance of Goethe's contribution to the Western mind, as the achievement of it is the significance of Rudolf Steiner's. It is perhaps still not too late to attend to these portents. The appearances will be 'saved' only if, as men approach nearer and nearer to conscious figuration and realize that it is something which may be affected by their choices, the final participation which is thus being thrust upon them is exercised with the profoundest sense of responsibility, with the deepest thankfulness and piety towards the world as it was originally given to them in original participation, and with a full understanding of the momentous process of history, as it brings about the emergence of the one from the other.

from *History, Guilt, and Habit*

History of Ideas: Evolution of Consciousness

Is there any real difference between what we mean when we use the word "evolution" and what we mean when we use the word "history"? It sometimes looks as if there is not. Whether you talk about the history of the earth or the evolution of the earth, or of mankind, makes no difference. On the other hand, the terms are not *always* interchangeable. No biologist would talk about the history of species, and no historian would refer to the evolution of the Peloponnesian War. This shows, I think, that there really are two different concepts involved, and that we should do well to keep them distinct in our minds, whether or not we allow them to overlap in the looseness of casual speech.

What then is the difference? It seems to me that the historian R. G. Collingwood was laying his finger on it when he argued in *The Idea of History*[1] that "all history is history of thought." Maybe, by putting it in just that way, he was spoiling a good case by overstating it; but whether that is so or not, he was drawing attention, and drawing it usefully, to the fact that, when we speak of history, we have in mind, or ought to have in mind, something that imports a consciously directed process. At least in some degree a conscious process. There may be, even in recent history (as Marxism for instance maintains), much in the process that is going on unconsciously, but in order to be historical, it must be in some measure a conscious process.

And that surely is what distinguishes it from evolution. By contrast with history, evolution is an unconscious process. Another, and perhaps a better, way of putting it would be to say that evolution is a natural process, history a human one; since nature, in its higher development, does of course include animal consciousness. I do not however think we can say it includes *human* consciousness—not, that is, unless we are happy to smudge our vocabulary. Nature, someone will say, includes human nature. Very well, but insofar as we treat man

1. Oxford: Clarendon Press, 1946; Oxford: Oxford University Press (Oxford Paperbacks), 1961.

as a part of nature—for instance in a biological survey of evolution—we are precisely *not* treating him as a historical being. As a historically developing being, he is set over against nature, both as a knower and as a doer, and we can no longer consider him simply as a part of nature—unless of course when we say "nature," we really mean "everything"; in which case the word ceases to be of much use to anyone. One of the disadvantages of being an out-and-out materialist is that you can no longer use the word "nature" with any consistency, because in your system it includes everything; just as one of the disadvantages of being an out-and-out idealist is that you can no longer use the word "spirit" meaningfully, because in your system it includes everything.

When Collingwood contrasted the *study* of history with the *science* of nature as sharply as he did, he was concerned primarily with historical *events*. Historical events (he gave as an example Caesar crossing the Rubicon) are different from natural events, inasmuch as they are always in some measure the result of, or accompanied by, *thoughts*. He went on to say that we only really experience history, and therefore we only study it properly, to the extent that we "re-enact" in our own minds the thoughts which preceded and accompanied the actions it records. As a theory of history in general this latter contention has been disputed, by historians and others; but that need not concern us now, because, whether or not it is true of history as a whole, it is certainly true of one branch of history. Whether or not it is true of the history of man as doer, it is self-evidently true of the history of man as knower—or, if you like, as would-be knower. You cannot study the history of thought without thinking the thoughts whose history you are studying.

This particular branch of history, which I am calling the history of man as knower, has been attracting increasing attention in the last few decades under the title history of ideas. What sort of discipline then do people usually have in mind when they speak of history of ideas, and perhaps create an academic department with that label on it? Maybe something like this: instead of wrestling, head on, with—let us say—the philosophy of Aristotle, and asking where he was right and where he was wrong, we trace how the ideas that constitute that philosophy arose as corrections, modifications, refutations of the philosophies of Plato and the pre-Socratics before him; and then we observe how those ideas were themselves corrected, modified, refuted by later thinkers; we arrive by that route at the Scholastic philosophers of the Middle Ages, and by the like dialectical progression on to Francis Bacon, Descartes, the English Empiricists, Kant and so forth.

Such a discipline is undoubtedly a very valuable one, provided it is conscientiously and not superficially pursued. But it is based on a certain assumption, which it is my principal purpose to question. It assumes that all these philosophers were asking themselves the same questions and then finding different answers to them; that they were talking about the same things, and merely reasoning differently about them. That means that the history of philosophy is treated, in effect, as though it were a dialogue between contemporaries.[2]

Of course history of ideas is not confined to the history of philosophy; but I think you will find this same assumption underlying the history of ideas, as it is commonly approached and treated, in other domains as well, whether it be ideas in religion or politics or science. To explain why I question that assumption, I must go back to the difference—and, arising out of that, the relation—between history and evolution. I have called one of them a natural process and the other a human process; and it follows from that that there is, to begin with, a simple chronological relations between the two. History is *later* than evolution. It only came into being after evolution had already had a long innings. The physical basis on which our thinking rests had to acquire something like its present form before there could be a dawning of what we call "ideas." Let me leave aside for the moment the question whether it is also a mutually exclusive relation; whether, that is, history must also be thought of as progressively *replacing* evolution, or whether the two processes can continue side by side. For, whatever we may think about that, the chronological relation raises another question which I would rather consider first. When—at what stage in the process of evolution— did thought first make its appearance, and history in its proper sense therefore begin?

Obviously we are taken back by such reflections into a long period which is sometimes loosely designated "prehistory"; a period when man, both as doer and as knower, must have been already active, although we have no surviving records of him. It is a period about which there has been any amount of speculation, and plenty of unsupported assumptions. There is however one assumption which I think *must* be made: that there is something else which made its appearance on the stage of evolution before thought could do so, and that is *perception*. I hope you will allow me to use that term rather loosely—more loosely than it could be used, for instance, in any epistemological theory of perception. I mean it to cover a wide gamut, ranging from what is better called "sensation" at one end of the scale to what is better called "feeling" at the other end. Because I want only to fix attention on that point in nature—whether we are speaking diachronically of evolution, or synchronically of the ascending scale of organisms in the present—or again, of individual mental development up to the beginning of self-consciousness—on that point at which nature becomes a duality: the point at which there is both an outer and an inner to be considered. Call it the point at which *consciousness* appears, if you like; but I have to eschew that term for the moment, because consciousness, *for us*, normally includes thinking; and the distinction between thinking and perceiving is just what I have now to emphasize.

2. A very unfair dialogue, since in the nature of things the predeceasing disputant had no right of reply. The point is that the ideas are taken as related in the *mode* of dialogue. The thread on which they are strung is a dialectical one only.

It is one of those distinctions which is obvious, without being sharp or clear. It is obvious, and remains obvious, to every normal mind, although when we come to analyze it, we may not be able to rule a boundary line. It remains obvious, as the distinction between day and night remains obvious, though, when we begin to analyze that distinction, we come up against such refinements as dusk and twilight. There is more than one way of characterizing the difference. Perception is essentially a passive experience, something that *happens* to us; thinking is an active one, something that we *do*. Or if you don't like this distinction, because of refinements such as the "intentionality" which some have detected (rightly, I would say) in perception, or on the other hand because of the passivity of that uncontrolled type of thinking called "reverie," then thoughts are something that comes from within; perceptions something that comes from without. The point is not how we choose to characterize it, but that we all realize the distinction as a matter of course and without any real difficulty.

Unless, of course, we go out of our way to lose sight of it, as some philosophers who ought to have known better have done. One of the most valuable lessons I learned from Coleridge was to detect that terribly obsessive, and terribly contemporary, fallacy which supposes that we must only *distinguish* things that we are also able to *divide*. It is closely allied to an obsession with space as the criterion of reality. When we divide things, we set them, either in fact or in imagination, side by side in space. But space is not the be-all and end-all, and there are many things that, by reason of their interpenetration—I repeat, because of their *interpenetration*—cannot be divided, though they are easily distinguished: acquaintance and friendship, for example, or envy and hatred. We shall see, I hope, that for human consciousness as it is today, thinking and perceiving come within that class.

Let me pause for a moment, before proceeding, upon this obsessive confusion between distinguishing and dividing. I call it an obsession because I see it as one of those ingrained habits of thought, of which it is difficult to say whether they are conscious or unconscious. It is that mental habit (and this also is something which Coleridge perceived so clearly) that has been both cause and effect of the whole direction taken by natural science since the Scientific Revolution; I mean the concentration of attention always on smaller and smaller units—molecules, atoms, neurons, genes, hormones, etc.—as the only direction in which advancing knowledge can proceed. The beneficial results of such a combination of reduction and concentration, for the purposes of technology and manipulation, need no stressing. But again, like space itself, technology and manipulation are not the be-all and end-all, not, at all events, for me. In any case their usefulness for the study of such matters as history and evolution is, to say the least of it, marginal. And my subject *is* evolution and history. I will only add, before returning to it, that, however impressive may be the practical justification for this atomic obsession, there is no evidential justification whatever for the conclusion, or rather the assumption, to which it so often leads, namely, that the parts preceded the wholes, and that the world was actually built by putting together the units into which our minds divide it, as a house is built by putting bricks together.

Interesting attempts have been made to arrive at the relation between thinking and perceiving by imagining them actually divided from each other. You may remember William James's supposition of a confrontation between, on the one hand, the environment—all that we usually mean by the word "nature"—and, on the other, a man who possessed all the organs of perception, but who had never done any thinking. He demonstrated that such a man would perceive nothing, or nothing but what James called "a blooming, buzzing confusion." Well, he was only expressing in his own blunt way the conclusion which always is arrived at by all who make the same attempt, whether philosophers, psychologists, neurologists, or physicists. Unfortunately it is also a conclusion which is commonly *forgotten* by the same philosophers, psychologists, neurologists, and physicists almost as soon as it has been arrived at; or certainly as soon as they turn their minds to other matters—such as history or evolution—but which I personally decline to forget. I mean the conclusion, the irrefragable consensus, that what we perceive is structurally inseparable from what we think.

In particular I decline to forget it when I try to fix my attention on such matters as evolution and history, and the relation between them. I refuse to forget, when I am in *that* room in the library, what all those philosophers and neurologists and so forth taught me in the other rooms, namely, that what we perceive is structurally inseparable from what we think. With what result? Here I must come, for a time, the nearest I hope I shall need to come to what is commonly disparaged under the name of "metaphysics." You will sometimes hear people say they have no metaphysics. Well, they are lying. Their metaphysics are implicit in what they take for granted about the world. Only they prefer to call it "common sense." And at this point in my lecture unfortunately I have to question rather radically what, under the present dispensation, the great majority of people do take for granted about the world. This involves putting the question: what do we really mean when we use the expression "what we perceive"? and putting it without, at the same time, conveniently forgetting that what we perceive is structurally inseparable from what we think. And the answer is that we can only mean the very world itself. Or at all events the macroscopic world itself. The physicists, as you know, have been telling us for a long time that, in addition to that, or somehow underlying it, there is the microscopic and submicroscopic world; moreover that it is only this microscopic and submicroscopic world that exists independently of ourselves; only that world that has an objective existence. Some philosophers[3] have added that it is therefore only knowledge of *that* world that can really be called knowledge at all.

3. Notably the group, including Bertrand Russell and G. E. Moore, who came to be known as "the Cambridge Realists."

Evolutionists and historians must think differently. The knowledge they are aiming at *is* knowledge of the macroscopic world. And that—as I have been emphasizing—*is* unquestionably both subjective and objective. When a historian, for instance, talks about Caesar crossing the Rubicon, or any man crossing any river, he does not mean by the word "river" simply a combination of oxygen and hydrogen; he means a rich assemblage of qualities like coldness, gurgling, flashing in the sun. When he is describing Napolean's retreat from Moscow, the word "cold" does not signify a thermometer reading; it means the felt quality "cold." And when an evolutionist refers to redwoods or red deer, he is not referring to vibrations or light waves, but the quality "red." All quality is subjective as well as objective, and the macroscopic world is compounded of qualities, as well as quantities. It *is* therefore what we perceive and, accordingly, is inseparable from what we think. I hope my vocabulary is not irritating anyone. It doesn't matter what you call it; whether you say "macroscopic" or "real appearance," or whether you borrow from phenomenology and speak of "the world as experienced" or the *monde vécu*—as long as you remember that what we perceive is the actual world, and not a kind of shadow-show pretending to be the actual world (with, of course, an actual world, consisting of particles, mathematical equations or something of the sort, hiding behind it).

Maybe that sounds obvious enough; and if anyone feels that I have merely been laboring the obvious at inordinate length, I can only refer him to George Orwell's observation that "we have now sunk to a depth at which the restatement of the obvious is the first duty of intelligent men." Obvious as it is, we have to exert a real effort to remember it when we go on to realize a certain consequence it entails. It entails, in particular, that when we speak, as I did a little earlier, about *consciousness*, about the point at which consciousness arose and so forth, we are speaking not merely about human nature, as we call it, but also about nature itself. When we study consciousness historically, contrasting perhaps what men perceive and think *now* with what they perceived and thought at some period in the past, when we study long-term *changes* in consciousness, we are studying changes in the world itself, and not simply changes in the human brain. We are not studying some so-called "inner" world, divided off by a skin or a skull, from a so-called "outer" world; we are trying to study the world itself from its inner aspect. Consciousness is not a tiny bit of the world stuck on the rest of it. It is the inside of the whole world. Or, if we are using the term in its stricter sense—excluding therefore the subconscious mind—then it is *part* of the inside of the whole world. That is why, although it is not divided from the outer world, it is so very easily *distinguished* from it. For what is easier than to distinguish the outside of something from its inside? It is just because men have come to distinguish so sharply the one from the other, an inner from an outer, that they have gone on (with some help from the philosopher Descartes) to imagine the inner *divided* from the outer.

I say with some help from Descartes. But the help should not be exaggerated. To say that what we perceive is inseparable from what we think is not the same as saying that what we perceive is dependent on any philosophy. What it *is* dependent on is a collectively and historically hardened *habit* of thought, of which we are no longer conscious. Two very different matters—as any convinced idealist who has just stubbed his toe on a stone will tell you—and as Dr. Johnson *failed* to realize when he thought he was refuting Berkeley by kicking one. And it is precisely because of the great difference between these two that there is a difference between history of ideas on the one hand and history or evolution of consciousness on the other. It is these passive habits of thought, not any ideas we are actively entertaining at the moment, that are inseparable from our perceptions; and it is the changes in *these* with which a history of consciousness must deal.

At this point I think I must forestall a possible objection. While I have been emphasizing—not to say reiterating—this fact of the inseparableness of perception from thought, some of you may have long enough memories to recall that, some time before that, I had observed that, in the longer perspective of human evolution as a whole, perception must have *preceded* thought. But if there could ever be one without the other, then they cannot after all be inseparable! Actually I rather hope this objection *has* occurred to you, because it brings up at once a fundamental difficulty of studying consciousness historically at all. The difficulty is this: you cannot study anything without speaking and reading and writing about it. And you cannot speak or read or write without using language, without using the language of today, as your medium. But the language of today is itself the product, the manifestation, of the very thing you are trying to undermine, so to speak, with your historical depiction of the way in which it came into being. You can dig into the earth with a spade in order to get beneath the surface. The spade is itself a product of the earth, but that does not bother you. But if, by some mysterious dispensation, the spade were part of the very patch of earth you were splitting up, you would be rather nonplussed, because you would destroy the instrument by using it. And that is the sort of difficulty you are up against when it is not the earth you are digging into, but consciousness; and when it is not a spade you are digging with, but language. Some people regard the difficulty as insuperable and reject any study of consciousness itself as impossible. Ludwig Wittgenstein for instance insisted that there are some things you can't say anything about, and that foremost among these is—*saying* itself. However quickly you turn around, you can never see the back of your own head. But I do not think it is quite so bad as that, and Wittgenstein, as far as I know, never tried the historical approach.

In fact, however, the historical approach is all-important. When William James experimented with fancying what perceiving would be like if it were divorced from thinking, he found it reduced to chaos, to that "blooming buzzing confusion" of his. This, I am persuaded, was because he was imagining it happening *today*; and therefore, when he thought or spoke of perception, he was thinking of perception as it is today. In other words he was merely demonstrating the impossibility of separating what *is* now in fact inseparable. It is otherwise how if we imagine inseparableness, not (as I think he was doing) in terms of a kind of molecular aggregation and interspersal, but in terms of interfusion or interpenetration. That need not mean losing sight of the distinction. The distinction between thinking and perceiving is, as I have said, fundamental and self-evident; and we can only lose sight of it by deliberately averting our eyes from it, as the philosopher Hume did, for instance, when he succeeded in persuading himself that ideas are nothing but faded sense-impressions.

If we go ahead with the study of the relation between the two—thinking and perceiving—in terms of real interpenetration, what sorts of results do we get? We shall find in the first place, I think, that it is not a fixed relation but a variable one, variable in terms of the predominance of the one ingredient over the other. The example of this that comes most readily to hand is the difference between poetry and prose; or perhaps (as it is not external literary forms I am thinking of) better say, between the Poetic Principle and the Prosaic. But I will go on saying poetry and prose for short. If we survey the uses that have been made, and are still being made, of language, we can hardly fail to observe that in general in the language of poetry the perceptual element is proportionately higher than in prose; while in prose the intellectual element predominates over the perceptual. Then, if we continue the survey, we shall find—or so I believe, and certainly many others have so found besides myself—the like variable predominance, when we compare language as a whole in its earlier stages with language in its later stages; or the earlier stage of any one language with its later stages. In the early stage the perceptual element is relatively greater; in the later stages the intellectual element. This is not so much in the *use* that is made of words as it is in the meanings of the words themselves. Thus, in our historical survey of consciousness, we find ourselves looking backward down a perspective which reveals more and more of perception and less and less of thought. And if, along *this* path, we allow our fancy to approach the kind of consciousness that would be all perception and no thought, what do we come to? We come to something that is perhaps equally hard to imagine, but is certainly very different from James's blooming, buzzing confusion. What sort of thing then do we come to? Can anything be said about it?

Let me return for a moment to poetry and prose, or let me now say to the language of imagination on the one hand and the language or abstraction and analysis on the other. There is a certain element in the best poetry, which critics of literature have sometimes striven to indicate and theories of imagination have struggled to formulate, namely, that in the language of imagination at its most powerful we are made to feel a kind of *union* between the observer and what he is observing. Charles Lamb, for instance, could speak of a level of writing at which "the imagination seems to resolve itself into the element it contemplates." If this accords with our experience of poetry—and it certainly accords with mine—then it also says something meaningful about that supposititious condition of consciousness, which would be all perception and no thought. In saying it we have found language itself, not a hindrance but a help. That is because it is a good deal easier to see that *language* arises from an interpenetration of thinking and perceiving than it is to see that consciousness itself does. So that to study language historically, taking into account not only its analytical function but also its poetic substance, is a good way of studying the evolution of consciousness. In doing so we are studying that evolution *from within*, and therefore studying consciousness *itself*; not, as the biologists do, studying the evolution of something else altogether and then, on the basis of that study, making all sorts of unwarranted assumptions about the evolution of consciousness. You will be satisfied with that way only if you are blandly convinced that consciousness is a tiny bit of the world stuck on to the rest of it.

Of course the difficulty is still there—the difficulty that made me say I was glad of the objection I envisaged. We have had to use the *word* "perception," because it is the only word we have. And we have had to go on using it about a kind of consciousness that must be so different from what *we* now experience as perception, as to be almost unrecognizable. I believe nevertheless that anyone who has taken the trouble to follow me must agree that, though I may of course be mistaken, I have not simply been talking nonsense. The alternative of using a different word altogether also has its disadvantages. What word? And at what point do we give up using "perception" and start using that other word instead? I myself have occasionally used the word "participation" to try and indicate a predominantly perceptual relation between observer and observed, between man and nature, and one which is nearer to unity than to dichotomy.[4]

I fear the amount of time I have expended on this topic may have given the impression that evolution of consciousness means for me simply a lot of speculation about its origin, or its very early stages. Believe me, it is not so. I have been expatiating on the evolution of perception for two reasons. First, because it gave me an opportunity to look at one of the objections that is sometimes raised to the whole project. And secondly because in doing so I had to sketch the broad conceptual framework within which I do feel the study has to be placed if it is to bear any fruit. The study of natural history at any point is going to be pretty useless unless it is pursued within the broad conceptual framework of evolution— not necessarily Darwinian evolution, but evolution in its essential meaning of the process whereby one form emerges from another—so, I feel sure, will the historical study of consciousness be pretty useless unless it is conceived of as

4. For example, in *Poetic Diction*, Middletown, Connecticut: Wesleyan University Press, 1973, chapter IX; and in *Saving the Appearances*, New York: Hillary House, 1957, passim.

within the longer process of evolution by detachment—emergence from identity with the inner workings of nature, through consciousness, to self-consciousness.

This, it may be worthwhile to observe, is the sequence presented in substance in a book published recently, which has made something of a stir in the United States—to judge by the number of people who ask me if I have read it: Julian Jaynes's *The Origin of Consciousness in the Breakdown of the Bicameral Mind.*[5] The author, it is true, seeks to fit in what he has to say with a theory of a varying relation between the two halves of the brain. But the book is not really about the brain. It is a valuable and well-documented account of the development of consciousness from the earliest times down to our own; and as such I found that it made no difference to the conviction it carried, whether one accepted, or ignored, or rejected the intrusive bits about the brain. Or no, that is not quite true; because they are incompatible with nearly all the rest it was much *more* coherent, and more convincing, if one ignored them.

Just as a book about biology or natural history, although presupposing evolution, is by no means necessary *about* evolution, so a book or study about the history of consciousness, although presupposing its evolution, need not necessarily be about it. On the contrary, it may well be concerned with the art, the literature, or the science of some particular period, including, last but not least, our own. The difference between reading such a book and reading the general run of books on the same subject will then be something like the difference between entering a shop that sells cut flowers and selecting one or more bunches (which is a perfectly sensible thing to do, but not the *only* thing one can do) and entering a shop that sells growing plants in pots and selecting one or more of *them.*

Let me try to indicate an example, and one that is especially relevant to the relation between history of ideas and history of consciousness. There is no time left in this lecture to do more than indicate. Referring to the history of *ideas*, I spoke near my beginning of its application to philosophy. In that domain history of consciousness must do something more than the sort of things I described. It must take into account the fact that philosophers have, and always have had, to begin from the world they live in—from what they perceive. And it will try to become aware of some of the habit of thought that is structurally inseparable from that world. As one single instance of this: when it has to consider references to the four elements, Fire, Air, Water and Earth in Aristotle's *De Coelo* or his *Generation and Corruption* or elsewhere, it will not be content to treat these terms as having nearly the same meaning that the corresponding words have in our own language today. It will be very much aware that the perception of these elements common to Aristotle and his contemporaries was much less a perception of something detached from themselves, much more a perception

5. Boston: Houghton Mifflin, 1976.

of qualities and processes to be found within themselves, within their own consciousness, as well as without in nature. *They* did not need lectures to remind them that qualities are both objective and subjective. The historian of consciousness will be even more aware of this when he comes on the same terms in the writings of earlier philosophers, Heraclitus for example.

From a background such as this the historian of consciousness may profitably go on to other and wider issues. He may for instance try to review and assess the essential difference between the two primary periods into which he will be inclined to divide any history of man as knower: I mean the period before the birth of philosophy and the period after it. For he will know that philosophy, and later on science, have always performed a dual role. They have operated both as effect and as cause: as effect, inasmuch as they start from and are limited by a mode of perception common at the time of their origin; as cause, inasmuch as, in the further course of time, they themselves help to bring about the formation and fixation of habits of thought divergent from those that prevailed before them. And it is from these divergent habits, from this different perception as their base, that subsequent philosophers will be starting in their turn. The philosophy of Immanuel Kant is based on a Galilean earth and a Copernican universe. He could never have produced it if he had been born a few centuries earlier in a Ptolemaic universe and on an Aristotelian earth.

This leads back to a question I raised nearer the beginning of this lecture, but without then pursuing it. There is no doubt that history, as I have defined it, came *later* than evolution. Are we also to assume that it has *replaced* evolution? Was, for instance, the change from a Ptolemaic into a Copernican world brought about solely by the Scientific Revolution? Many people think so. But I am sure they are oversimplifying a much more complex process. Changes in perception (evolution-of-consciousness changes) are indeed brought about over a long period by changed ideas (history-of-ideas changes). But ideas themselves had begun changing long before the Scientific Revolution: for example, when Nominalism gained the ascendancy over Realism in Scholastic philosophy.[6] Nevertheless not all the changing had been of that kind. Professor Herbert Butterfield in his *Origins of Modern Science*[7] has no doubt that evolution-of-consciousness changes had been going on as well. Let me conclude by reading a brief passage from that illuminating little book:

> Through changes in the habitual use of words, certain things in the natural philosophy of Aristotle had now acquired a coarsened meaning or were actually

6. Realism in Scholastic philosophy is not to be confused with the "realism" of the Cambridge Realists (note 3, above). This is one of the rare instances from historical semantics where a word has not only changed its meaning a great deal but has actually changed into its opposite. "Subjective" is another such instance.

7. London: G. Bell, 1949; New York: Macmillan, 1951.

misunderstood. It may not be easy to say why such a thing should have happened, but men unconsciously betray the fact that a certain Aristotelian thesis simply has no meaning for them any longer—they just cannot think of the stars and heavenly bodies as things without weight even when the books tell them to do so. Francis Bacon seems unable to say anything except that it is obvious that these heavenly bodies have weight, like any other kind of matter which we meet in our experience. . . .

Again a little later the text continues:

Between the idea of a stone aspiring to reach its natural place at the centre of the universe—and rushing more fervently as it came nearer home—and the idea of a stone accelerating its descent under the constant force of gravity, there is an intellectual transition which involves a change in men's feeling for matter.

You can call it a change in men's feeling for matter, or a change in their "reality principle" or common sense, or what you will. But if Butterfield is right, the change into our present world, and out of an older one, has been at least as much an evolution-of-consciousness change as a history-of-ideas change. And if the Scientific Revolution has played a prominent part, as no doubt it has, in strengthening and ingraining our present habit of perception, we shall do well to remember that it is an effect as well as a cause of that continuing change.

Lastly, you may have noticed that, in spite of the pointed antithesis in the title of this lecture between *history* of ideas and *evolution* of consciousness, I have been referring in the course of it sometimes to the evolution and sometimes to the history of consciousness. This was not because I regard them as merely synonymous, but because I also feel that the two processes, the one unconscious and the other deliberate, do continue side by side. Reflections of that nature can lead into far-reaching questions. What is the nature of the forces that are determining our evolution in addition to those that we rightly classify as historical? I raise this question now at the very end without attempting even to begin to answer it. I will only add that, in my opinion, the true answer is much more likely to be found by investigating the evolution of consciousness, and its relation to the history both of ideas and of consciousness itself, than in any exclusively biological theory, extrapolated into the past from the natural science of the present, however popular and however deeply ingrained such a theory may have become.

from *Romanticism Comes of Age*

Thinking and Thought

There is a difference between 'thinking' and 'thought'. One way of grasping this difference (which is of the utmost importance) is to consider the *history* of thinking and see how it differs from a history of thought. The following is intended to be a kind of digest of notes for a possible history of thinking—not of thought, but thinking—as it has developed in the Western world from the beginning of Greek civilisation down to our own day.

If we examine reflectively the manner in which we Europeans think to-day of the world about us, one of the first things we notice is that the concept of 'Law', explicit or implicit, as the case may be, plays an absolutely fundamental part in it. We might say that our thoughts take their whole shape and colour from this concept. The whole of what we respect as 'science', for example, is nothing but the investigation and revelation of 'laws', which are assumed, albeit with somewhat less universal consent, to govern such regions as human behaviour, economic intercourse, etc. The familiar 'law of supply and demand' will do for an example of the latter kind. Nor is the idea merely one of those abstruse hypotheses which are deliberately adopted for the convenience of an accurate scientific method. It is fixed, as a reality, quite as firmly—perhaps more firmly—in the head of the proverbial man in the street than it is in the specialised mind of the professor expounding logic or the expert pursuing scientific research.

When we have realised the ubiquity of this idea in modern European thought, we may for that reason be inclined to stop and ask ourselves more precisely what is meant by it. What do we all mean? Do we, for example, think of a law of nature as corresponding at all to a Hebraic 'Law', that is to say, as being a definite *command* of the Almighty? I believe that very few modern Europeans and Americans conceive of the laws of nature in that light. Do we think of it, then, as a kind of custom or tradition, which Nature keeps tactfully agreeing to follow, as though, when she was bringing to birth a litter of puppies, she would say to herself: Well, I suppose I had better make them as like the parent dogs as possible—after all I always *have* done so? It would be absurd. No, it is only when we think of nature, life, reality, or whatever we call it, as being *obliged* to behave as it does, or—to translate the same idea from Latin into English—as being 'bound' to do so, that we begin to speak of 'laws of nature'. A law of nature is to us a something, an *x*, which binds or connects together otherwise discrete phenomena.

Now a history of thinking differs from a history of thought in that, not content with observing *that* men began to think thus and thus at a certain time, it goes on to ask *how* they became able to think so. Enquiring on these lines, it is quite easy to discover that the concept 'law' arose out of human practices and institutions and was only afterwards transferred, by analogy, to nature, or to processes in general over which the human will is conceived to have no control. But human laws have been created and conceived of very differently at different times and places; so that we have still to enquire what particular kind of human law it was, which was adapted by analogy and became such an indispensable instrument of modern thought. Now, just as the Hebraic 'Law' was much more of a command than a law, as we understand it, so the Greek law, as the word *nomos* suggests, was rather in the nature of what we understand by 'custom' or 'tradition'. It is only in the Roman *lex*, with its etymological derivation from 'blinding' (ob-*lig*-ation, etc.), that the modern meaning really begins to appear in human consciousness at all. Here at last, distilled as it were from the formidably practical activity of generations of Roman soldiers and statesmen, we have the true legal conception of a relation between human beings, not based on blood or affection or religion, but upon a purely abstract something which is 'binding' on them. This could be illustrated in an interesting manner from the meanings of all sorts of Latin words and English words derived from Latin. It could also be demonstrated, from such records as the writings of Augustine and Aquinas, old pictures of the Last Judgment, etc., that, as Steiner has pointed out, the peculiarly Roman conception of, and feeling for, law crept into all kinds of thought during the Dark and Middle Ages. But at the moment all this must be passed over. The question is, when did men first begin to think, in something like the modern manner, of 'laws of nature'?

As far as I am aware, the first writer to draw the analogy in England (though it was not in the English language) was the lawyer-philosopher, Francis Bacon.[1] Moreover, Bacon's place in the history of European thought makes it pretty certain that he was at least *among* the first to draw it at all. So that, in the history of thought, we have here a fairly definite point—round about the beginning of the seventeenth century—at which the concept 'laws of nature' first begins to reveal itself as working in human minds. But now, if we wish to go on from a history of thought to a history of thinking, we shall have to ask ourselves: then, how did

1. For the *lex naturæ*, or *naturalis*, of the Schoolmen meant always the law of God implanted in the human reason for the guidance of human conduct.

men think nature before they had acquired this concept? I purposely avoid saying, how did they think *of* nature, because (as I hope to show) to think *of* nature, as we do to-day, the concept of 'law' must to some extent have been already absorbed by the thinker at first or second hand. History of thought is illusory just because we tend to *think back* in this way *in our own terms*, to project into the minds of our ancestors a kind of thinking which was only made possible by the subsequent events of that very history. For history of thinking we have to be much more conscientious; and, once having perceived that such a concept as 'law' in its application to nature only entered into human consciousness at a certain period, we must try for all previous periods, as it were, to *unthink* that concept together with all its intellectual and psychological implications and consequences. This requires a very real effort of the imagination, besides a fairly intimate acquaintance with the customary processes of our own intellects.

Now one of the most significant passages in which Bacon makes this strikingly novel use of the word *lex* (for he was writing in Latin) runs as follows:[2]

> It may be that nothing really exists except individual bodies, which produce real motion according to law; in science it is just that law, and the enquiry, discovery, and explanation of it, which are the fundamental requisite both for the knowledge and for the control of Nature. And it is that law, and its 'clauses', which *I* mean when I use (chiefly because of its current prevalence and familiarity) the word 'forms'.

The writer has just been vigorously condemning the scholastic science of his day, which consisted almost entirely of efforts to discuss and expound these 'forms' of which he speaks. It will thus be seen that he actually substitutes the meaning of the word 'law' for the meaning then commonly attached, in philosophical circles, to the word 'form' (*forma*) and only refrains from substituting the word itself because of its unfamiliarity. But subsequently—from about the time of the Restoration—this was actually done, with the ultimate results which we have just observed; and the word 'form' was dropped altogether in that connection. Thus, there is some reason to suppose that, if we wish to grasp imaginatively the way in which men thought, before they had this transferred concept of 'law' both to help and to hinder them in their mental processes, it may be worth while to investigate the old meaning of the term for which, in effect, it was substituted—I mean the word 'form'. As soon, however, as we attempt to do this, we find ourselves plunged into the world of Greek thought, for the meaning attached to the word 'form' in the Middle Ages was a definite relic of Greek philosophy. And in the kind of history which I am attempting to sketch Greek thought takes its place as the *result*, or product, of Greek thinking. We must consider the latter, therefore, first.

2. *Novum Organum*, II, 2. Author's translation.

The pervasive quality of Greek thinking, and of Greek consciousness as a whole—the characteristic which distinguishes it most from our own and most delights us—is that it was in a certain sense *alive*. As a thinker or knower, the Greek tended to be at home, as it were, in the coming-into-being, or becoming; whereas our own thought, built as it is on the secure but rigid framework of *logic*,[3] (which the Greeks did not succeed in evolving for us until Aristotle's day), can only deal with the 'become', the finished product—except, of course, where it is willing to bring in the aid of poesy and metaphor. Ontologically— and dismissing all moral and aesthetic values—it is quite legitimate to corre- late 'alive' with 'becoming' and 'dead' with 'become'; and it is in this sense, as will appear more clearly, that I characterise Greek thinking as *alive*, when compared with our own. One casts about for a way in which one could try to convey this living quality of Greek thinking to those who had not had the op- portunity of discovering it for themselves; and it must be confessed that it is not altogether easy. To take, however, a very homely example: the man of to- day knows quite well, of course, whether his hair is long or short; but if he ex- amines this knowledge more closely, he will find that it is only knowledge of a *result*. Thus, he may look in the glass, he may see the snippets lying on the kind of surplice in which barbers envelop us, he may find that his new hat is now large enough to include his ears, or he may feel cold round the back of his neck as he goes out into the street. On the other hand, he may feel the heat or weight of long hair. But if we try to imagine that, instead of this way of knowledge, we could actually be conscious *in* the growing of our hair, could feel it as *move- ment* in something the same way that we still feel our breathing as movement, we should be making an approach towards the difference between Greek con- sciousness and Greek thinking, and our own. Consciousness and thinking are practically interchangeable here; for thinking, in this living sense, differs from thought in that it is not merely an intellectual operation connected with the brain, but involves the whole consciousness. Thought is only the *result* of this consciousness.

For this reason, history of thinking is often better revealed by the meaning of individual words (the study of which has been called *Semantics*) than by the parallel history of literature or philosophy. For the individual word is, in a sense, the point at which thinking becomes thought. Like thought, it is the product or *result* of thinking, and literature (apart from its redemption by poetry) and our thought, too, in so far as we have to think in words, is a kind of synthesis of these products. "It is only by recording our thoughts in language," says a recent writer on Logic,[4]

---

3. This is true of the average modern European, whether or no he is really capable of thinking with logical accuracy. There is all the difference in the world between the illogical and the pre-logical. The point is that he thinks *in the logical mode*.

4. Carveth Read: *Logic Deductive and Inductive*.

that it becomes possible to distinguish between the process and the result of thought. Without language the act, and product of thinking would be identical and equally evanescent. But by carrying on the process in language and remembering or otherwise recording it, we obtain a result which may be examined according to the principles of Logic.

Thus, if we try to enter imaginatively into the meaning of many Greek words, comparing them with apparently similar words in our own language, we get all sorts of interesting results. In the case of long hair, for instance, we find that, besides the static, analytic method of statement, which arises from a knowledge of results only—'to *have* long hair', the Greek language in its early stages actually had a single *verb* to express this physical condition, a verb which is *ex hypothesi* untranslatable in modern English, and to which the nearest approach would perhaps be 'to become long as to the hair', 'to bristle', etc.

The important thing is to realise imaginatively *the kind of underlying consciousness* which have expressed itself in such terms. I mention these few words less as evidence than as *examples* of the fact that the Greek manner of thinking was determined by direct experience of *natura naturans*, whereas *our* direct experience is always of *natura naturata*. The proposition that Greeks did in fact think in this manner is no more capable of experimental proof than the proposition that a manuscript of *Hamlet* contains something else beside a certain weight of paper plus a certain weight of ink. Those who combine, let us say, a dram of imagination with some knowledge of Greek art and literature must take the responsibility of deciding for themselves whether or no they can venture to agree.

The Greek youth of Homer's day, as he approached manhood, did not 'have a beard', he did not even 'grow a beard'; he did not require a substantive at all to express what was happening—he 'foamed'! And again, in order to attribute youth, the Greek language did not require, as we do, the static, logical mode of copula and predicate—"So and so—is—young"; it could say "So and so 'blossoms' or 'blooms' ", using the same word as it used for the flowers of the field. It cannot be too often insisted that this was not a poetical metaphor, but a bedrock element in the Greek language; it is *we*, when we use such expressions to-day, who are trying to get back, *via* poetic metaphor, into the kind of consciousness which the Greek had and could express quite naturally and straightforwardly.[5]

Nor is it merely a poetic fancy to connect in one's mind the whole flavour and freshness of Greek thinking with a blossoming flower—a flower that is still moist, alive, in movement, becoming; and our own thought (again, in so far as it

5. For an interesting discussion of the true meaning of the words ἄνθος and ἀνθεῖν and its distortion by the lexicographers' insistence on 'metaphor', see now *Greek Metaphor* by W. Bedell Stanford (Oxford, 1936).

is not redeemed by the poetic) with the withered leaf and stalk of Autumn, the hard rind of the seed, the motionless, the dead, the 'become'. We can even take the connection in its most literal sense, when we find that the *popular* names of so many English wild flowers—*anemone, daffodil, bryony, celandine, cherry*, etc.—the names by which we instinctively call them when we see them blowing in the field, are traceable to a Greek origin, while the same flowers only acquire Latin labels, when they begin to appear, as dead, dried up specimens, in the botanist's scrap-book. In the same way one could consider all the medical terms that have come to us from Greek, or again the unsurpassed vitality and perfection of living form which breathes to us from the Elgin marbles, as revealing the manner in which Greek consciousness as a whole tended to be at home in the physically living, in the process of becoming.

It is only as a natural growth from this pre-existing soil, this instinctive *kind* of thinking, that the world of Greek *thought* proper can really be understood. Philosophy may be defined as the most *wakeful* part of a people's consciousness. We find, accordingly, early Greek philosophy concerned precisely with this problem of 'coming into being' or generation. The kind of question which the first philosophers set themselves to solve would be expressed by us somewhat as followers: where, they would ask, is the flower's 'form', the shape and beauty which our eyes will see clearly enough when it blossoms, now that they can see nothing but the bare earth or the dry seed? It is not too much to say that all the famous puzzles of Greek philosophy, the puzzles about the One and the Many, about Being and Not-Being, and whether Not-Being *is*, and so forth, begin to be intelligible in the light of this underlying 'becoming' quality of Greek thinking. Now it is one of our four fundamental 'Laws of Thought' that a thing cannot both be and not be, and so obvious does this appear to us that when we find Heraclitus maintaining the opposite, we are inclined to stigmatise him as a verbal quibbler. This is because we can only think 'is'; we cannot really think 'becomes', except as a kind of cinematographic succession of states or 'is's'. Consequently Dr. Karl Unger, in an interesting article, has recently urged us to regard these so-called 'laws' of thought rather as subjective limitations to be overcome, and not as laws of Nature, in which sense they are sometimes accepted. We may thus compare them if we will with St. Paul's conception of the *Torah*, whose strict observance at one time was not more necessary than its supersession at another by a new impulse of Life.

With the Greeks themselves there could be no question of having to overcome such laws of thought; for no such laws had been formulated. Even by the end of Plato's career Greek consciousness had not yet succeeded in distinguishing either of the two opposed concepts of 'being' and 'becoming' from a third concept of mere logical 'predication', as we do. The struggle to achieve this can actually be overheard, at an acute stage, in the dialogue called the *Sophist*. And if we go a little further back, we come to a period when the Greek mind had not even succeeded in distinguishing 'being' from 'becoming'. For up to this point Greek consciousness had actually *lived* in this experience of 'becoming'. And because of this the Greek mind could not at first be conscious of it as such. Thus, although the early Greek philosophers were indeed occupied with a problem which we are now able to *name* as that of 'coming into being' or 'becoming', they themselves could have no such name for it, for being conscious *in* it, they could not get outside it and be conscious *of* it. So that, in a sense, this too was the problem of early Greek philosophy—to acquire, as far as possible, the *idea* of such a world of becoming. And it began to do so, when Anaxagoras set over against the for-ever-changing world of growing and decaying substance (the 'universal flux' of Heraclitus) the other principle of *Nous* or Mind. This was the beginning of the antithesis (hitherto unapprehended) between Spirit and Matter,[6] and if enforced brevity may excuse a somewhat amateurish expression, it may be said that by Plato's time the central problem of philosophy was how spirit, or *nous* 'becomes' matter, or how matter, at certain times and seasons imitates or takes the 'form' of spirit. It is no wonder that the Greeks were a nation of artists!

Note that our own problem tends to be the reverse of this: for we ask how (if at all) matter becomes spirit, and enquire into the 'origin of reason' which we often conceive of as having arisen at a certain point of time, in a world which previously consisted entirely of material substance.

We are therefore in a position to ask ourselves once more the question which was asked a few pages back: what were the 'forms' of which Bacon speaks, and which, by altering the meaning of the word, he wishes to eradicate from the men's minds, putting in their place his own abstract 'laws'? They were nothing else than the memory, so far as it had been retained by European thought since Plato's and Aristotle's day, of those elements, as it were, of *nous*—of the mind—or spiritual world, which the best Greek thinking could still apprehend in its time as living Beings. They were a faint, shadowy recollection of those Thought Beings, neither objective nor subjective, which Greek thinking could actually enshrine within itself—Beings, by whom the part of Nature which is perceptible to our senses is continually brought into being and again withdrawn, in the rhythm of the seasons and of life and death.

But by Bacon's time most, if not all, men had already lost the power to think these Forms. They could only think *of* them, filling their minds with the abstract, subjective 'ideas' of modern thought, which are at best no more than their shadows. Bacon transformed these ideas, already abstract in men's minds, to the still more abstract idea of 'laws'; and modern science has grown up since

6. The idea of 'matter', however, was not really crystallised out into anything like its modern form before Aristotle's day.

his day entirely as a system which deduces from sense-observation these laws, or rules for the changes which occur in the sense-perceptible part of nature.

Now to the most typical Greek thought this part of nature, as we saw, was itself but the sum of the accomplished deeds of another invisible part—that of the 'Forms' as we will call them. Indeed the Greek tended to lose interest in the Nature which had *become*, dwelling only on the Nature which was still in process of becoming. We may even characterise this as its weakness. The 'law' type of thought, on the contrary, if strictly observed, can only deal with a nature that has already, in the physical sense, become. To it, the seed is a congeries of minute particles, which are disposed in a certain relation by the 'laws' of their being, and which, as the year proceeds, draw other particles towards them, building up, again according to certain 'laws', the leaf, the blossom, and so forth. And the flower is nothing else than these particles—apart from the mysterious 'laws' which determine their changes of position.

But now if we ask again, as it was asked at the beginning of this chapter, what these 'laws' are, no scientist with a sense of his responsibilities can admit them to be more than the fact *that* certain changes *have been* constantly observed. He may, of course, add other ideas out of his religious or aesthetic convictions as a private individual, but that is the definition of 'law' which he has to observe in his work. He must deal with *facts*, and facts, alike in their real and their etymological significance, are simply—*facta*—'things which have been done'. Natural law is observable in its effects only.

The result is, of course, a purely static type of thought which can deal adequately only with the most static part of nature—the mineral, the inorganic, the dead. With that part it can deal in a marvellously skillful manner. The most elaborate machine which the Greeks ever even attempted would look like a drawing by Mr. Heath Robinson if it were placed beside the electrical installation that hums to-day in the power-house of a tiny Alpine village. That is the first result.

The second result is the modern civilisation which has arisen along with this static thought and the machinery which it has produced. But for those who see clearly how the *institutions* which make civilisation possible are but the bodies or husks of concrete creative thinking in the past, there is also a third result, as inevitable as the other two. It is the imminent disruption of this same civilisation. For this static, abstract thought has death in it. As far as being is concerned, it can *give* nothing; it can only classify what is there already and re-arrange somewhat its component parts.

For a long time our systems and institutions, grown up out of the ancient world in which this real thinking was still operative, have gone on working, as it were, by their own momentum. But the period which culminated in the Industrial Revolution and the Great War has altered the world out of all recognition. Is it not painfully obvious on all sides that, if the continuity of Western civilisation is to be preserved, we need fresh creative thinking, the power to create fresh forms out of life itself, that is to say, out of the part of Nature which is still coming into being, the spiritual world?

Not that this power to think life into the world has ever been wholly lost from Europe. As religious inspiration, as art, as poetry, it has continued to manifest itself sporadically right down to our own day. But it is a very long time since it appeared anywhere with strength enough to be *operative* in the practical, scientific sense. And it is the development of scientific thought with which I am here particularly concerned; when we want to cure a man of tuberculosis, we go today, not to religion or art, but to science.

By the end of the eighteenth century, then, apart from these isolated exceptions, the power to think in a living way may be considered as having died right out. The man of the eighteenth century lived in a clockwork cosmos. And because this static, clockwork cosmos which he had spun out of his abstract, scientific fantasy was remote from the truth, and because he was honestly seeking for the truth, he had at last to dislodge it from its repose with the idea of 'evolution'—an attempt to get back again, in a new form, to the old notion of 'gradually coming into being'. But it was as yet no more than a notion—even in its Lamarck-Bergson-Shaw evening-dress of 'creative' evolution it is not much more than an abstract shadow of the real life force, the true creative Logos, which was once not an idea for men but an experience and a Being. If 'evolution' to-day were not merely a *theory* for men, but an actual experience, it would be impossible for them, when speaking of it, to omit all reference to its meaning—which is the evolution of *consciousness*. The spell-bound teachers and parents, who must go on inculcating this lifeless, repressive dogma, do not introduce Shakespeare to their children by repeating what psychologists have said about the causes of the impulse to clap hands. This is because the genius of Shakespeare is, not somebody else's theory, invented to explain the repeated phenomenon of hand-clapping, but a concrete *experience* of the individual soul. There is no such experience of evolution.

How are we to get back this experience, this which will alone enable us to impart fresh life to our decaying civilisation? There is no question of going backwards and trying to be little Greeks. The Greeks are not to be our models; they are merely interesting examples, historically close to us, of a people who possessed something which we need desperately ourselves, though in a different form. Indeed, our problem is essentially different from theirs. The task which their philosophers instinctively set themselves was, as we saw, to get outside a plane of consciousness in which they normally lived, so as to be able to conceive of it: to turn thinking into thought. Our problem is the converse of this. We *are* outside it already. Our task is twofold, first to realise that it is still there, and then to learn how to get back into it, how to rise once more from thought into thinking, taking with us, however, that fuller self-consciousness which the

Greeks never knew, and which could never have been ours if they had not laboured to turn thinking into thought. Thus, being normally outside it, it follows that we shall also be conscious *of* it as a different world, a world into which we can plunge at will.

The first part of the problem has already been solved. Rudolf Steiner's comprehensive work is enough and more than enough many times over to enable any real unprejudiced, unobsessed mind to realise that this great world of formative thinking is still there, awaiting us, if we have but the will to reach it. His book, *The Philosophy of Freedom*, for example, is a bridge, itself compacted of ordinary, logical thoughts, which leads beyond and away from such thoughts right up to this other world of creative thinking. And the name which, in other books, Steiner has given to this world is 'etheric'.

But the second part of the problem is not solved, and it depends on ourselves, the men of this generation and the next. This is the problem of actually *reaching* the etheric in fully conscious experience of thinking. The preservation of continuity in Western Civilisation depends on how many and how active may be the spirits which shall succeed in doing this. For the futile inadequacy of our method of knowledge to the rapidly changing realities by which its dignified Roman nose is being tweaked on all sides at present simply shouts at us. We understand what is at rest and what has become, and we can deal with it as never before; but when we try to grasp what is in motion or alive, we merely gibber fantasies in a vacuum hermetically sealed from the truth. Thus, in Medicine, the whole of the *surgical* branch has reached a point little short of perfection; but when it is a question of treating malignant growths and, in general, diseases of the living organism, where are we? In this country, no one who has been brought into contact with even the outer fringe of medical controversy on these matters (I mean, of course, outside the wide area over which the British Medical Association extends its virtual censorhip) will need to wait for an answer. Indeed, the healthiest sign of all, probably, is the increasing number of doctors and others who are beginning to realise, and in some cases to admit, their helplessness. Not to admit it is to be led blindfold into a grotesque world of superstition in which our posterity will hardly be brought to believe, a world from which the sense of humour eloped long ago with the sense of proportion.

In 1924, when Cancer Research on orthodox bacteriological lines had been going on for more than twenty years and had already absorbed thousands and thousands of pounds, the Medical Correspondent of *The Times* (September 13th), in an article on a lecture, enumerated the following results, as "an important addition to knowledge":

(i) The first time a carcinoma has ever been produced in a guinea-pig.

(ii) The first demonstration that a mechanical irritant *can* produce cancer.

(iii) The first time a cancer of the glandular type has ever been produced experimentally.

(iv) The first demonstration that a pathological substance developed wholly within the living body (i.e. a gall-stone) can produce cancer by prolonged irritation or injury.

But, as though his readers might feel almost too triumphant at these startling results, he prefaced them with the remark that:

> Rash conclusions cannot and must not be drawn. While mechanical irritation does cause cancer in the gall-bladder of the guinea-pig, there is no assurance that it will do this in other sites or in other animals. In all disease we have to consider the pathogenic agent on the one hand and the susceptible or refractory tissue on the other. Thus, if tar is applied to a mouse's skin, a skin-cancer will eventually develop, but no amount of tar-application will cause cancer on a rat's or a guinea-pig's skin. . . .

We must also, he said, face the fact that tar applied to the inside of the bowel in a mouse does not produce cancer. It is as though he held up a warning finger: Steady! Do not be too optimistic, my friend. We can produce cancer in some of the animals some of the time, but, remember, we cannot yet produce cancer in all the animals all the time! Not a word, be it observed, of any *remedy*! But this is the sole method of investigation open to a mode of thought which can only perceive the formative forces in their effects: first produce similar effects, and then hope you will somehow chance on a remedy; ignore throughout as irrelevant all specifically human impulses of decency and compassion.

Or one could take Economics. The economic life is to-day the real bond of the civilised world. The world is held together not by political or religious harmony, but by economic interdependence; and here again there is the same antithesis. Economic theory is bound hand and foot by the static, abstract character of modern thought. On the one hand, everything to do with *industry* and the possibility of substituting human labour by machinery has reached an unexampled pitch of perfection. But when it is a question of *distributing* this potential wealth, when it is demanded of us, therefore, that we think in terms of flow and rate of flow, we cannot even begin to rise to it. The result is that our 'labour-saving' machinery produces, not leisure, but its ghastly caricature, unemployment,[7] while nearly every civilised and half-civilised nation of the world sits

---

7. So, in the '30s, when this article was written. Since then the problem of over-production has been temporarily masked by the vast expenditure on industrial expansion that accompanied World War II and the vastly increased wage-distribution which that entailed—*plus* uneconomic 'consumption' of a large part of the product in the form of armaments. It has also (it is good to record) been partly remedied by 'giving away' programmes such as Marshall Aid and its successors.

helplessly watching the steady growth within itself of a malignant tumour of social discontent. And this increasingly rancorous discontent is fed above all things by a cramping penury, a shortage of the means of livelihood, which arises, not out of the realities of nature, but out of abstract, inelastic thoughts about money!

It is a startling thing to go back to poetic writers such as Ruskin or Shelley and to find them forestalling already, out of the living thinking that was in them as artists, the most advanced and intelligent criticism that is being directed today upon the financial mechanism of distribution in our industrial civilisation. It is startling, but it is not very consoling. For what effect did their intuitive foreknowledge have on the problems upon which it was directed? About as much as Cassandra's. It is no longer enough that an occasional artist here and there should see his parcel of truth and speak it out, while the actual direction taken by civilisation continues to be wholly determined by a *soi-disant* scientific method of knowledge. Science must itself *become* an art, and art a science; either they must mingle, or Western civilisation, as we know it, must perish, to make room for one that may have spirit enough to learn how to know God's earth as He actually made it.

It is intoxicating to go on repeating the word 'must', besides giving one a very pleasant sense of superiority. But this time it was not the result of ignorance. Flirtations, it is true, are common enough, but it would be difficult to exaggerate the repugnance with which artist and scientist alike are generally inclined at present to contemplate any such spiritual marriage as anthroposophy desiderates for them. Indeed, for those few who have as yet been brought by the circumstances of their lives to comprehend how desperately Europe needs what anthroposophy can give her, it is an experience more moving and at the same time very much more bitter than the spectacle of high tragedy to see the indifference, misunderstanding, antipathy, and cold suspicion, with which Rudolf Steiner's work meets on every side. A kind of bigotry and arrogance is sometimes imputed to anthroposophists for their exclusive emphasis upon his work and their movement in so many different departments of life. The answer is in the facts themselves. Those who have accepted Steiner's priceless gift are not the choice and picked ones of the earth: they are simply those who have felt out of the depths of their being the fearful need of this living, creative thinking. They are only too glad to take and use such thinking wherever they find it. But where do they find it? Does the traveller, dying of thirst, stop to complain because the torrent gushes from a single spring instead of oozing up out of every stone beneath his feet?

from *The Case for Anthroposophy*

Concerning the Nature of Spiritual Perception

Perceptions in the field of noetic reality do not persist within the psyche in the same way as do representations gained through sense-perception. While it is true that such perceptions may be usefully compared with the ideas of memory, . . . their station within the psyche is nevertheless not the same as that of its memories. This is because what is experienced as spiritual perception cannot be preserved there in its immediate form. If a man wishes to have the same noetic perception over again, he must occasion it *anew* within the psyche. In other words the psyche's relation to the corresponding noetic reality must be deliberately re-established. And this renewal is not to be compared with the remembering of a sense-impression, but solely with the bringing into view once more of the same sense object as was there on the occasion of the former impression.

What *can*, within the memory, be retained of an actual spiritual perception is not the perception itself but the disposition of soul through which one attained to that perception. If my object is to repeat a spiritual perception which I had some while back, it is no use my trying to remember it. What I *should* try to remember is something that will call back the psychic preparations that led me to the perception in the first place. Perception then occurs through a process that does not depend on me.

It is important to be very conscious of this dual nature of the whole proceeding, because it is only in that way that one gains authentic knowledge of what is in fact *objective spirit*. Therefore, it is true, the duality is modified for practical purposes, through the circumstance that the *content* of the spiritual perception can be carried over from the intuitive into ordinary-level consciousness. Then, within the latter, it becomes an abstract idea. And *this* can be later recollected in the ordinary manner. Nevertheless, in order to acquire a reliable psychic relation to the spiritual world, it is a very great advantage to cultivate assiduously the knowledge of three rather subtly differentiated mental processes: 1, psychic, or soul, processes leading up to a spiritual perception; 2, spiritual perceptions themselves; 3, spiritual perceptions translated into the concepts of ordinary consciousness.

Selected Short Passages

Nature and Imagination

The Greek philosophers, as the Greek spirit emerged from that more thorough-going intermingling with the Spirit—or Spirits—of nature, which gave rise to the rich Imaginations of their Mythology—the Greeks evolved their doctrine of the Logos . . . the creative Word, which informs both man and nature. The nature-poetry of the Romantic tradition does indeed reflect this older tradition in many ways; but it is also very different from it.

There is little, if any, evidence that the Greeks were moved by the beauty of nature, or, more precisely, little evidence that they were ever moved in such a way as to be aware of themselves as moved by it.

Yet that is the very essence of the Romantic Inspiration in the aspect of its response to nature. It imports a *reciprocal* relation between the spirit of man and the spirit of nature, which the Greek, and later the Roman, exponents of the Logos could never have understood.

It is rather as if a musical instrument, which was being played on . . . an Aeolian harp perhaps, played on by nature herself . . . fell silent for a while. And then, after an interval, when it began to sound again, it was no longer merely an instrument, but had become aware of itself as such . . . and could itself take part in the playing of itself.

from *Romanticism Comes of Age*

Natura Naturans and *Natura Naturata*

We may speak of *natura naturans* and *natura naturata*; or we may say that, in addition to the phenomena, there are the so-called 'laws' of nature, without which it is impossible to understand the phenomena. The laws themselves are not phenomenal and we only become aware of them in their effects. But we have, all the same, to distinguish them from the phenomena themselves. They are not the less real because they are not things.

Thus, the distinction between *natura naturans* and *natura naturata* reveals itself as resembling in quality that distinction between the act of thought and its product, . . . *natura naturata* being "the productive power suspended and, as it were, quenched in the product."

. . . .

We cannot comprehend nature without first having grasped that the whole may be "in" each part, besides being composed *of* all its parts. We cannot comprehend imagination, or revelation, in literature without first having grasped that that very fact provides the distinction between a symbol and a metaphor. We cannot understand the Old Testament, for we cannot comprehend *any* significant historical record, without first having grasped the fact that particular events, or particular stretches of history, may themselves be symbols of the whole. And we cannot comprehend the New Testament, unless we have also understood that we are confronted with the paradigm of all symbol both in space and in time, when not merely *natura naturans* becomes manifest to the understanding and the senses as *natura naturata*—which was and is happening all the time and everywhere—but also the one voluntary origin of *natura naturans* itself became manifest as *natura naturata* in the body of a single human being.

from *What Coleridge Thought*

Instinct

The plain fact is that if we really *look* at nature—if we really observe her without the tabu at the back of our minds—there is nothing whatever to suggest that she has "no inside." Indeed, there is everything to suggest the contrary. The concept of "instinct," however it is taken, alone implies as much. For instinct cannot be understood, cannot honestly be conceived, otherwise than as a superindividual wisdom at work in nature.

from *Speaker's Meaning*

Dashboard Knowledge

Take a clever boy, who knows nothing about the principle of internal combustion or the inside of an engine, and leave him inside a motor-car, first telling him to move the various knobs, switches and levers about and see what happens. If no disaster supervenes, he will end by finding himself able to drive the car. It will then be true to say that he knows *how to drive* the car; but untrue to say that he knows the car. As to that, the most we could say would be that he has an 'operative' knowledge of it—because for operation all that is required is a good empirical acquaintance with the dashboard and the pedals. Whatever we say, it is obvious that what he has is very different from the knowledge of someone else, who has studied mechanics, internal combustion and the construction of motor-cars, though he has perhaps never driven a car in his life, and is perhaps too nervous to try. Now whether or no there is another kind of knowledge of nature, which corresponds to 'engine-knowledge' in the analogy, it seems that, *if the first view of the nature of scientific theory is accepted*, the *kind* of knowledge aimed at by science must be, in effect, what I will call 'dashboard-knowledge'.

from *Saving the Appearances*

The Universe as Motor-Car

I believe the difference between the two theories of knowledge may best be presented in a parable. Once upon a time there was a very large motor-car called the Universe. Although there was nobody who wasn't on board, nobody knew how it worked or how to work it, and in course of time two very different problems occupied the attention of two different groups of passengers. The first group became interested in invisibles like internal combustion; but the second group said the thing to do was to push and pull levers and find out by trial and error what happened. The words 'internal combustion', they said, were obviously meaningless, because nobody ever pushed or pulled either of these things. For a time both groups agreed that knowledge of how it worked and knowledge of how to work it were closely connected with one another, but in the end the second group began to maintain that the first kind of knowledge was an illusion based on a misunderstanding of language. Pushing, pulling and seeing what happens, they said, are not a means to knowledge; they *are* knowledge. It was an odd sort of car, because, after the second group had with conspicuous and gratifying success tried pushing and pulling all the big levers, they began on some of the smaller ones, and the car was so constructed that nearly all of these, whatever other effect they had, acted as accelerators. Meanwhile the first group held their breath and began to think that their kind of knowledge might perhaps come in useful after the smash.

from *Poetic Diction*

The Darwinian Hypothesis

There is no more striking example than the Darwinian theory of that borrowing from the experimental by the non-experimental sciences, to which I referred at the beginning of this chapter. It was found that the appearances on earth so much lack the regularity of the appearances in the sky that no systematic hypothesis will fit them. But astronomy and physics had taught men that the business of science is to find hypotheses to save the appearances. By a hypothesis, then, these earthly appearances must be saved; and saved they were by the hypothesis of—chance variation. Now the concept of chance is precisely what a hypothesis is devised to save us from. Chance, in fact, = no hypothesis. Yet so hypnotic, at this moment in history, was the influence of the idols and of the special mode of thought which had begotten them, that only a few—and their voices soon died away—were troubled by the fact that the impressive vocabulary of technological investigation was actually being used to denote its breakdown; as though, because it is something we can do with ourselves in the water, drowning should be included as one of the different ways of swimming.

from *Saving the Appearances*

Evolution of Consciousness

In my own field of study everything points to an evolution of consciousness, which, up to as recently as three or four centries ago, has mainly taken the form of a contraction of meaning and therefore of consciousness—an evolution from wide and vague to narrow and precise, and from what was peripherally based to what is centrally based. Further, that if this predominance of contraction is demonstrably true of the historical period up to now, it was even truer of the pre-historic period.

from *Speaker's Meaning*

Mere Perception

Mere perception—perception without imagination—is the sword thrust between spirit and matter. It was the increasing predominance of that kind of perception without Western humanity that enabled the philosopher Descartes to formulate his partition of all being into the two mutually exclusive categories of extended substance and thinking substance—which is another way of saying: between matter and spirit. But mere perception is not what normally occurs when we look at, or listen to, a fellow being. When we do that, we see his body, or hear his voice, not only as matter, but also as expression. We see his body and his countenance as a material picture of the immaterial. I say that is what normally occurs, and I think it does normally occur to *some* extent every time one human being observes another. But of course it may occur to a greater or lesser degree. And the extent to which it does occur will depend a good deal on ourselves. We may—or may not—make up our minds that it shall occur, in our case, to the maximum degree of which our imagination is capable. 'Tis not in mortals to command success, and the result will be uncertain. What seems certain is that something very important will depend on the extent to which we *are* successful. For what will depend on it is precisely what I suggested just now is the most important thing in a meeting between two human beings—that it should be not simply a relation between two phenomena, but a relation between two spirits.

Now it is possible to look not only at a fellow being, but also at the world of nature in that way, that is to say, not merely as matter but also as expression. It is possible, but for most people it is no longer normal and instinctive, to do so. It has been becoming less and less normal in the course of the last three or four hundred years. And the great discovery made by the poets and philosophers of the Romantic Movement was just this: that, although it is no longer normal, it is not impossible. This is the discovery that found expression and became embodied in the aesthetic and philosophical concept of imagination, as it was developed especially in England and in Germany in the second half of the eighteenth and the first half of the nineteenth century—that it is to imagination, in the first place, that we must look for the healing of that Cartesian sword-thrust between matter and spirit.

Thus, for all these reasons I have long felt that, whether by way of the so-called inanimate world of nature, or whether by way of our fellow beings, a strengthening and deepening of the faculty of imagination—or better say the activity of imagination—is the only way in which we can really begin to have to do with spirit. I think I would put it this way: we *live* in that abrupt gap between matter and spirit; we exist by virtue of it as autonomous, self-conscious individual spirits, as free beings. Often, in addition, it makes us feel lamentably isolated. But because our freedom and responsibility depend on it, any way that involves disregarding the gap, or pretending it is not there, is a way we take at our peril.

Now imagination does not disregard the gap; it depends on it. It lives in it as our very self-consciousness does, in this case not as a small helpless creature caught in a trap between the two, but rather as a rainbow spanning the two precipices and linking them harmoniously together. The concern of imagination is neither with mere matter nor with pure spirit. It is thus a psychic, or a psychosomatic, activity. On the other hand, if we are seeking to have to do with spirit, it is worse than useless to try to approach it by way of scientific investigation—at least as the word "science" is used today, for science is avowedly based on *mere* perception, and in mere perception it will always be matter we are having to do with and never spirit. Indeed *mere* perception *is* itself the gap between matter and spirit and, whatever else one can do with a gap, one cannot use it as a means of crossing itself.

from *The Rediscovery of Meaning*

Threefold Organism

Sanderson: We think of [man] as in all respects—physically as well as spiritually—a threefold organism. He is not always thinking and he is not always awake. He thinks and feels and wills; and he wakes and dreams and sleeps. Even while he is awake, he is still a sleeper in his will. What does he know of his volitional process—except its results?—and he is a dreamer in his feeling life. It is only in his thinking that he is really awake. And all this is reflected in the form itself of his physical structure. If, that is, you really *look* at it. . . . He has his brain, for his waking life, swelled out into a bubble in his head, but radiating in the form of nerves through the whole organism. In all this, but especially in the head, he can be psychically active, because he is physically passive. He has, at the other pole, his motor organism—limbs and metabolism—which also reaches up into the head, in the form and function of mouth and lower jaw. And between the two poles his heart and chest, his breathing and his blood circulation—which also permeate the whole body, but are focused in his heart and lungs.

We say that, when he is asleep—and also, even during the day, in his unconscious, from which his impulses of will spring so unaccountably—his relation to the spirit is still that of the first period. In his dreaming, and, in the half-conscious goings-on of his emotional life, he is still really living in the second period. It is only when he is wide-awake, and actually thinking and perceiving that he is wholly up to date.

from *Worlds Apart*

A Literature of His Own

As *A Barfield Sampler* makes clear, Owen Barfield wrote a considerable number of imaginative pieces throughout the years when he was producing his better-known nonfiction works. Although his first published work was a poem, and his early literary aspiration was to be a poet, Barfield reached his main public by other writings, even while continuing to write creative pieces. The *Sampler* provides a substantial selection of Barfield's poetry, three short stories, and two "nouvelles," most of the material being previously unpublished or of difficult access. Except for the poem "Fifty-Three," the following selections do not duplicate any in the *Sampler* but instead mainly reflect Barfield's fictional and quasi-fictional works. Selections range from an early fairy tale through three highly individual, serious but sportive, quasi-fictions to end with two personal reflective poems. Titles (except "Tabula in Naufragio") have been supplied by the editor.

from *The Silver Trumpet*

The Wedding

This fairy tale was Barfield's first published book. It tells the story of beautiful twin princesses, one good and one wicked, who live at Mountainy Castle. The good princess Violet is wooed and won by Prince Courtesy who enters the kingdom sounding his silver trumpet. The trumpet is hidden and the kingdom thrown into disarray by the wicked princess Gamboy. Various intrigues follow, and harmony is not restored for many years until the trumpet is found again and sounded throughout the land. Violet returns to life, Gamboy is slain, and a new young prince, Peerio, weds Violet's daughter. The story incorporates many traditional fairy tale and mythic elements and thereby anticipates the later interest by other Inklings in myth and fairy stories. The following chapter tells of the wedding of Courtesy and Violet before the loss of the trumpet.

And now the story must hurry on, for there are many more things to be told yet, so many, that if you knew all that is still to happen you would say it had scarcely begun. Therefore you must try and imagine to yourself what took place in the next few months; how happy the Prince and Violet were together in spite of Gamboy's ill-nature; how for a long time she refused to speak to either of them, and how unhappy this made Violet, though the Prince didn't care a rap. But although she wouldn't speak to them, neither would she leave them alone. You see, it would have been very little pleasure to her to sulk alone in her room and from her window see them walking and whispering together down in the garden. So she contrived to be always waiting round the corner, and as soon as they came near, she would get up from her chair, pull her skirts about her, and march away with her head in the air without looking at them. Or if they came into a room in the Castle, she was sure to be sitting there already, and she would get up and go out, slamming the door after her. This always made poor Violet feel unhappy for quite a long time, and even the Prince would feel uncomfortable, which was just what Princess Gamboy wanted. You may be surprised that she should still have wanted Violet to feel unhappy, when she loved her better than anything else in the world; but there are two ways of loving people: one is to like seeing them well and happy, which was Violet's way of loving, and the other is to like them to do what you tell them to, which was Gamboy's way.

One day Princess Violet stopped Princess Gamboy and asked her why she was so angry with her, and Gamboy raised her eyebrows and answered coldly:

"My dear child, I am not in the least angry with you. Why should I be angry? I am only concerned for your own happiness. I am sure I hope you will *always* be as happy as you are *now*." And she swept out of the room and left Violet crying. But the Prince frowned and said:

"Stuff!"

Which was quite right, because it was all lies from beginning to end, and he knew it.

And you must also imagine to yourself how the preparations went forward for the wedding, and how the Prince began to feel horribly nervous lest, in the excitement of the moment, he should find himself *married to Gamboy instead of Violet*. How dreadful that would have been! But remember that the two Princesses, in accordance with the law, were dressed exactly alike, and both wore their hair hanging loosely down their backs *and* well keemed. It might happen, you know. So at last in his perplexity the Prince went for advice to the Little Fat Podger. And when he had told him his trouble, the Little Fat Podger stood thinking for awhile and then skipped away with three great grasshoppery, jiggery jumps, looking back over his shoulder and crying out at each step,

"Twiddlem
Twaddlem
Twenty-one."

How puzzled the poor Prince was, till suddenly he remembered having been told that the law about the Princesses only held good till their twenty-first birthday, and then he understood what the Dwarf meant. So he delayed the preparations for the wedding, in spite of his impatience, and arranged that they should be married on Violet's twenty-first birthday, when she would be able to wear what she pleased.

At last, at last, the longed-for morning came, and at breakfast-time everybody waited to see what kind of clothes the two Princesses would wear. Of course they had both looked forward very much to the day when they would be able to wear what they pleased, and each of them, without saying a word to the other, had been secretly preparing her new dress for a month past. Yes, even Gamboy was pleased and excited about this, for, as she said, it was not the clothes themselves that mattered, but *the liberty to choose them for yourself.* By which she meant the liberty to make yourself look as ugly as you pleased.

Gamboy came down first, and everybody gasped to see how different she looked from yesterday. She had put on a narrow, straight, skimpy black dress, which was no wider at the bottom than it was at the top, so that she looked like an umbrella-stand; as for her hair, she had just taken hold of it with both hands, pulled it back as far as it would go over the top of her head, and tied it there with three pieces of string. But she had tied it so tightly that her eyes looked as though they were starting from her head with surprise. She did look funny. And when they saw Gamboy's hair, all the ladies-in-waiting at the breakfast-table put down their knives and forks and let their bacon get cold, while they giggled and tittered to each other:

"She's done it in a bun, she's done it in a bun!"

"What's that?" said Gamboy sharply. And everybody dropped their eyes and picked up their knives and forks and went on eating in silence. But then the door opened and Princess Violet came in! She was dressed in white from head to foot and her skirt fell spreading from her waist so lightly that she seemed to float on air. And her beautiful long hair was piled and piled on top of her head up against a marvelous comb, made of old silver, which rose above it at the back like a tower on the top of a rocky hill, or like St. Michael's Mount in Cornwall. And once again everybody put down their knives and forks and stared. They stared at her in amazement, for yesterday she had been a pretty little girl and now it seemed she was a beautiful lady. How glad Prince Courtesy was that he had waited till her twenty-first birthday! And even the King, who had come down-stairs in a bad temper, because he was to go to the wedding that day instead of going hunting, even the King smiled with delight, and rose and kissed his daughter and was most sweet-tempered all the rest of the day. "No fear of mis-taking them *now*," thought Courtesy to himself, and indeed it would be hard to imagine two more different people. Their very faces no longer looked the same, though of course they were exactly the same really; and if Princess Gamboy cared, she could have made herself look as beautiful as her sister.

When Violet and Gamboy had opened all their parcels (for people receive more presents on their twenty-first birthday than on any other), there was a tre-mendous bustle throughout the Castle, and everybody, from the Lord High Teller of the Other from Which (who no longer had any work to do, but still went on drawing a high salary for it from the King's Treasury) to the smallest and dirtiest of the stable boys, began to scrub himself up and put on his best clothes in readiness to start for the Church. At eleven o'clock every soul in the Castle started off in a long winding procession, some in chariots, some on horseback, some in sedan chairs, and some afoot, to go to the Church, which lay a mile off.

The wedding, too, you must imagine for yourself, and how Princess Gamboy, in her skimpy black dress, sat in the front row and glowered at the bride and bridegroom all the while it was going on. She would have frowned as well, only she had tied her hair back so tightly that she couldn't move her forehead. But as the party came out of the Church, the Prince's herald, who had been stationed at the door, put the Silver Trumpet to his lips and blew. And the sound that came out of the mouth of the trumpet was

Rooty tootity tootity tootity tootity $^{too.}$ Too tootity tootity tootity $_{too.}$

Rooty $^{too.}$ Rooty $^{too.}$ Rooty $^{too-oo-oo.}$

And Gamboy, who was just passing him as he blew, started and smiled in spite of herself, and ran as best as she could in her narrow dress to Violet and kissed her on the lips. But then the sound of the trumpet died away out of her ears, and she fell back ashamed of herself, glowering at everybody near her, and walked on in moody silence at the tail of the procession.

But when they reached the Castle, there was still another surprise in store for them. For the old King came up to the Prince and suddenly fell on his knees before him, offering him the hilt of his sword and saying:

"Homage to King Courtesy and Queen Violet!" Then Violet, who could not bear to see her father akneel, put her arms round his neck and raised him up, whereupon he explained that he and the Queen had decided that they were too old and too tired to reign anymore, and they wished King Courtesy and his wife to govern the realm from now onwards. So Courtesy humbly thanked the old King for his kindness and vowed he would strive to be worthy of so great an honour. He and Violet took the oath there and then, and, as they mounted the throne, everybody in the Castle shouted aloud with one great shout:

"Long live King Courtesy and Queen Violet!" till the old stone walls echoed to the sound. And, as they mounted the throne, the Silver Trumpet rang out again, high above the shouting and the din:

Rooty tootity tootity tootity tootity $^{too.}$ Too tootity tootity tootity $_{too.}$

Rooty $^{too.}$ Rooty $^{too.}$ Rooty $^{too-oo-oo.}$

and then died slowly away, while Princess Gamboy walked, as in a dream, to the foot of the throne and bowed her head, doing homage to the King and to her sister, the Queen.

That night lights blazed from every window in the Castle, so that far away on

the hills the shepherds, gathered around their fires, saw three unbroken rows of little twinkling lights like stars. And they took off their caps, crying:
"Long live the King and Queen!"
Nor did they know that it was a new King and Queen they were hailing.

But inside the Castle a great ball was afoot, with Japanese lanterns in the courtyard, and strawberries and peacocks for supper, and the Great Throne Hall blazing with candles. All the while the Little Fat Podger danced madly in and out of the throng, leaping higher and higher: "Up—up—up—and *again!*" he shrieked and turned two somersaults in the air, because Violet was happy. Nor was the new Queen herself too dignified to dance a little dance of her own in the centre of the hall, while everybody looked on. And when she had finished everyone applauded clamorously, not because she was Queen, but because she danced like a leaf in the wind. Everyone, that is, except Princess Gamboy. She sat alone and aloof at a corner of the supper-table, eating, eating, eating, and drinking, drinking, drinking. She had not even changed her clothes. And all the time she grew more and more jealous of the Prince and spiteful towards everybody; for this was not the kind of music that made her dream.

from *Orpheus*

Orpheus's Lament (Act II, scene ii)

The verse drama *Orpheus* was written in 1937 but not performed until 1948 when there was a six-night run at the Little Theatre, Sheffield, England. Forty-five years later John Ulreich edited it for publication and included a Foreword by Barfield and a reprint of Barfield's program notes for the original production. The play is based on Virgil's account of the myth of Orpheus and Euydice presented as what Barfield called a "mystery drama, not a 'problem' one." The passage below is a speech by Orpheus immediately after the death of Eurydice.

(*Darkness.* **Orpheus** *is seated beside a glowing fire, alone.*)
Orpheus
    Dark!
    The very sun is dark!
    How shall I go on breathing here in space
    Dark with the vanished brightness of her face?
    (*Sings:*)
        Eurydice! Eurydice!   5
    Smooth-gliding nymph, bright wife,
    Who floated down the river of my life
    Sleeping and waking by my side,
    Clothed in her beauty's seamless vesture
    And slipping liquid without pause   10
    From gesture into lovely gesture!
    Lovely in motion, beautiful in rest,
    She filled with light the light
    But filled more full the night,
    When all my round horizon was her breast.   15

Come back, oh Queen, oh bride,
Whose kisses are my only laws!
Hateful my heavenly birth!
Flesh—of my flesh the monarch and the thrall—
Be in my veins my life, my blood, my all!   20
Again
Be thou possessed!
      Thine arms about me placed
Melt me in streaming ocean: mine around thee pressed
Draw down my music spirit to the earth,   25
To be the girdle round thy waist,
And lo!
My mother and the Muses and their train
Troop from above below
And are enchanted in the solid sphere   30
And caught down here!

Hush! Said I so?
This dreaming with the streaming blood
Leads me on, and leads me to no good.
Back! Orpheus! Back! for fear.   35
Oh traitor bard! Oh sacrilegious Son!
What! like some gross ox trampling holy ground!
I will be steadfast in my misery.
      I see her gazing as she used—oh, song!
Out of my misery   40
Pass thou into a strain more high and strong,
Where thou shalt of Eurydice be found
Worthy in sense and sound:
(*Sings*:)
Sing me, oh Muse, how once I groped for hours
      Brooding in anguish on my coming years   45
When, like white dew that falls on purple flowers,
      A silence fell athwart my storm of tears:
The iron band across my breast was broken
      And for a time such grief was its own balm:
It was evening; "Orpheus!" my name was spoken,   50
      "Lift up thine eyes and in the blue find calm!"
I gazed intense and rose into wide ringing
      Fields of bright ether where Apollo sings
And saw the solid earth beneath me swinging
      Soft in the shadow of the spirit's wings . . .   55

Her soaring ended,
  My soul descended
With folded wings
  In humbler wise.

Oh, lovely Creature!   60
  Oh holy Nature!
Now first I saw thee
  With open eyes!

One came to meet me
  And soft did greet me   65
A blue-robed goddess
  Out of the night.

Crowned with the stars,
  Her feet on flowers
Her dark eyes shining   70
  With beauty bright.

And without ceasing
She breathed out blessing
Upon all creatures
  Brought to birth.   75

Those that could kill me
  With love did fill me!
No thing was hateful
  In all the earth.

Quenched was my yearning   80
  And I all burning
To fall before them
  In sacrifice.

Persephone!
  I gazed on thee   85
And thy great Mother
  With open eyes!

Persephone!

(**Orpheus** *observes for the first time that he is surrounded by a ring of listening animals.*)

Encircled by my listeners once again!
Dear creatures, sitting crouching at my feet,   90
Dear friends, who come to help me ease my pain
With your still presence! Say, what can I do?
You have saved me from madness. My pent soul
You have set free, calling it out of prison
Into you on the wings of its own song;   95
What would you have me do in recompense?
How shall I serve you? Answer me!
            They cannot answer me—save with my voice.
It is their bridge. I will sing to them again.
And listen while I sing:
(*Sings:*)
                         Eurydice!   100
Smooth-gliding nymph, bright wife,
Who floated down the river of my life
Clothed in her beauty's seamless vesture
And slipping liquid without pause
From gesture into lovely gesture—   105
Lovely in motion, beautiful in rest—

from *This Ever Diverse Pair*

Tabula in Naufragio

This "high and sharp philosophic comedy," as C. S. Lewis described it, tells of the activities of a London solicitor whose psyche is so divided between the pedestrian, quotidian world of his profession and the literary, imaginative world of his desiring that his two identities have different names. Burden is the humorless one, Burgeon the inventive one; Burden always sticks to business, Burgeon is forever screaming silently inside to get out. The story is told in the first person by Burgeon, who always speaks of Burden as of another person. The opening chapter that follows sets the stage for a series of encounters and struggles between Burden and Burgeon, as Burgeon sees his situation as that of a plank (or even, in a play on words, a writing tablet) in a shipwreck. The title is Barfield's.

Of course he already keeps a diary in a sense, like any other solicitor—a great fat thing bound in coloured boards and buff leather, which looks rather like a sporting bible and doesn't tell you anything about him. What it does tell you about is costs, stamp duties, the name and addresses of other solicitors and the formalities preceding cremation. All this is in very small print, while the blank pages of diary proper contain laconic and virtually illegible pencil entries of the nature of "10.30 Mackenzie Summons" or "Mrs. Parsons" or simply "15/2"; with a sprinkling of occasional intimacies like "Call for G's shoes" or just "toffee".

If this partner of mine kept a real diary, there would be no need to write all this about him. As it is, you can take it that *this* is his, or rather our, true diary—in exactly what sense will appear, I hope, as it proceeds. It will certainly not be a diary in common form.

But first let me make it quite clear that I am not writing it out of any love of the man. Quite the reverse, in spite of our long and close connection. I am doing it simply because I must now write about something or die. If I *do* die—but we come to that later. I would much rather write about something else, but, as a painter can paint only what he can see, and, if there is something which girdles and confines his entire horizon, must paint that or nothing, so a writer, if there is somebody who exacts his unremitting attention during waking hours, must either write about that somebody or hold his peace.

Over and over again I have started writing about something really interesting or useful—classical stuff, matters of public interest, the Lord knows what—only to be pulled up with a jerk. Just as I am getting absorbed in it, up comes Burden. "Hi!" he says. "I want you! You must stop that!" I stop with a wrench and an abiding grudge against him. And when five or six weeks later there is a chance to start again, I shrink from re-absorption—remembering the wrench. You can't really write with any force about anything on which you are never allowed to fix your attention. But the only thing on which I am allowed, and indeed expected, to fix my attention, is Burden. So I am writing about him.

Let me do him justice. It was *my* doing that we ever went into the law at all. I, Burgeon, am responsible for the present constitution of the firm of Burden and Burgeon. I am responsible for the professional existence, almost for the existence at all, of Burden. I deliberately called him forth from his obscurity—summoned him, as it were, from the realm of the Mothers, and set him up in space and time. It is not the fault of either of us that we have since become involved in a complex of responsibilities from which there may be no way out until the shadows lengthen, the busy world is hushed and our work is done. It may not be the fault of either of us—it is certainly not his—that he is turning into a sort of Frankenstein. But in all my present bewilderment I am at least certain of this: that if, without injuring anyone but him, I can do anything to arrest the process and keep my own end up, I ought to do it. So I am going to try keeping his diary, and see what happens.

This is my declaration of independence. I always thought I should be able to keep that, but now I am afraid. The original idea was, that he was to earn the bread and butter and I was to support him as a sleeping partner. I was to put in exactly as much *time* at the office as he did, but nothing much else; and in my spare time I was to carry on as before. I admit I also had the ineffable idea that, I being (at any rate by inclination) a poet and he a business man, the association might in some undefined way work out for the benefit of both poetry in general and business in general, and thereby contribute to the gaiety of nations and the amelioration of society. (Romeo and Juliet were to do as much for the Montagues and Capulets.) But this wasn't the essence of the contract; alternatively it hasn't worked, there is a total failure of consideration, the contract is frustrated and under the Law Reform (Frustrated Contracts) Act 1943 I am under no obligation to him of any sort whatever.

How could we possibly foresee that in 1931, less than six months after we joined forces, the pervasive strain on the whole economic system would begin, that it would get tenser and tenser until it culminated in the War, that life in a solicitor's office would be like life in an understaffed telephone exchange? It was quiet enough, at least in externals, fifty years ago, I am told. How could I have foreseen that by 1941 both the other members of the firm would be *hors de combat* and we too, inadequately equipped with experience, still half green, carrying on the whole business alone? Take a Rugby football player, knowing the rules of the game well enough, having learnt it well at school, having perhaps played once or twice for his college (notwithstanding a slight lameness in one leg); drop him by parachute into the middle of the scrum at an International Match, informing him casually, as you press the release-button, that he is captain of his side: he will have an idea of our position.

It is odd to reflect that only a few years ago I made a stern and deliberate resolve to abandon all writing on personal subject-matter. It seemed to me, and it still seems, that this particular romantic vein is thoroughly worked out. I don't like it even when the raw material is transmuted into first-rate lyric. True, many of the poems which have given me the keenest pleasure are made of it. The best of the few lyrics which I myself have put up were all of this type, written to relieve my personal griefs and in fact relieving them. That made no difference. It began to disgust me. I wanted, above all, to be objective, to write about Nature and events and quite other people, using my own feelings solely as instruments of perception and fountains of diction, sacrificing them like the glass in the window, to let in the light and the warmth of the outside world. And now here I am, at it again!

The whole trouble is that the sleeping partner doesn't get enough sleep. I don't mind having to be in Burden's room while he is doing his work. I expected that. After all, I am invisible, and no one else knows I am there. (At least, I imagine not.) As long as he is jogging away at routine work without interruptions, I would as lief be there as in any other place where I am not allowed to be actually about either my own or my Father's business. What I object to is the unexpected degree of *attention* he demands. I can't call it exertion. If it were, it mightn't be so bad. But in practice there is very little routine work without interruption, and every time he is interrupted he calls for me. Every time the telephone bell rings, *I* have to answer it, ascertain who is there and what he is talking about, and then, if I am lucky, I can hand over to Burden. The systematic 'waking' of witches in the Middle Ages is usually referred to by modern historians as just an instance of barbarous torture. I don't believe the infliction of pain was the main object of this procedure—which involved the systematic prevention of sleep for days at a time by pins, pinches or other light nervous shocks. The object, and the necessary object, was to keep the other part of the woman *there*; I mean the sleeping partner who had other things to do in her spare time, and who perhaps would have been off on the very mischief they were seeking to prevent if they had merely used the rack.

Was it a *hundred* times today
I nodded and began to sway,
Drowsed, and the blank walls dropped away?

Faces and voices merge; the glare
Softens to dusk; the live black air
Bosoms me: *Whisk! my broomstick there!*—

Hey up the chimney!—sharp the pin
Of gaoler jerks me back to skin:—
"Pardon me, is your *partner* in?"

Worst of all, I find that nearly all *decisions* have to be made by me. And this part of the work is not even confined to office hours. He tells me to take them home with me and (the supreme imposition) to *use my imagination!* Why on earth should imagination be necessary for these fiddling problems? And then there are the awful times when he is so tired that I have to keep *him* awake!

Of course, someone will say that all this is a subtle form of exhibitionism or narcissism or some nastyism or other. It might be if I were writing to please others. But in point of fact it's a matter of complete—well, almost complete—indifference whether anybody else ever reads it or not. I am doing it for my own salvation. Burden is eating me up, my time, my wit, my memory, my 'shaping spirit of imagination', my whole *me*. Take poetry, for instance. The other evening he was so exhausted and spiritless and devoid of hope that he asked me to write a poem about *his* feelings. That's the sort of thing he does—calls on me to exert the very abilities he is destroying. I produced the following quatrain for him:—

How I hate this bloody business,
Peddling property and strife
While the pulse of Europe falters—
How I hate this bloody life!

And he paid me the last insult of *praising* it. He thought it was good. In fact the silly ass was so pleased with it that he kept saying it over and over again to himself, in the train going home, till he fell asleep and overshot his station!

It may be that there is some impropriety, or even danger, in writing about anyone as closely connected with me as Burden is. So close that, until twelve months ago, I had never even dreamed about him. As I hesitated, pen in hand, before I began to write all this—pondering the very doubts I am now trying to express—my mind went back to that perhaps prophetic dream. I was sitting at a concert in a full hall, when I caught a glimpse of him walking down the middle, looking along the rows for a vacant seat that wasn't there. In my dream it was a second or two before I established the identity of that intelligent, anxious, tolerably ugly face under the bowler hat, though I know it well enough, and the moment I had done so, I woke up—feeling a little frightened. It hasn't happened again. Frightened or not, I have got to try some remedy beyond those I have tried already, and the homeopathic one is the only one that suggests itself. A hair of the dog that bites me. Kill or cure. Perhaps it may be cure, for, to be honest, I feel a bit better already.

from *Worlds Apart*

Discourse by Sanderson

Subtitled "A Dialogue of the 1960s," this Socratic symposium brings together over a three-day period seven representative modern intellectuals whose fields include theology (Hunter), rocket science (Ranger), physical science (Brodie), teaching (Sanderson), biology (Upwater), linguistics (Dunn), and psychiatry (Burrows), along with their host, Burgeon, "a solicitor with philological interests." Their spirited exchanges cover many of Barfield's favorite topics, making this work, in T. S. Eliot's words, "an excursion into the seas of thought which are very far from ordinary routes of intellectual shipping." What follows is a portion of the discussion on the third day when the retired schoolmaster Sanderson discourses on experience and thinking in a vein that suggests both Barfield and Rudolf Steiner.

Sanderson: I had better begin by referring back to the human trinity, the three-fold nature of man, as we see it thinking at one pole and willing at the other—and the resulting tension between them. If that is all right, the problem of making the unconscious conscious, or at all events *more* conscious, can be seen as the problem of getting our will into our thinking activity. We have somehow to acquire, or re-acquire, the faculty of thinking and observing not merely with the brain and the senses, but with the whole threefold organism. You remember I claimed that this polarity, and the resulting threefold nature, is also implanted in our *physical* organism. So far from denying our psycho-somatic unity, therefore, we have deliberately to make use of it. But to do that we must first achieve it. That is something quite different from leaving it to achieve itself in us. For then *it* makes use of *us*. Then it degenerates to mere instinct.

Burgeon: You would distinguish psycho-somatic unity from somato-psychic unity?

Sanderson: The one is instinct. The other is spirit. But we do not achieve this unity by forming new *ideas* about the nature of the unconscious, or even about what is going on in our own unconscious, because all that still remains in the one sphere of thinking. I mean something quite different. To some extent we most of us do it already—when we force ourselves to attend closely to something we are not interested in. But it is possible to raise this faculty of attention to a higher power by systematically exercising it—rather as we strengthen the muscle by repeated exercises. To some extent we do strengthen the muscle by ordinary use. But we need special exercises if we decide to develop it to an enhanced and special strength. You do that with willed thinking, if you practise attention to other objects than a *train* of ideas; if you practise regularly, over a long period, concentrating the mind on one single concept or one single object, to the exclusion of all else. Of course it must be a concept without emotional overtones.

That is one thing; and of course it is only the very beginning. I don't see how I can hope to do more than give some sort of crude and fragmentary idea of the *sort* of thing I mean, in case it's really quite unfamiliar to you. To take another example—I stressed the fact that the tension between the two poles of the human being is the basis of his emotional experience, his whole flickering life of feeling. The pursuit of the kind of knowledge, the knowledge in extended experience, which I have argued for, also requires a systematic cultivation of feelings—feelings evoked by selected images and symbols, for instance, and feelings about the process of nature and her appearances. One must take pains to become able somehow not merely to feel but deliberately to *use* one's feelings as a means to perception; to treat *them* as a precision instrument for investigating quality, just as we take enormous pains to develop external precision instruments for investigating quantity.

. . . .

One of our commonest experiences of the face of nature is what I might call the spring and autumn experience. The different forms and colours and smells that we perceive on the one hand in growing and on the other hand in decaying things. To some extent we already 'read' them rather than merely perceive them, for the inner processes of growth and decay which they express are qualitatively part of our perception—unless we are idiots. Now we *may* choose, instead of casually noticing all this and perhaps poetizing it, really to concentrate on the qualities and on the processes they betoken, and then deliberately to cultivate strong feelings about them. I don't of course mean emotions of melancholy or hopefulness, but something much more impersonal—more akin, perhaps, to our experience of the minor and major keys in music. Again, we can experience, both in observation and feeling, the alternate expansion and contraction, which characterizes the growth-process itself—most noticeably in plants—to which Goethe drew attention with such delicacy in his book on *The Metamorphosis of Plants.* (I confess that condensing it in this shorthand way gives me a feeling of nakedness— still, one *can* do so.) Of course it is only a first feeble step, but eventually, as a result of that and of many other steps in the same direction, one may come to a direct experience of those formative, structure-bestowing forces from space, of which I tried to speak before. One becomes, to use a metaphor, really acquainted with Huxley's 'invisible artist' and able to study his modelling movements in detail. And you can use these detailed observations, as is already being done, for quite practical purposes—therapeutic, agricultural and so on.

. . . .

And yet it is surely obvious that we cannot closely approach familiar nature in any other way. There is no other road to a science of the qualitative. Take colour, for instance. You can treat it spectrally (in both senses of the word!) as waves or vibrations. But in doing so you lose colour itself altogether. For we never actually experience the vibrations. If you want to investigate colour as a quality, you are obliged to approach it—as Goethe did— without forgetting our normal experience of it as a sort of bridge between the outer world of perception and the inner world of feeling. That is why the people who are practically concerned with the *quality* of colour—because their bread and butter comes from colour-printing or colour-reproduction— are at present busy studying Goethe's theory of colour, or rediscovering it for themselves.

. . . .

Burgeon: Then what about the objection, Sanderson?

Sanderson: Our time's getting very short, but I'll do my best. You must remember the position I start from: that the material world is condensed from a spiritual origin and that the individual self has evolved from that same origin. Now those who believe the opposite get at any knowledge they have of the remote past—how shall I put it—*vestigially.* They try to observe the past in its present outcome by examining the geological and fossil 'record of the rocks' and so forth. We both agree that the present substance, form and condition of anything is the outcome of its past development, but it must make all the difference of course whether that past is wholly material or whether it is also immaterial. If what I was saying earlier is right, it follows, I think, that the objects of the natural world will be vestiges of their primeval spiritual origin as well as of their subsequent physical development. This will apply to all objects phylogenetically speaking and, in the case of living organisms, it will also apply ontogenetically. For both of us nature is, in a manner of speaking, history displayed; only the histories are very different. For more recent periods I suppose both views may be to some extent right; but go far enough back and one of the two must be wrong.

Secondly I have maintained that the immaterial realm from which the material is derived is accessible to direct observation by a human being who has trained himself adquately to the task.

Now I have still to try and meet the objection that this does not explain how anyone could actually observe the past. And I think here I can only refer back to what I said yesterday—that the whole relation of past and present, the whole nature of time, is different in the spiritual, or if you like, in the unconscious realm. I suppose that sounds rather bald. But really *everything* changes its aspect as soon as you start from somewhere else. Most people feel that their mental experience is a kind of replica of nature; but *we* feel nature herself as a replica of mind. Burgeon at least seemed to agree with this in theory, when he was talking about symbolism and the origin of language.

Need we go again into the relation between 'thinking' and 'I think'? To say that nature is history displayed is really to say that nature is man's unconscious being, displayed objectively before him. I don't think it matters much whether you put it that way or whether you say, with Goethe—and to some extent with Chardin and perhaps even Upwater—that human consciousness is that mirror in which nature surveys herself. The point is, that in the unconscious, whether you call it man's or nature's the whole relation between past and present, the whole nature of time, has to be conceived differently. We get a hint of it in dreams. The past remains latent in the present, perhaps in something the same way as it does in the meaning of a word. I don't think I can be more precise. I could not be without beginning to speak of hierarchies of creative beings, and there is obviously no time for that, even if you wanted it.

When I speak of experiencing, or observing, the past, rather than theorizing about it, I mean roughly that it is possible with trained powers to reconstitute nature as history—to reconvert it, as it were, from history displayed into history remembered. Remembered in the detailed manner of its display. Of course it is memory in a somewhat different sense from ordinary memory; but even ordinary memory is nearer to observation than it is to theory or inference.

Burgeon: I am interested to know whether all this applies only to what you called the 'primeval' period, or whether these 'trained powers' have direct access also to the pre-historic period—perhaps even to the historic.

Sanderson: They are not necessarily limited to the remote past. And I have already said that emergence from the immaterial into the material is ontogenetic as well as phylogenetic.

Burgeon: I was thinking more particularly of the present furious interest in archaeology. From what little I know of it, if ever there was an example of a precariously inverted pyramid of theory on a very slender apex of fact, there you have it. When I compare the sort of theories that are put forward about the consciousness of primitive man with the indications you get, by pursuing

a more internal route—myth and the study of language, I confess it has sometimes seemed to me that there *must* be a more satisfactory way of getting
back into our own past than all this measuring of potsherds and arrowheads.
Sanderson: Believe me, there is. It is not a question of having to jump suddenly back to the *remote* past. I have already said that the human physical organism reproduces as it were all three periods; it is the lower organs that embody our most unconscious part and it is these you will study if you want to
experience the remoter past. But you may also study, for instance, the brain
and nerves.

Perhaps I shouldn't have used the word 'study'; though you would certainly have to study them in the ordinary physiological sense as well. But it is
more a question of rendering conscious the unconscious element in you, of
which your different organs are functions. Brain, heart, liver, spleen, have
been built into your body by the world, by the whole history of the world,
and if you 'study' one of them in that intensive way, you have access to the
relevant period of world-history. Access, first of all, to the building that was
going on before your birth and, through that, back into their remoter phylo-
genesis.

You see—or at any rate I have argued—that if evolution has indeed been
fundamentally the evolution of self-consciousness, there cannot be that
sharp break between ontogenetic and phylogenetic development, which the
positivist picture of evolution assumes. The one must merge gradually back
into the other.

from Unancestral Voice

Flume's Lecture

In this, his most esoteric fiction, Barfield again presents the reader with the experiences of Burgeon, this time in communication with a spirit called the Meggid, a variation on the similarly named Maggid from the sixteenth-century Jewish rabbi and mystic Joseph Karo. Burgeon, with Burden in the background tending to everyday matters, listens to and exchanges thoughts with the Meggid on a vast range of contemporary intellectual issues of the kind that most engaged Barfield throughout his life. The dramatic highpoint is a lecture given by a young physicist, Kenneth Flume, to the dismay of the conventional members of the Physical Society and to the fascination of Burgeon. The main part of the lecture is given here.

It was at this point in the evening that one of the visitors present, the lecturer's own invited guest seated in the front row, suddenly grew more alert. Not that his attention had exactly wandered. The reading he had undertaken since his last encounter with the Meggid, and indeed on the Meggid's persuasion, had enabled Burgeon to follow most of what had so far been said without too much difficulty. But it must be admitted that his attention had lately begun to flag a little. *Now* he had the pleasure of recognition to enliven it, as his mind went back to a long talk he had had with this interesting young man a few weeks ago. Kenneth Flume was the nephew of an old friend. Though Burgeon had known him slightly from boyhood, it was on that evening that the two had, properly speaking, 'met' and, in doing so, had discovered how, underlying all their differences, of age, of background, of interests, of assumptions about most things that are important, they acknowledged one passionless passion in common. Now, by his choice of words, Flume was delicately, in his presence, bearing witness to it. Perhaps it was flattering; certainly it was touching; and the listener felt himself strangely and strongly drawn to the speaker.

To return, Flume continued, to this question of models. There was a feeling in many quarters that they should now be abandoned altogether. No single model had been devised, and none apparently could be, with which quantum mechanics would fit; and quantum mechanics was so effective, it was said, that there was no *need* for one anyway. Others took the opposite view; and one strong argument for it, which must appeal to all physicists, was this: how was it possible to make any substantial further advance without them? Fruitful research, if it was to have any directedness, any coherence, must be based on *some* new hypothesis, however, tentative, and (they added) however mistaken. You had to have something to work on. In the history of science it had often been the ardent attempt to prove a new but false hypothesis which had led to the discovery of the new and true one. He instanced Kepler's almost accidental discovery of the ellipse as the true basis of planetary astronomy. How could any new theory ever swim into our ken if we continued to have simply no way whatever of representing to our minds what actually goes on at the sub-microscopic level? He personally felt that there was only one answer to that question; and this had led him to give some thought to the whole question of the nature and function of the model in the process of scientific enquiry.

The model was a moving system—nowadays generally a notional one only—of objects within the ordinary range of perception by the unaided sense, by means of which the mind represented to itself the operation of a natural process. Generally the process so represented was itself beyond the range of the unaided senses, because otherwise no model was needed. It was when the process was either too big or too small for the senses to perceive it as a whole that scientists had had to recourse to the model. Thus, to help us to grasp the working and proportions of the solar system, we imagined a collection of spherical objects varying in size from, say, a football to a pea, revolving round each other in some space not bigger than a fair-sized room. At the other end of the scale—when they had wanted to think about the molecular motions of gases, or the inner structure of the atom—it had been much the same. Billiard balls, for some reason, had been a strong favourite here. He suggested that there was another essential feature of the model, which had perhaps not yet been so fully appreciated. Characteristically, the model was a moving system of a kind which, given sufficient skill, *we could ourselves construct*. The objects we selected were of a size and nature that we could handle as well as perceive. The model system was accordingly one which we could at least *think* of ourselves as constructing. A moving system constructed by man is, of course, a machine, and classical physics, in the development of which the model played such a leading part, perhaps inevitably culminated in the general theory known as 'mechanical causality'.

'The reason,' said the lecturer, 'why I am troubling you with all this is that I am one of those who are convinced that, unless we do succeed in solving this problem of representation, there is no way forward for us. No doubt we shall improve in accuracy, we shall fill in some gaps; but of another leap forward, such as occurred with the transition from classical to nuclear physics, I see no prospect whatever. For in order to be led to *new* ideas, we really must be able to imagine—or at least apprehend in *some* way—what is actually happening. And that is just what, apparently, we have ceased to be able to do.

'I am anxious that, before we give up the struggle, before we settle down to the conviction that field and particle represent the last limit of what the human brain is capable of conceiving, we should seek to explore this problem of representation a little more exhaustively. At the moment, we have, on the one side, our quantum mathematics, to which the existence or non-existence of its subject-matter is a matter of indifference, and, on the other side, those models which we look like having to abandon. And there is no connection between them. Or, more precisely, there is only a *historical* connection between them. In this situation the only fruitful line of enquiry I can see, the only possible *starting*-point, is to ask ourselves the question: Is there some conceptual sphere which lies between mathematics at the one extreme and the "model" type of thinking at the other? Is there a mean between the zero-representation which characterizes the mathematical symbol and the solid, constructional representation aimed at by the model? In this connection, and to indicate one possible starting-point for such a line of enquiry, I would draw attention once more to the particular circumstances that have led up to the collapse of the model as a mental support for scientific research. It began when Niels Bohr convinced us that, if we insist on having a model at all, then we must have two complementary ones, which cannot both be used at the same time: the wave model and the interacting-particles model. Now you will notice that these two so-called models differ from each other in one important aspect. Only the second, the interacting-bodies one, answers to the definition, which I hazarded, of a model as a system which we could in theory ourselves construct. We do not think of ourselves as constructing *waves*; their structure—if structure is the right word—and their motions and interactions are an immediately "given" experience made available by nature herself, so that in this type of model, if we should so call it, we are using nature herself, macroscopic nature, nature as normally experienced, as our means of representing sub-microscopic nature. It is possible that this distinction may turn out to be an important one.

'But above all I ask myself if our predicament is not one which obliges us to look for help in any direction where it might conceivably be found. Would it not be wise, for instance, to pray in aid some of the results arrived at in other disciplines than our own? We could at least try the experiment. Here I will suggest one possibility, and I put it forward as an example only. There are those who have studied with some care the whole process of representation that normally goes on between the mind and nature. Forgive me if for a few moments I speak of matters of which I know almost nothing, and know even that from hearsay! I am told that the nature and function of the human imagination has received a lot of attention in the last few decades; that it has been examined as a mode of inter-action between the observing mind and the observable—or conceivable—ob-ject, which underlies both thinking and perceiving. But that is not all. By some at least of those who have researched in that field it is claimed, I am told, that the element of imagination, which is present in a slight degree even in normal per-ception and normal thought, can be isolated, as it were, for the purpose of deter-mining its attributes, and that when that is done there is a considerable measure of agreement about what is found. For example—once again I am told—imag-ination as such is especially adapted for apprehending a relation between a whole and its parts different from that of aggregation, and different again from any kind of relation envisaged by classical physics, but not altogether unknown in the organic realm. It has been said that imagination directly apprehends the whole as "contained" in the part, or as in some mode identical with it.

'Secondly, it is said to be characteristic of imagination that it apprehends spatial form, and relations in space, as "expressive" of non-spatial form and non-spatial relations. A third attribute which is claimed for it is that, operating as it is said to do, anteriorly to the kind of perception and thought which have become normal for fully conscious modern man, it functions at a level where observed and observer, mind and object, are no longer—or are not yet—spa-tially divided from one another; so that the mind, as it were, becomes the object or the object becomes the mind.

'Now it seems to me that the first two claims alone—if there is anything in them—*might* be of some significance in our problem. For this question of the actual relation between whole and part and the closely allied question of spatial relationships, and of the nature of space itself, is very much the heart of our matter. Perhaps, when we are considering the relation between field and parti-cle—or rather, as at present, considering how to consider it—we should be rash to leave such claims altogether unexamined.'

Returning to more familiar ground, the lecturer said they would know he was not the only physicist who was being led by the recent developments to which he had referred to reflect on the whole treatment of space, both mathematical and non-mathematical, in physical theory. He supposed the overall goal of physics, apart from utilitarian considerations, was to determine, as precisely as possible, the structure of matter and, through that, the structure of the universe. To this end it had been consistently striving to resolve matter into its ultimate elements. Originally the chemical 'elements' had themselves been regarded as ultimate; but with the advance of science these had increased in number in a dis-concerting way, as more and new elements were discovered. At the same time they were discovered to be unstable, because capable of changing into each other. It became necessary, therefore, to investigate the *structure* of the chemical element; and that search had soon become a search for elementary particles. With the triumph of the atomic theory the atom was for a time accepted as the elementary particle—until it, too, was found to be unstable, and capable of transformation. It was therefore assumed, rightly, that the atom was not, in fact, an elementary particle but a micro-object with a structure which itself called for investigation.

'Now, in our own time, the same process is being repeated with the sub-atomic particles, into which the structure of the atom has been resolved. There is the same menacing increase in their number; we have had to add to the original and, as it was hoped, ultimate electron, not only protons and neutrons, but positrons, neutrinos and many different kinds of mesons and hyperons. Nor is there any sign of an end to the process. We might have assumed from this symptom, even if we had not actually found, that the sub-atomic elementary particle would turn out itself to be unstable. In fact, we have found them capable—at very high energy-levels—of being transformed into each other or, in the case of the newer particles, of "decaying" into neutrons, protons and electrons. We have, moreover, to assume that these bodies can be "created" in collisions of other particles with nuclei. Putting it shortly, the new "elementary particle" turns out to be more "ultimate" than did the atom into whose structure it combines, or than the chemical element into whose structure the atom itself combines.

'Logically, therefore, our next step can only be an investigation of the inner structure of the sub-atomic particle itself. But it is here that the difficulties I have been reminding you of this evening arise. My time is running out and I shall remind you now of one of them only—the awkward fact that, for mathematical purposes, what we at present regard as the elementary particles have to be deemed of zero size. This does seem to raise in an acute form the question, which has been raised by others before me and for other reasons, whether we are not being called on to revise our whole notion of space; or, if you prefer it, of space-time. But I would prefer, as far as possible, to simplify by leaving time out of the reckoning this evening.'

Maybe, he continued, they had not yet appreciated the full implications of introducing the 'field' concept at all into physical theory. That had already constituted a striking departure from the classical framework of the universe. Newtonian mechanics postulated that things were constituted of bodies interacting according to specified forces; and perhaps a Newtonian space had followed from those mechanics. But the whole scheme had been found inadequate by the end of the nineteenth century. They had to introduce a new set of entities, the electric and magnetic fields. Now, the mode of existence of a 'body' had required that it be localized in some definite region of space, whereas the fields, consisting of energy without mass, had to be conceived of as *continuously* distributed throughout the whole of space. One could only speak tentatively and with great hesitation; but the sort of question that arose, for him, was: had they perhaps to abandon the assumption that *structure*, as such, was exclusively 'inner'—'inner' in terms of Newtonian space? Was it nonsense to conceive of something like an 'external' structure? Alternatively, or implied, if the increasingly constricted hunt after the inner structure of matter was not to be abandoned altogether, were they obliged to take in conceptually, in addition to the 3N dimensional space of their equations (to which no sort of actuality could be attributed) a—what should he say?—a negative, or perhaps a potential, space, for which they had no model and therefore, as yet, no equations; for in the history of science up to now the equations had always followed the model, even if they subsequently abandoned it? That such a space would have some very unfamiliar features was not in itself an objection; for everything suggested, as he had tried to remind them, that it would be of little use in their present predicament unless it did. If they hoped ever in any way to imagine the kind of field which is represented 'mathematically' by the ψ field of Schrödinger, it might involve, nay, it *must* involve, learning to think, in an unaccustomed way, of such fundamental relations as inner and outer, centre and periphery. Actually it had happened at about the time when he himself was first venturing on this highly speculative flight, that his attention was drawn to those studies in the psychology of imagination to which he had briefly alluded. He had mentioned them this evening on the footing that, in a really tight place, any way out might be worth trying; and that, however unlikely it might look, it was better to try the only one in sight than to sit still and do nothing. But he perhaps owed to that accident a notion that had also occurred to him, that the elementary particle for which they sought might be conceivable, might some day be conceived, as the detectable moment of transition from structure, or potential structure, in negative space to ordinary 'inner' structure in Newtonian, three-dimensional space—with the electric and magnetic fields affording perhaps some slight tantalizing evidence of the anterior process leading up to it. It might, he suggested, be in some such direction as this that they would have to look for the answer to what he himself regarded as the crucial question for physics: What keeps the nuclei of atoms together?

The lecturer concluded with a further apology to his audience for the highly speculative nature of some of the considerations he had placed before them. If he was right in calling the present state of physics a 'crisis'—and he was not the first to do so—then it might well be that any further advance depended on the discovery of new entities—of entities as new to contemporary physics as the electric and magnetic fields had been to classical physics. He himself did not think—and here again he was not alone—that there was any foreseeable future at all for their science, unless they at least *explored* new ways of thinking. Whether there was any value in the particular suggestions he had made would be decided by others than himself and he hoped, up to a point, would be discussed in the time that remained to them this evening.

Three Poems

While Barfield's poetry is often personal in terms of experience and perception, it is rarely explicitly about himself. The two poems that follow "Day" are exceptions that give insight into his self-assessment and his humility. The first, written when he turned fifty-three in 1951, finds him at what would be the mid-point of his extraordinarily long life, though of course he could not have known that at the time. The second poem was written in the very last of his life as he confronted with characteristic forthrightness the end that could not be far away.

Barfield wrote poetry throughout his life but published very little of it. One early exception is the poem "Day" that first appeared in the magazine The Challenge and was anthologized in The Best Poems of 1923. It shows Barfield in a lyric mode as inspired by his love of nature and of England and reflects also his awareness of the power that animates nature. That awareness had become a conscious and potent reality for him in the turning-point year of 1923 when he accepted the tenets of Anthroposophy, and it would influence all that he wrote thereafter.

Day

Down in the fens of Lincolnshire a bird
Threw up his head and uttered (like some word,
Spoken in hope, that very softly falls
Upon the silence of despair) two calls.
He waited: and innumerable trills
Filled the old darkness. . . .
                    Over Malvern Hills
A lark went twittering up into the sky. . . .

One seagull down the cliffs of Anglesey,
Even as the dawn-song of this lark was dying,
Called, and the coast was filed with swooping and crying.

    A tiny pool of light that slid and spread
In shots and runnels over the flat lead
Face of the chill North Sea: then colour came:
The pool of light turned to a pool of flame
That smoked up into a purple and red mass,
Where—like a face behind a darkened glass—
A circle faint out of the dimness grew,
And, flown with the wine of dawn, looked strangely through
At island hill-tops rising warm and green
Out of the blind white seas of mist between.
Chiltern and Costwold's upland grasses glistened,
Colouring the light with dew: the clear air listened

    Silent He rose out of that dreamy pall
And hung in the blue ether clear and small,
Till, underneath, the hills left dry and bright
Drew closer, and the valleys ran with light. . . .
Silent He rose and arched up over, and soon
The golden languor of the afternoon
Slept over meadows and sheep-dotted downs
And danced upon the pavements of the towns. . . .
Silent He fell, and east to meet the van
Of night the great Welsh mountain-shadows ran,
Rippling over undulating miles
Of English counties. Piles upon deep piles
Of crimson pageantry were slowly heaped
Against the West. Birds sang. The air was steeped
In memory. Dusk flittered like a bat
Down over England, hovered, and then sat
Darkling upon her, till she cast aside
Her twilight vestments, like a calm young bride,
When love himself has broken down his bars,
And spread her bosom to the quiet stars.

Fifty-Three

Now comes the time: shrewd autumn is on to me:
These mists of late September, what augury
    What's past and in store? What accompt, now
    Destiny opens her autumn budget?

Old strains of wars, reined passion, repulses, woes;
Breakdowns—at arm's length poised by tenacity;
    Will (maugre too much, undeflected)
    Paid with collapse of the fibres ruined:

Blown safety-valve—one morning the lump appears:
Fresh air and outdoors blanch to a memory:
    Scene shifters—hey presto?—the tale's all
    Hospital walls and the reek of ether . . .

Or shroud they harvest, practical, extrovert,
Soft self contained warm summer collected in
    Dew fallen, rime, crisp like a biscuit.
    Gemmed on the blades in a bright of morning:

Moist underneath, fecund, merry, innocent
Of sultriness, no longer preoccupied,
    No longer introspective—like these
    Quinquagenarian ruminations?

Owen Barfield

What is his proper name, that alien man,
The one that through time's telescope I see,
When the departing century I scan?
I ask and ask. He only answers: *Me.*

Those meannesses, deceptions, tricks to please,
Those hours and days of trifling—*In my scales*
What can you bring to counterbalance these?
Asks the Accuser, as my courage fails.

Watching him stand, the unalterable Past,
Naked before those stern unbending looks,
What will he say, if anything . . . at last
He mutters, scare above a whisper: *"Books?"*

Is that revealing stare a thought less grave?
And does He pop in his ascending pan
Before it kicks the beam: "Tis true they gave
A light lurch to the journeying Soul of Man"?